BEYTH YAHUSHUA, THE SON OF TZADOK, THE SON OF DAWUD

By Messianic Rabbi Simon Altaf

Copyright Forever-Israel International 9th September 2010
Second Edition

Edited 8, March 2018

Excerpts can be used from this book without modification for study or reprinting purposes with the set condition that as long as reference is given back to the author and this book.

For contacting us the USA Rabbi Lamont Clophus, Forever-Israel, 8111 Mainland, Suite 104-152, San Antonio, Texas, 78240, USA

For contacting us Rabbi Simon Altaf for forever-israel International congregations or please contact us via e-mail through foreverisrael777@yahoo.com or phone Rabbi Lamont in the USA: Tel 1-210-827-3907.

Visit our website at: www.forever-israel.com

Acknowledgments

All quotes are from the Hidden-Truths Hebraic Scrolls unless otherwise stated. We encourage you to buy these scriptures from the above website or www.amazon.com. Hardback can be obtained from www.lulu.com/simalt.

Preface

I was asked by my African student and friend Rabbi Dr Melech Mikhael Ukahson to write a book to clear the confusion about Yahushua's identity and His family background that has been obscured for so long. The time has now come to know who He was so that we know why is it that we worship Him because He is no ordinary man yet He is seen as an outcast by many who read the testimony of Yahushua written in the gospel accounts. Some historians looking back place Yahushua simply as an ordinary human stripping Him of His divinity at times making it look like he had no family background and no power or wealth.

While others try to remove Him from His Jews environment and make it seem like that He was a Torah breaker and it did not matter to Him and He held the laws of the Pharisees in contempt as a lone wanderer.

Many people to this day are uneducated in rabbinic customs and Scripture misinterpret Matthew chapter 23 in which Yahushua had a discussion with one group of Pharisees. Christians view this discussion in a negative way trying to prove that all Pharisees were corrupt. However they never really address the fact that if all the Pharisees hated Him then why were there so many Pharisees who were followers of **The Way** another name for the faith of Yahushua the Torah based faith which derives its name from the Tanach.

Nicodemus was a very well known Pharisee and a ruler plus teacher in the Temple he was one of the staunch followers and a man of wealth and influence as you will learn in this book. There were many staunch followers of Yahushua in the Temple who were also Pharisees and even priests. Rabbi Paul was a Pharisee and remained one to His death.

Modern theologians and Christendom in general have

little understanding that the tensions between some Pharisees were caused by the school of thought they belonged to or Rabbi they came under which explains the various disputed teachings one such being the resurrection which was denied by the Sadducees.

Mattityahu (Matthew) 22:23-24 The same day came to him the Sadducees, which say that there is no resurrection, and asked him, **24** Saying, Rabbenu (our great teacher), Musa (Moses) said, If a man dies, having no children, his brother shall marry his wife, and raise up sons[1] to his brother.

We show this in the Abrahamic-Faith Nazarene Hebraic Study Scriptures, now known as the Hidden-Truths Hebraic Scrolls Complete Bible so that people can see that the Christian Church ran away with many ideas that were and still are unscriptural today because of a lack of understanding of first century rabbinic culture, customs and practices. The lack of knowledge extends into all areas of modern forms of Christianity producing gross ignorance amongst the congregations, contradictory statements and strange beliefs alongside undue hatred for people of Hebrew blood. Their under education in Hebrew its idiomatic usage its colloquialisms and the application thereof continue to breed the Messiah Yahushua devoid of His culture, people and heritage.

Christendom has no real idea or instructions on how to interpret various Halacha (instruction of Torah) according to rabbinic understanding. Ask a Pastor what the term "virgin" means and how was it applied in the first century Judaism then you will see what I mean. They will all answer with "an unmarried woman who has no sexual contact with her husband."

However the term is not applied like that always because there are different categories for women who come under the term "virgin." One category is where a woman is married and can still be called a "virgin" even after sexual contact with her husband. She can still be called a virgin even if she is very advanced in old age and barren, Sarah the wife of Abraham fitted this category before she beget Isaac. See the HTHS Bible for more on such types of issues.

This is why the people who reject the oral Torah are the least educated and the most ignorant amongst the groups out there.

When a person does not know what he or she is talking about then it is advisable that he or she should really find a good Rabbi and go and learn the things they need to know and not obscure their understanding this is a command in Scripture.

[1] This is commanded polygamy in the Covenant writings as instructed in Torah.

Mattityahu 25:8-9 And the foolish said to the wise, give us of your oil, for our lamps are gone out. **9** But the wise answered, saying, not so; lest there be not enough for us and you: but you go rather to them that sell, and buy for yourselves.

The term oil for Our Lamps: These were akin to lacking Torah instructions and were quoting verses from here and there all over the place but had no real understanding as the wise ones. You only become wise if you obey Torah, which is the simple allegory and truth. Proverbs 1:7, wisdom will begin when you fear YHWH by obeying His commandments.

When you do not obey the Torah your works are worthless as Ya'acob pointed out 'show me your faith and I will show you my works in James 2:26.' The lamps or Torah scrolls of the foolish were on their shelves like some Christians have Bibles in their homes on their shelves eating dust. The first five books of Moses are also amongst the same bibles sitting on the shelves which they never pay attention to.

Buy for yourselves: How can the foolish go and buy Torah works, you cannot purchase them. The drash or allegory is showing something really amazing. It shows that on this Sabbath when the lamps are trimmed the wise have sent off the foolish ones and the foolish ones have gone to merchants who are selling on the Sabbath. The only people, who sell on the Sabbath, are not going to be Jews strict Sabbatarians but gentiles who trade on Friday night to Saturday night and shut their shops on Sundays for their services, which was the day of the sun. So we see clearly that the church is doing the buying and selling which is a sin that even Yahudah was once caught in (Nehemiah 10:31).

Although in the last forty years Christianity has branched out into many offshoots with the messianic congregations but due to the lack of good leadership congregations continue to be divided on many issues. These groups lack in understanding, e.g. many even today though claim to follow Torah but reject circumcision of the flesh yet this is an everlasting covenantal commandment that has no way of annulling it unless you had some physical or medical condition.

Many continue to argue and ignore because they are blind leading the blind but they forget and that this command also formed part of YHWH's voice and it is YHWH who decides people's salvation and not committees eating biscuits and tea on weekly meetings in churches.

They also reason Noah did not circumcise and was saved so why should we. This once again shows their lack of knowledge to say that Noah did not circumcise therefore I won't either because for one Noah was a righteous man before the sight of Elohim and obeyed His voice fully on top of that Christendom does not realise that Noah was born <u>circumcised</u> supernaturally so did not need it.

In fact even the Egyptians were circumcising their priests and Egyptian women marrying priests, if then men were uncircumcised they were considered unclean and this was before YHWH made the covenant with Abraham. While YHWH's use of circumcision was a binding covenant but for the Egyptians this was simply an act of being ritually clean and wholesome as the uncircumcised people were looked at with disrespect.

These types of Messianism groups who reject circumcision and key Torah principles also fight about feast dates arguing over things with no understanding of accepted Jews halacha accepted by thousands of Rabbis in Judaism for over two millennia. Some women in the west in these groups are even worse who think they know better and come up with new ideas of feast dates with no authority or rabbinic backing. Many men folks in these Messianic congregations do not realize YHWH does not need them to redefine His feasts but has already given that authority to Yahudah and has rejected Christendom from appointing feast days and dates or even future Temple services yet they continue to fight like little children with no divine authority. They continue to pervert set halacha coming up with new ideas of what day to keep the Sabbath as some lunar Sabbath groups have done. In the recent past many are being corrupted aligning themselves with some of the Karaites or the old corrupted Sadducees with the Pharisees who started counting their day from sunset opposed to the Torah sunrise day that was even mentioned by Yahushua the Messiah.

John 11: 9 Yahushua answered, are there not twelve hours in the day? If any man walks in the day, he does not stumble, because he sees the light of this world.

Tehillim (Psalm) 78:67-68 Moreover **he refused the tabernacle of Yosef**, and **chose not the tribe of Ephraim** (Christianity): **68** But **chose the tribe of Yahudah**, the Mount Tsiyon which he loved.

The Ten tribes were not chosen to run the Temple or run YHWH's governance but Judah was as he still holds the sceptre, see Gen 49:10 but which Judah? Not what most think?

One such feast where we see interesting arguments amongst the Messianics is the rejection of Yahudah's usage of Rosh Hashana which usually occurs in September or October. The Messianics argue without any authority insist on just calling it Yom Terua (feast of Trumpets) not realizing in their ignorance that the Jews know this but Rosh Hashana is the accepted civil year for madinat Y'sra'el (State of Israel) and has been for two millennia with Yahushua even following it which was accepted by the school of Hillel and Shammai.

So if you are following any form of Christendom unless they obey Torah you are simply following the dictates of men with no authority from Elohim. Just because somebody builds a church and puts a cross on it and then tells you to worship Elohim does not make that authority from YHWH since His ways requires one to obey Torah and teach Torah while the church today is miles away from Torah. We also look back and do not find the disciples of Yahushua building churches with crosses upon them but they stayed inside Hebrew Synagogues with the star of Dawud, Menorah and the Torah scroll as their Symbol and the Temple worship for at least one hundred years after Yahushua's death and resurrection followed by them being removed from Y'sra'el in 135 CE.

This book's aim is to show you who Yahushua was and fill the gaps in your knowledge and you will learn about the real Yahushua. Who were the people He was related to and why some people wanted to kill Him? The real Yahushua is the Master of heaven and earth revealed in the flesh and I will expound on His real personality later, He called me out of Islam twelve years ago one day in an international merchant bank in England right next to St Paul's Cathedral.

It is an honour for me to serve Him and to represent and teach the true faith of Y'sra'el. He answered my call after ten years of calling to Allah who never replied or responded to my call but the One who responded was Yahushua when I said creator of the earth speak to me. I asked Him what should I do for Him now. He said to me 'follow me' and then He said to me to set up a website. Subsequently He told me that He had a big plan for me and to focus
on what is ahead and not to worry about my life that He will direct me through all things.

I learned many years later that my family is from the tribe of Kohen (Levi) from Iran the nation once ruled by King Cyrus son of Esther. My family is connected to Musa the great prophet and to Abraham biologically. My ancestor Musa (Moses) who took the commandments of YHWH, giving it to Y'sra'el and the rest of the world. He also took my people Y'sra'el from Egypt in the first Exodus back home. While in like fashion I am called to make way and prepare for the House of Y'sra'el for a great journey back to Y'sra'el for the second Exodus yet to come. YHWH told me in 2004 that I am like Moses in other words He told me my lineage, and my job for the coming days is to prepare the people for the second Exodus through Torah and the Messiah and await in the nations for His directions. No we are not to sell our houses and run to the mountains but simply wait.

In 2004 when I asked YHWH at the Mount of Olives facing the holy of holies should I go up to Eretz Y'sra'el to stay there? He told me no, that I was needed outside Y'sra'el. Later He revealed to me that my forefathers had taken three oaths and we are not to go to the land permanently yet because it's a grievous sin to disobey YHWH until He takes us back by the hands of the Messiah Himself and this is what the Master Himself told me to stay out until I call you back. He told me clearly to stay in the Diaspora because He has unfinished business with the nations of the world and to restore the House of Y'sra'el.

I have faithfully done what I can to the best of my ability and have lost much family in the process but I thank my Master Yahushua to faithfully carry me and help me in many areas of my life. I did not give up when my first wife (Muslim) did not want to walk with me in my faith and I did not give up when my second wife (Christian) rejected me for Torah obedience and refused to be obedient to YHWH and His words. I was made a mockery, laughed at, made fun of and slandered but these things did not deter me from obeying the everlasting Torah only confirming my true faith and that in like manner the servants of YHWH were reviled and I count myself to be in such a place in which few are chosen to be placed. My Master Yahushua was also hated for no reason and it is He who said you will be treated likewise.

Matthew 10:22 And you shall be hated of all men for my name's sake but he that endures to the end shall be saved.

Suffering and Persecution is good because it refines you and builds your faith and brings you closer to YHWH so I see it as a gain to be refined.

I will serve Him faithfully and if the Master tarries His return then I will continue to the end of my life awaiting the marvellous resurrection looking forward to the coming age in Y'sra'el.

I thank Master Yahushua for taking me from the darkness to the marvellous light. I thank all of you for reading this text and commend you all to be faithful to the voice of YHWH which is Torah. You need to be steadfast because we have a sure hope and reward from the Master. Do not be swayed by public opinion or criticism by other unlearned of our faith but if I can be of any assistance to you then you only need to write to me at shimoun63@yahoo.com.

My title of Rabbi came from the Master and He sent his servant to anoint me from Jerusalem so I am not ashamed to be called a Rabbi and also note Christians who do not understand usually misapply the reference in Matthew 23:7-8 which is not a forbidden use for the title of Rabbi misapplied and misquoted by Christendom as usual which lacks knowledge of the Hebraic Scriptures. See the HTHS Bible translation for the correct usage.

Table of Contents

CHAPTER 1 — 14
Jesus who? 14

CHAPTER 2 — 39
Yahushua The Son of Tzadok 39

CHAPTER 3 — 53
Has YHWH changed the way of Salvation? 53

CHAPTER 4 — 81
Who are all the Miriam's? 81

CHAPTER 5 — 163
Is Yahushua the Messiah? 163

CHAPTER 6 — 215
Yahushua the Divine Son of Elohim? 215

CHAPTER 7 — 246
Understanding the two Houses of Y'sra'el and who are the Gentiles? 246

Chapter 1

Jesus who?

I have heard of a Dr Who a TV Character but who is Jesus? Ah he must be the invention of Rome; this is the corruption they have left behind. Many people in the churches have utterly failed to understand the person of Yahushua and do not have the correct knowledge of the man from Nazareth because they are searching for a person by the name of 'Jesus' who does not exist hence my remark Jesus who. If we were to make enquiry and go back just six hundred years we may discover that this name did not exist. In the early seventeenth century this began to crop up in people's vocabulary but before that the title or name 'Jesus' was not used anywhere in antiquity. If we cannot find it six hundred years ago because the letter J was not invented then what hope do we have of finding a man by the name of 'Jesus' in the first century? And if you cannot even find His real name what hope do you have of finding his family and ancestry?

Here is a quote from a King James Version Bible the original 1611 edition.

Matthew 1:1, 25
CHAP. I. 1 The genealogie of Christ from Abraham to Ioseph. 25 And knewe her not, till shee had brought forth her first borne sonne, and he called his name <u>IESVS</u>.

Note in the 1611 version of the King James Bible there is no letter J but it was common practice was to use the letter I instead to pronounce the name as Iesous. Note other letters in the alphabet were also missing so the name is not written as Iesus but IESVS.

The unfortunate truth is if we went back to the first century and made enquiry of a person we were searching for by the name of "Jesus" then those living at that time will tell us no such person exists therefore there is no way we could trace him or his family under this Greek name.

The veil that covers the eyes of the churches worldwide is this blindness not knowing His real name yet making bashful claims that they have a relationship with him. Can I make a claim that I know the queen of England and have a relationship with her when I am
not allowed to enter Buckingham palace? I certainly know of the queen of England but we do not reference her by a modern changed name such as Queen Joanna. What hope do we have of finding a queen by the name of Joanna if we went enquiring to the Buckingham palace, the guards will chase us out that there is no such person there.

If I do not even know her real name then how can I make bold claims to know her personally? If I knew her personally would she not tell me her real name at some point of our relationship?

Mishle (Proverbs) 30:4 Who has ascended up into shamayim (heavens), or descended? Who has gathered the wind in his fists? Who has bound the waters in a garment? Who has established all the ends of the earth? What is **his name**, and what is his **son's name**, if you can tell?

Yet millions of Christians do not know the name of the Son nor the Father and make vacuous claimed relationship with Him and only help spread the deception further. One Christian was adamant to me because of miracles he knows him. These are the kind of leaps of blind faith that many such people take. There are people in this world who do miracles some true and some false, can we then ascribe those people as divine?

YHWH Himself tells us the relationship with Him only comes about when we obey His voice and even in the

Covenant it is confirmed in the same way.

First John 2:4 He that says, I know him, and does not guard his commandments, is a liar, and the truth is not in him.

John tells us that anyone who claims to know Him but refuses the commandments of Moses which is Torah is a liar. These are the words of the first century disciple of Yahushua who was a Torah keeper and a Torah teacher.

If Christianity had practiced the truth as it was given in the first century we would not have so much corruption and liars in the churches. Churches are full of these kinds of people. I know because I met some of these types on my journey of faith. I met many other Christians very sincere in their heart and who wanted tolearn and practice Torah truths as it was laid down but their clergy refuse to teach them the truth because they have given over to greed to stay with the status quo by teaching a faith devoid of its real tenets and Hebraic roots. I regularly receive calls from ex-Muslims who have come to faith who are utterly disdained by the church system and no lack of Torah teachings and the utter lack of teachings for defence of our faith against other religions such as Islam that try to take people into the Muslim religion. I have and continue to mentor several of my ex-Muslim students because my house and my doors are open for all the congregations of YHWH and is the bridge to connect the House of Y'shma'el and Yahudah.

Please feel free to leave me a message and I can usually connect people to various shuls (places of worship) where the Torah is respected and taught and Messiah is loved and cherished. I also teach many people directly through videos, tapes, CDs and audios at my site www.forever-israel.com and even some of my personal students come home to receive the nuggets of wisdom YHWH has given me.

Although there are many Christian TV stations out there

but I guarantee like pop culture in the West the American brand of Christianity is very popular with name it claim it and get yourself very wealthy type Christianity. Usually they will tell you to sow a seed, put hundred dollars or put one thousand dollars and get ten times back, let Elohim bless you variety. However I know of several people who gave tens of thousands of dollars in the hope of multiplying it by ten and ending up with nothing.

However this brand of Christianity is as false as the fake brands of Rolex watches coming out of Taiwan.

Most of these TV Channels are worthless garbage because hardly any teaches you how to obey Elohim and to serve Him. All they talk about is smoochy love which is also worthless. This brand of Christianity produces self-centred greedy people who are simply after how to be rich. Many sincere Christians are sucked into these kinds of games and plots and end up penniless, beware of such talk and ideas.

Usually you can tell a Christian from the way he or she behaves with money. In my case I have often found that if I had a piece of work that I wanted to translate into another language such as the
HTHS Bible then the first thing you are asked is "how much are you going to pay me." This shows that the intent of the person is not to be pleasing to YHWH but simply on just how much money they can make from this project. This is not that we are trying to avoid payment but it shows the greedy heart of the such people. I have seen the most sincere people in the field of translators to be ex - Muslims who will never ask you for money or rates but ask you to send the work and let them do the work. I have personally struggled to find translators for the HTHS Bible into other languages and the most problems were in Pakistan in the Urdu translation where every other Christian wants to become rich from the translation work. How then can a person appointed to get the work done finish the work if each person out there is only after

money? I have so far failed to get the work done losing money from at least two people because there only interests was how much money can they make. I have found that this kind of shameful behaviour is quite common in Christendom to treat Elohim's work like a money making idea.

Of course we would pay any translator the going rate but I have found the most problematic to be Christian background people who keep changing rates quarter way through the project and I have found people who come from other backgrounds such as a convert to be the most reliable and sincere in completing the work at hand without complaints or trying to get rich. Usually money shows the worst in Christians. I often receive e-mails from Indian Christian Pastors who claim to run orphanages and these are usually in the Andra -Pradesh area of India and believe me majority of these are 100% fraud. These people simply rent a house, gather some poor children from the street take their pictures then they write to big name organisations to help them feed the children and claim to be serving the Creator. In essence they are only after making a quick buck and this is what Western style greedy Christianity has done to these people on how to be rich either by miracle making or running orphanages. A well known evangelist in India who has little knowledge of the Bible just goes around making miracles to collect money and now a days he has his young son on the prowl who also has been trained in this kind of deception to claim miracles and of course the goal is to make money.

I was watching a TV program where his miracles failed to come to light and he was asking the woman can you hear out of your bad ear which he claimed to have healed in the titles of Yahushua while the woman was saying she could not hear, he was confused by pointing to the wrong ear to be healed and the woman who was still deaf in her diseased ear could not answer him. Such shameful behaviour is quite common in India and other places where Christianity claims to be the truth. Therefore I have termed India like the western spaghetti movie "For a few dollars more." Both in India and Pakistan when the Christian community has no jobs they become Pastors and miracle workers so they can make a "Few Dollars More" chasing after dollars.

In Nigeria where we have churches practically every hundred yards I have labelled the famous Clint Eastwood Western movie the Good, the Bad and the Ugly. There the Good are those people who are striving to obey the Torah such as the Netzarim, and some Christian congregations learning the ways of Yahuweh, the bad are those who claim to be serving YHWH but are not, the ugly are those Pastors and Bishops who sit on big money and claim to be serving Elohim but they are only building wealth for themselves and their children with big houses and many cars. The end result for such people is separation from Yahuweh and a place in Hell unless they repent and so far this does not seem to be coming.

In the West if you switch to any of the Christian channels of which we have many today the dominant theme is we are in grace and not under the law. They define the law as the Torah of Moses. This is the most devilish and perverted doctrine in the church today to put down YHWH's law as unnecessary for faith and living while the way Rabbi Paul used the term under the law he was not referring to the Torah of Moses but to man's or human law. This has been misunderstood and perverted by Western Christendom and this idea of the devil is also being spread in the East where many families have been corrupted. This is why the Muslim religion and its followers are very successfully thwarting this type of Western Christianity and defeating Pastor after Pastor in debates clearly because there is no foundation and the house built on sand cannot stand.

The solution is to return to the real faith of Torah and Messiah the real Rock or face annihilation by Islamic radical adherents spiritually where they do not control the territory and physically where they have control over the territory they will literally kill you if you do not listen to them. This is the judgment from YHWH.

Debarim (Deut) 28:25 YHWH shall cause you to be defeated before your enemies: You shall **go out one way against them**, and **flee seven ways before them becoming an object of terror** and shall be removed into all the nations of the world.

A good way to understand this text is by mystical analysis. The Hebrew is quite interesting in the above text, going out
one way against them the Hebrew is thus בדרך אחד תצא אלי.
(B'drekha Akhad Tetza alee)

The Hebrew word B'Derekh means to go in the way or to go out but the interesting mystery here is in the word Akhad, which in the primary sense means "to be united" or as one group but how can the Y'sraelites be defeated if they be one in mind and body. In order to understand the ancient thought the text is used in a variety of ways so really the text we focus on is Akhad and here is how we understand this thought behind it.

Akhad was the ancient region of Northern Iraq ruled by King Sargon or kings who worshipped false deities. The North section of the world in Kabbalah thought is the numeral one which is associated with the Father in heaven the source of all things. This is for all goodness in the world but the reverse of that one is Satan who stands for all evil at the same section of the North. So you choose one or the other.

The north is the place of YHWH's throne but also where Satan has setup a pseudo throne. In the Bible this place is in Turkey not far off from Sargon's ancient capital.

So what YHWH is trying to show us is that when you

have left Him and turned away from His Torah (His throne) you have actually joined with Satan who is trying to thwart the Northern sections with his pseudo false throne which normally is the place of YHWH's throne. In affect the reverse application of Akhad is that you are no longer united in the Torah but united with false doctrines and united with Satan therefore you will not stand and fail and run into seven directions.

In Kabbalah Akhad is equal to alef =1, Khet = 8 and Dalet = 4 which equals 13 which is the same numerical value for love (Ahav),

Romiyah 3:19 (HTHS) Now we know that whatever things the Torah said, it said to them who are under the *human* law: that every mouth may be stopped, and all the world may become guilty before Elohim.

It is obvious Rabbi Paul is comparing between two "laws", the first "Law" he used is clearly referring to the Torah of Moses and the ones who are under the second "LAW" which is human whose mouths may be stopped are those people who have taken it upon themselves to be saved through man made laws, institutions such as Rabbinic Judaism, Christianity or whatever or even some other type of societal institution but in the context of Rabbi Paul he was addressing first century institutions of Rabbinic Judaism, which had their own ideas of how one can become part of the community of Israel and be saved.

The text in Romans 3:19 is clear that the entire world is guilty before YHWH because of His Torah. So what is YHWH going to use to judge the world since by the Anglican Church reckoning the Torah of Moses is abolished which was given as eternal? See the contradiction in this doctrine? If YHWH is going to use New Testament only then what about the 325 year period when there was no New Testament compilation as one unified book but there were only just as separate scrolls and letters? Rabbi Paul tells you that the whole world is guilty before YHWH because of His Torah since this is what identifies sin and also points to life here (How to live on the earth) and also to know about the expected Messiah.

See how many texts in the Scriptures are misinterpreted and perverted which end up destroying Torah which is a sin. But I am going to put you straight that without YHWH's TORAH/LAW there is no GRACE. Grace is only for those who accept His law because within that law (Torah of Moses) are eight covenants and if you reject the law then you have already rejected grace, which is tied to those eight <u>highly important life changing</u> covenants which all faithful have to accept listed below.

10. A Covenant with the animals also in the millennium in Israel Hosea 2:18		
9. Covenant of peace with Israel yet future in the millennium Ezek 37:27		
Deut 29:1 - The New Covenant Repeated in Jeremiah 31:31		
8. The Davidic	Covenant	Second Samuel 7:10-16
7. The Renewed	Covenant at Mount Nevo	Deuteronomy 29:1
6. The Sinaitic	Covenant	Exodus 24:7
5. The Abrahamic Covenant (Circumcision)		Genesis 12:3,7; 15:4; 17:7
4. The Noahic	Covenant	Genesis 9:1, 11-13
3. The Adamic	Covenant of Relationship	Genesis 3:14-17
2. The Creation	Covenant of the Sabbath	Genesis 2:3, Exodus 31:16-17
1. The Edenic	Covenant of Relationship	Genesis 1:26-28
Not ratified by blood.		

Though Christendom loves to use the term 'saved' but they do not understand what the term actually really means other than misapplying it to Church made creeds. Any person 'saved' is that person that has accepted YHWH's Voice, His Torah, His Torah (voice) which embodies a total of ten of His covenants each granting a measure of grace, protection, freedom and everlasting life to us. When we reject the Torah of Musa (YHWH's voice) we also reject grace and therefore are then only deceiving our self and others by living a distorted lie.

Is there any way we can tell if a person is 'saved' in the modern term? Yes we can tell one hundred percent accurately if that person has a love for the Torah which reveals the person's salvation and his heart for YHWH.

Jacob (James) 2:17 Even so faith, if it has no works (Torah deeds), is dead, being alone.

So if you reject Torah your faith is dead anyway because your works or (deeds) are defined by Torah which are acceptable to YHWH.

One example of such type of 'work' is to celebrate the seven feasts. Another example is to feed the poor. A third example of Torah works is to lend money to someone in need without interest. So if you deny Torah your faith is of no use. For me then faith without Torah is nothing but a dead donkey which Christianity should stop beating. Whoever told you that the Torah deeds are not necessary have lied to you because every deed that is not of Torah will be burned and the Torah deeds will be weighed, judged and your future will be decided using them. Here is proof.

Revelation 20:12 And I saw the dead, small and great, stand before The Throne,[2] and the books were opened: and another scroll was opened, which is the scroll of life: and the dead were judged out of those things which were written in the books, **according to their deeds**…

Torah deeds are used to judge people. So if your deeds are not according to Torah then they are according to Satan. These will be adultery, idolatry, whoring, unclean living, lying, cheating, usury, hatred etc, etc. If these are YOUR DEEDS then you are beating a dead donkey and claiming faith which has no value.

A person who has real faith and provident grace may not know how to fully obey the Torah but will have a sure love for it and that is a sign that the person is indeed under grace and 'saved' and if the person hates the words of YHWH (Torah) then we can be sure that he or she is not 'saved' at all. Such people are of the devil because it is the devil that rejected YHWH's voice. What testimony does YHWH give of those rejecting His voice?

Revelation 20:15 And whosoever was not found written in the **scroll of life** was cast into the lake of fire.

The devil and the angels who rebelled with Elohim are not written in the scroll of life. Some of the rebelling angles are tied with one leg upside down in She'ol (place of the dead) and will be in such a position until Judgment day when they are thrown in the lake of sulphur. If you have lived a rebellious life then that is the fate that awaits you because a cell is already reserved for you in She'ol. The choice is now yours if you want to remove your name from the book of the wicked dead, the time is now to repent and walk in Torah and Messiah.

The books in heaven are opened at the feast of Yom Kippur annually and people's names are written into them. If you do not even know what is the feast of Yom Kippur (Day of Atonement) what hope is for you to have your name written in the book of life? It is not by chance but by choice. All the disciples of Messiah in the first century believed and practiced these feasts understanding the ramifications.

Those people not written in the scroll of life will be

destroyed and this is the majority who reject YHWH's voice for this is YHWH's testimony. So if you are reading this and did not realise this then wake up from your slumber and repent and turn to YHWH as the hour is late and you do not have a moment to lose. Connect with us using the information page at the front of the book to start experiencing real grace and the love of YHWH in your life opposed to the false man-made grace you have traded for the truth.

We can test each individual using John's definition to test every person out there claiming to be a believer. In short any person who does not believe or refuses to obey YHWH's voice, His Torah is a liar and deceiving himself or herself and by John's definition tested to be 'unsaved.' This is the testimony of John one of the pillars of the Hebrew faith of the Netzarim assembly the disciple who was loved by the Master. I do not need to show you further proof to prove who is saved or not because it is right here and the same John then confirms it by saying this in First John 2:6.

First John 2: 6 He that says he abides in him is himself obligated also to walk, just as he walked.

John has said the one who claims to be in Messiah must keep the halacha (Works of Torah) as Yahushua kept them. Are you keeping them like Yahushua and walking in the halacha of Yahushua. He agreed with everything that was appointed by the school of Hillel. Are you?

Yahushua used His piercing words that NO MAN is His disciple who does not obey the Torah.

John 8:31 Then said Yahushua to those Yahudim (Hebrew
people) which believed on him, If you continue in my word, then are you my disciples indeed

Note you are only His disciple if you keep the Torah of Musa. If you do not then stop wasting your time and other people's time. By now you should be shaking in your boots to know that you face eternal demise and the gates of hell await you and your foolish talk will not save you alone but in order to receive the salvation on offer from Yahushua you must agree to the covenant terms which is to be obedient to the Torah to the best of your ability. Mistakes are allowed but disobedience is not. If you agree then the next verse of John follows that the Torah will set you free. The word "truth" is the idiomatic expression for both the living and written Torah of Yahushua. Well if Yahushua is Elohim then why are you not obeying His voice?

John 8:32 And you shall know the truth, and **the truth** (Torah) shall make ye free (Liberate you from bondage).

The TRUTH here refers to Torah, and when you start believing and acting on the written Torah you are no longer under any bondage and are FREE indeed and will be part of the millennium resurrection.

If the truth be told I have seen many deceivers in the churches and people who have no love for the Elohim of Y'sra'el but simply are there to make money while there are those in churches who want to know the truth but the truth is hidden and suppressed by the false orthodoxy of Rome and Anglicanism. Beware of Isms because they all lead to eternal death such as Catholicism, Christianism, and Islamism etc.

So for our quest and in order to trace the real Yahushua who many in the Western world do not know while some call him the name Yeshua even make a mistake not knowing this title was not his real lingual name given by Gabri'el unless Gabri'el spoke Aramaic and ascribed an Iranian name to the Son of Elohim. If you went back to the first century there were many such people called 'Yehoshua' as it was a common name but to seek the man we are searching for you would have to search for

Yehoshua or correctly spoken Yahushua. So what was His name and is there any proof that we can furnish before we go to investigate such a man? His real name was Yahushua and we have conclusive proof of this while the churches continue to make new doctrines the one thing they cannot get straight is what was the name of the Saviour. Just as the Muslims do not budge from calling the name of their deity Allah and superimposing him as the Elohim of Abraham likewise Christians superimpose 'Jesus' as the name of Elohim. This is simply living in ignorance and introducing the seeds of idolatry in a congregation.

This is why when someone makes a claim to me that 'Jesus' is the saviour I usually ask a question. Jesus who? They look very perplexed and then I usually give them a list that follows;

Jesus of the Mormons, Jesus of the Jehovah's witnesses, Jesus of the Catholics, Jesus of the Anglicans or Jesus (Isa) of the Muslims? Take your pick, which one are they talking about.

When the reality sets in none of these will turn up but only one and His name is not 'Jesus.' This is not a game of semantics and syntax but salvation is a serious business both in the eyes of the Creator and equally for man.

Did YHWH (Yahuweh) say that the name 'Jesus' is the Saviour? You will find no such text that the Jews hold and neither in the hands of Christendom if you search in the original copies of the texts such as the Hebrew, Aramaic or even Greek texts.

Let us hear it from YHWH.

Yeshayahu (Isaiah) 43:11 I, even I, am **YHWH**; and beside me there is no Saviour.

So who is willing to challenge YHWH that another man by the name of 'Jesus' is the saviour and took over from being YHWH?

Who dares call YHWH a liar?

The only way the first century Yahushua the real one could be true is either if he pointed back to YHWH as the Saviour or **was Himself YHWH** revealed in the flesh and unless He did this requirement He would be simply a false prophet.

His name is important because the name 'Jesus' does not mean what the name Yahushua means and Yahushua's name has the power and authority from heaven while 'Jesus' is a man-made PERVERTED title. The early Netzarim disciples of the Master only spoke in the Hebrew name of Yahushua and no other. The name means '**Yahuweh is salvation**' and more appropriately **Yahuweh has become salvation of Y'sra'el**. The term 'Jesus' if translated back to Hebrew means a "war horse" and in Scripture "war horses" are not seen as good things.

The people who teach that Yahushua did away with Elohim's law are already disqualified and the English title of Yahushua's name they use to lead people astray by telling them that the Torah of the creator is no longer valid. Is that not what Churches teach, I did not make this up in a vacuum because this is what I have heard and seen for the last 12 years since my salvation came about? So can the churches claim to be in the place of a prophetess? A whoring prostitute yes a prophetess no. Why would they be a whoring prostitute is that not a strong condemnation? This is because they teach YHWH's Torah is no longer applicable to them. The only one who rebels openly against the Torah was/is Satan so the churches which teach this are indirectly accepting to be the bride of Satan and the bride of Satan is a whore and not a chaste bride so let that be clear to you. The chief principle teaching and way of life of this bride is rebelliousness. Any woman on this earth that rebels against her righteous husband who obeys not the Torah also fits the title of a whore. Many people equate the title of whore with physical adultery but the reality is that the title whore alongside physical adultery is much more ascribed to mixing so if you mix or introduce a new way of salvation or new Saviour then you fit the title of a harlot or whore.

The Church could only have been in the position of a prophetess if they taught Torah and pointed back to YHWH. But right now they are a false prophetess because the teachings of the real Yahushua have been distorted and new ones made that have no relevance in the Bible such as pre-tribulation rapture and salvation by remaining in sin namely not obeying any Torah commandments which is the bulwark of the Covenants that the creator formulated. This is what Yahushua said about this ecclesiastical authority that she is Jezebel because Jezebel was the only one who taught the servants of YHWH not to obey Torah and not to circumcise in the flesh and break the covenants.

Revelation 2:20 Notwithstanding I have a few things against you, because you tolerate that woman Izebel (Jezebel), which calls herself a prophetess, to teach and to seduce my servants to commit whoring, and to eat things sacrificed to idols.

Did I just not say what whoring is and now you hear it from the Master's mouth?

Jezebel here is described as any system of religion such as Christendom that does not obey the voice of YHWH. This incorporates all versions of Christendom such as Jehovah's witnesses, Mormons, Catholics and any other variety. I am told that there are thirty eight thousand denominations, some suggest up to one hundred and twenty eight thousand but I do not know if these figures are accurate but that is what we are looking at.

The 'woman,' drash (allegory) has been used to describe all the various assemblies out there that teach to disobey Yahushua/YHWH's teachings, not to keep His Torah, to eat unclean foods such as pork and crabs, to not do His feasts the seven YHWH has established in Leviticus 23 and to reject circumcision as of the Jews.

We cannot claim one Covenant as ours by picking and choosing while ignoring the rest. It's ALL or NOTHING. If Christians believe the bible why have they not adhered to the seven annual feasts of the Bible? Why have they not circumcised their male children according to the Abrahamic eternal Covenant written in the Torah the Christians allege to accept yet deny in reality? Why have they ignored the LAW of the creator given at Sinai?

Luke 1:31 And, behold, you shall conceive in your womb, and bring forth a son, and shall call his name **Yahushua** (Yahushua).

Now let us examine if this is the correct name. If anyone went making enquiries they could even find in the King James Version the true name of Yahushua.

Here is proof:

When the translators were busy translating these texts they made a big mistake they mistranslated the name of Joshua from "Yahushua" in the Hebrew to the modern vernacular 'Jesus' and this is one way to know with absolutely certainty that in 1611 AD in the King James version this change occurred.

Hebrews 4:8 (KJV) For if Jesus had given them rest, then would he not afterward have spoken of another day.

This is the mistake from the 1611 AD KJV because here it was not the term 'Jesus' there but "Joshua" who led the Israelites out of Jordan. The Hebrew form of the name Joshua is **Yahushua** while some pronounce it as

Yehoshua. This is who the translators confused the term of Yahushua to Jesus.

We can check in the Hebrew and see that the English name Joshua is actually the Hebrew equivalent of Yahushua.

Let me show you.

Exodus 17:9 (NKJV) And Moses said to Joshua...

Exodus 17:9 in Hebrew

עשוהי־לא השמ רמאיו

V' Yomar Mosheh Al Yahushua

Note names do not translate but always <u>transliterate</u> from one language to another. One such proof is the Hebrew term Hellelu-jah which can be found in every nation. If you note this is the phrase for the Hebrew words Hallel-lu-Yah and it is very close to the Hebrew transliteration while this phrase is proof that it carries in every language of the world whichever nation you go to. No one says hallel-lu'jeh just to show you that the hybrid form Jehovah was also incorrect in its transliteration which a German author came up with in the 16th century.

If we take the English name <u>James</u> and if I was to pronounce the name James in Urdu the national language of Pakistan it will remain <u>James</u>. Peter would be pronounced Peter with no change of translation. However in Urdu the name James is correct as Yaqub and Peter is not correct calling him Patras which is his Greek title. We can see the Hebrew is correct in Urdu carrying forward Yacov to Yaqub which is the ancient Hebrew while Patras is Greek and it should have been Kefa and not Petros or Patras. This shows us that the names have been corrupted in many translations.

The name James in the Bible especially the letter of James is actually the <u>letter of Jacob</u> because his name was switched to the English name of the King James who had the bible translated in 1611 AD. The same things happened with Yahushua over many years of change. You may wonder why the form Yeshua is not correct either. Remember what I said earlier about a name carrying forward from language to language? Well Yeshua is the Aramaic form of the name but it's not correct in spelling nor in its meaning and we can be <u>certain</u> that the angel Gabri'el did not come speaking Aramaic. Ecclesiastical language in its usage and written form was always proper Hebrew and not Aramaic or Greek.

Many people confuse the name <u>Yeshua</u> with Hebrew and think it means "salvation." It does not mean anything unless you append a Heh (H) in Hebrew to it so then it means "salvation", which is the Hebrew word Yahshua**H**, note it is the Hebrew <u>feminine</u> form of the world while Yahushua is applied to a male (masculine) and only in this Hebrew spelling it means salvation.

Without the ending character of heh it would be neither here nor there it's like taking my surname "Altaf" and removing the ending F then calling me "Alta" so it's neither here nor there and becomes a wrong name altogether but here we are talking about the name of the Master Messiah and not little me. My name's meaning is a "warrior" and it also has a dual meaning of plural for thank you. However if you knocked off the letter F in my name then it would be "Alta" and it no longer could mean a 'Warrior' or the plural for thank you. This is what many have done to the Saviour's name.

It only means salvation by adding the heh at the end such as העושי or the Hebrew letter tav for the plural form would be
Yeshuot. Don't be fooled by cheap doctrines of men because there are many who claim to know Hebrew yet still do not know ancient rule of Hebrew.

Have you ever thought how would anyone on this good earth find the name "Jesus" in the writings of Moses? They would never find it and is guaranteed to fail. We must understand that if it was OK from a human stand point to call Him 'Jesus' when you did not know this to be the case but from a divine perspective then why assign an angel to deliver the name? Indeed Abbah YHWH assigned an angel to take the name down. There was a kinship pattern that had to be maintained but also to connect Him back to this ancestors as you will read in this book.

It is always more holy to address Him by His actual name which was hand delivered by a heavenly messenger. Do you see the importance? Did the heavenly messenger hand deliver the name 'Jesus' or Yahushua?

Are you not then contradicting the name that came from heaven from the Father? Do you hold more authority or does the Father? Be afraid for the day that you will die and then you will have to stand for judgment to answer for these things. Flesh and blood cannot compete with the Light of lights.

If you did not know this then it has been OK up until now but now that you know the times of ignorance are over and I would not condemn you for not knowing this but now that you have been educated you need to change your behaviour because if you stay in the old camp then you hold fast to idolatry because you hold to a name that has been taught to rebel against Adonai to break His holy law.

What about the title YESHU? The Indian Christians call him either Yeshu or Eshu, this term Yeshu was a clever ploy to devise an acronym by some of the orthodox Rabbis in the first century (note not all of the Orthodox Rabbis hated Yahushua, only some from the School of Shammai hated him who were zealots and wanted to kill Yahushua), which goes something like this;

Yimakh sh'mo v'zikh-rono

The above Hebrew means "May his name and memory be blotted out."

In the Greek the name is written as ee-sous. Both the

Hebrew form which is Yahushua and Jesus' name Yahushua come out as ee-sous. Since Greek has no consonant y, so it uses the initial I that should theoretically come out sounding like a y. The Greek alphabet has no letter to pronounce the sound of the letter S or Shin in Hebrew so it is replaced with the transliteration of sigma or s the softer sound.

The final vowel point is an oo sound or a long U sound like in the word flute but the guttural consonant of ayin a vowel has been added. The s on the end is part of a standard conversion from other languages to Greek. Since Greek nouns almost always have case endings, including names, the s is added to give the name the right feel. So we can see how in Greek we end up with something completely different to Yahushua such as ee-sous.

A friend Robert Young quotes in his book **Name above ALL Names** page 75/76 as follows:

As one author put it, "Once the Jews came under Greek influence, we note the tendency to replace or to translate Hebrew names by similar sounding Greek names." (My highlighting) [From a quotation of E. L. Sukenik Journal of Palestinian Oriental Society 8-1927, pgs, 113-121, given by Gerhard Kittel Theological Dictionary of the New Testament,
vol. 3, page 286.] The Universal Hebrew Encyclopedia has this entry: "Jason (Greek form of the Aramaic of the name of Joshua)." [Vol. 6, pg. 42, 1948 copyright]

On page 110 of The New Schaff-Herzog Encyclopaedia of Religious Knowledge we read, "JASON: A Greek name borne often by Jews of the Maccabean or later times and by Hebrew Christians. On account of its resemblance to the Hebrew- Hebrew name Jesus or Joshua, it was often assumed by the Jews inclined to Greek culture or living in a Greek environment." (My underlining)

Of course, one has to overlook their saying "Jesus or Joshua". What they obviously mean is the Hebrew name commonly called "Jesus" and "Joshua" in English usage. Their scholarship is too good for them to mean that "Jesus" or "Joshua" are the correct sounds of this one Hebrew name found written in the English both as "Jesus" (when referring to the Messiah) and "Joshua" (when referring to the son of Nun). In dealing with the subject of what "JASON" is, they are not trying to be exact about the pronunciation of the Hebrew, but merely using "Jesus or Joshua" so the public, in their limited knowledge, will understand the main point.

In other words Robert says that the Name was never pronounced Jesus but from Iesous to Jason by the Greeks which later got transliterated into Jesus with the advent of the J in the English alphabet.

Robert beautifully sums it like this on page 77 of his book **Name above ALL Names**

So the sum of the matter is this. The Hebrew name of our Savior was a name first developed by Moses through combining the name of our Creator, "Yah", with the name of his servant – the man today commonly called "Joshua". He changed his servant's name, which meant "Salvation", by calling him "Yah-Salvation." Therefore, the significance is primarily in the sound of this name that Moses "called" him so that when a Hebrew heard that name spoken he would be hearing "Yah is Salvation". The written form of the name in Hebrew (or any other language) is primarily a group of symbols used to portray the sound wherein the real significance exists.

How do we know the pronunciation of Yahushua or YHWH is correct with a long oo sound as in the world **FLU**te. We only need to look at the prophets names such as Eliyahu who carried the name of Yahuweh also reflecting the NAME of the Saviour. ELI-YA-HU so we can see that it is YA-HU at the end because it contains the letter Vav and that spells in the ancient to a W giving us the long U sound. How about Yesha- YAHU (Isaiah) so from at least two prophets' names we can prove that the correct rendering of Yahuweh or Yahu -eh with an

aspirated U sound and the Saviour's name with an aspirated U as well such as
Yahushua. Some choose Yeshua or Yahshua though I do not criticize such transliteration usages because they are simply the shorter post exilic names but I will caution that Yeshua does not mean "salvation" without the missing heh but nevertheless its a start to switch from the traditional English form of 'Jesus' to 'Yeshuah.'

The Bottom line

We have transliteration of the sacred name in the ancient cuneiform script with written vowels of this language. In 1898 A. H.Sayce transliterated three cuneiform tablets dating back to Hamurrabi that clearly said "Jahweh is God."[1], Hammurabi was the 6th king in the period 1792-1750 BC.

[1]See Halley's Bible Handbook, p. 62

In addition the cuneiform inscriptions known as the Murashu texts dating back to about 500 BC leave no room for any further debate give it away that the term Yahuweh is correct and even the term Yahushua is more accurate with clear pronounceable vowels. This means the Masorets change is a very late change and when we go back to the older evidence, we can get an accurate transliteration of the most set-apart name thus we should use it with reverence and to protect it too with Titles where possible so we do not desecrate it amongst the nations by mistake.

What about the people who say that the name of the Creator should be pronounced Yahuwah or Yahuah?

Look at the evidence in the Hamurrabi tablets going back to 1792 BC that was many hundreds of years before the birth of Messiah which says the name of the Creator was called Jahweh. Let's stop here. Going by the linguistic rules of the ancient Hebrew language
we have 4 letters here Yud, Heh which give us the sound of Yah. If we then add the ancient W which has the

modern U sound then we pronounce it as Yahu the long U similar to the sound of the word flu-te followed by the Heh gives us the clear transliteration of Yah-- oo-weh thus we can see why Hammurabi's written Jahweh would be correct. Note Hammurabi did not write Jahweh with English that is just the modern characters used to explain the ancient text. One caution for those who suggest we should call the name of Elohim Yahuwah. Yes it can be Yahuwah at times as it was done once a year in the Temple but if you use the word Yahudah which has the Hebrew letters Yud, Heh, Vav, Dalet and Heh then the people who opt for Yahuwah suggest that if you remove the U that is the Vav character in the word Yahudah then it pronounces the word Yahuwah.

I am not going to explain here in detail why this will not work because this is a very lengthy discussion but I want to concentrate on the topic of Yahushua and his family in this book but the idea that Yud, Heh, Vav and Heh removing the character of Dalet from the Hebrew word Yahudah (Judah) in the Hebrew tongue forms the word Yahuwah in my opinion is inaccurate and not true although only appears to be true on the surface but really is not using the ancient Hebrew set of characters without the vowels. I can easily prove to you that this will not work but I want to point out that it is not a sin to call Him Yahuwah so I will leave it here.

So in essence if we are correct then the Hebrew would be rendered Yahu-weh and not Yahu-wah. However saying this it is not entirely incorrect to use Yahuwah since the High Priest used to pronounce the names three ways one form of this was this annually on the Day of Atonement in ancient Y'sra'el. One thing to note is that there is a difference between Ya-hu- wah and Ya-ho -wah. The term Ya-ho-wah or Ya-howah when split into its Hebrew counterparts is <u>incorrect</u> based on syntax grammar and meaning. The term Hovah in Hebrew does not have good meanings such as the destroyer, mischievous, perverse, calamity and wickedness hence we cannot attribute these terms to the Creator the reason why those who like to pronounce his name as Yaho-wah are in error still. If you pronounce it as Yahuwah (Yahoowah) there is a marked difference as noted above. In order to check the Strong's reference please look at H1942 for Hovah.

Note also the form Jehovah is incorrect because it too carried the bad root word of Hovah.

So now that we have the correct name nailed down we can edge closer with our investigation to discover the family of Yahushua and find further insights revealed in the New Covenant (NT).

Chapter 2

Yahushua The Son of Tzadok

We will examine the details surrounding why Yahushua needs to fit this genealogy and if he does not then we have a big issue at hand. Note the Eternal One tells us that Yahushua entered the Holy of Holies and paid the price of sin in one payment which lasts forever.

Ibrim (Hebrews) 2:17 So in everyway he had to be made like to his *Y'sra'elite* brothers, that he might be a merciful and faithful **Kohen Ha Gadol** (High Priest) in things pertaining to Elohim, to make reconciliation for the sins of the people.

Note the letter of Hebrews does not say Yahushua is LIKE a Kohen ha Gadol (High Priest) but that **HE IS THE HIGH PRIEST**. Well if He is Kohen ha Gadol then He must also be the Son of Tzadok else He cannot be the Kohen Ha Gadol (High Priest).

A: Son of Aaron

The question then remains is how can Yahushua enter the holy of holies unless He is the High Priest? On top of this the only person who would legally be a High Priest would be the son of Tzadok as specified by King Dawud.

First Dibre ha yamim (1Chron) 29:22 And did eat and drink before **YHWH** on that day with great gladness. And they made Sulahmon the son of Dawud king the second time, and anointed him to **YHWH** to be the chief governor, and Tzadok to be kohen (priest).

Note Y'sra'el had two offices running side by side the office of the King and the office of the Kohen ha Gadol (High Priest).

Unfortunately most believers never think about the legal

implications that the Eternal One himself has stipulated and put in His Torah yet most think Yahushua can somehow waltz into the holy of holies just as kohen MelechTzadik (Priest in the order of MelechTzadik) which He cannot without the right qualifications and birth credentials since the Torah of the Eternal One is clear that only the High Priest can enter of the order of Aaron and later it became the order of Tzadok who was the son of Aaron so legally

Yahushua has to be the Son of Aaron (Levi) for the High Priest and the Son of Dawud to be the King of Y'sra'el in the future.

Let us piece this important evidence to answer the question of Yahushua being of the tribe and lineage of both of the above.

We have strong evidence to believe through the documents discovered in the Dead Sea scrolls that the sect living in Qumran known as the Essenes were not necessarily there at their onset of leaving the Temple and Jerusalem. In fact through the discovery of the Damascus Document we discover that the sect had at first confined itself to Damascus but later may have built a community at Qumran. The Damascus document is dated earlier than the Dead Sea Scrolls and that is when they would have moved to Damascus followed by going to Qumran with a community there.

A man known by the name of Solomon Schechter discovered the Damascus Document in 1896 in Cairo in Egypt and later translated it in 1910. He was correct in pointing out that the title used in the Qumran scrolls and the Damascus Document for their leaders was the Teacher of Righteousness which really is the Son of Tzadok. In English this title passes us without notice but the Hebrew is clear to understand that indeed these people at Qumran were from the line of Tzadok and also Hassids.

How do we connect this with Yahushua?

We know from the Covenant Covenant that Elizabeth was the wife of Zechariah and she was from the House of Levi.

Luke 1:5 There was in the days of Herodes, the king of Yahudah, a certain Kohen (Priest) named Zechar'yah, of the course of Abi'yah: and his wife was of the **daughters of Aharon**, and her name was Elisheba (Elizabeth).

Note Elisheba (Elizabeth) was the **daughter of Aaron** which connects her with the Levite tribe.

So who was John her son or Yochanan the immerser? He was the cousin of Yahushua which clearly links Yahushua with the Levitical tribe. This is our first piece of evidence to connect Yahushua with the line of the sons of Tzadok. Yahushua was not only the son of Tzadok but a Hassidim or the Hebrew word Hasid or Chesed where the term Hassidm comes from for "loving-kindness" or "mercy."

B. Who were the Hassids?

The Essenes were actually the Hassids because the term Essenes was given by people who examined their documents many centuries later after their death which happened in 1948 and onwards but the people at Qumran did not call themselves Essenes as this title was given by the scholars who were examining the documents discovered in the Qumran caves after 1948.

In First Maccabees 2:42 the Hasmoneans were called Assideans, which were mighty men of Y'sra'el.' This connects forward to the Essenes or Hasidim and John the son of Zechariah was from the House of Aaron so likewise Yahushua was also from the House of Aaron but you may wonder how this helps us connect Yahushua. Bear with me as we piece the evidence together. Yahushua was indeed a Hasid the term in Hebrew stands for Loving-Kindness or for mercy.

Although Yahushua was from a very powerful family as you will learn but He distanced himself from wealth and fame and lived like a Hasid.

The person commonly known as James who really was Jacob and was known as the brother of the Master Yahushua described by Rabbi Paul (Gal 1:19) was killed by the High Priest Ananus[1] who was later deposed by King Agrippa.

Note Jacob the brother of the Master or half brother was one of the High Priest's in the Temple. That is correct he was a High Priest in the Temple after believing in Yahushua as the Messiah.

---

[1] Ant. 20, 9:1

Now this may come as a shock to you but this is clear cut evidence of Yahushua being from the House of Tzadok. Basically Judah and Tzadok had mixed so it was very difficult to separate one from the other unless genealogies were mentioned. When the Eternal One described His servant Zechariah it is not just a casual reading on a lazy day that we are told Elizabeth was the <u>daughter of Aaron</u> but this is serious reading connecting Yahushua back to His original family and the line of Tzadok.

Now my question to Christian churches who pervert the way of YHWH by ascribing a new way of salvation which is not even remotely true that if Jacob (James) was a High Priest then do you suppose He gave the sacrifice the year he was High Priest on Yom Kippur (The Day of Atonement) and asked for the forgiveness for the whole people of Y'sra'el or not? We do not read any history of this Jacob (James) kneeling beside a cross and praying for forgiveness. That unfortunately is the habit of the prophets of Ba'al. What about the other seven annual feasts in which the High Priest took part? The High Priest would be present to attend the sacrifices and pray for Y'sra'el and bless them collectively.

Indeed Jacob (James) did do the sacrifice for atonement and present it to YHWH in the holy of holies. He was also the Nasi or leader of the first assembly of believers to form in Y'sra'el. They were not seen as Christians as most historians try to distort the historical picture by calling them Christians. If you pickup most Christian books today they are <u>always</u> called Christians incorrectly or Hebrew Christians but this is deceptive to superimpose upon the truth a cult that really started in the late first century. The adherents of the Christian cult were people like Thebuthis, Marcion and Ignatius.

The original assembly was Hebrew and they believed in Messianic Judaism and were people of colour. There was no Christianity as most believe today. The only Christianity that existed then was an offshoot of the cult of

Serapis whose followers were called Kristianos in Greek. The term Kristianos meant "good men".

These were confused with the Netzarim believers while the ones who formed a Christian sect under the auspices of Marcion that was very popular until the 5th century CE hated anything to do with Torah and you will find the same attitude today in most churches. Marcion was called a heretic but there were others who were doing similar things and calling the keeping of Torah commandments a yoke or punishment given to the Jews such as Justin Martyr in 165 CE.

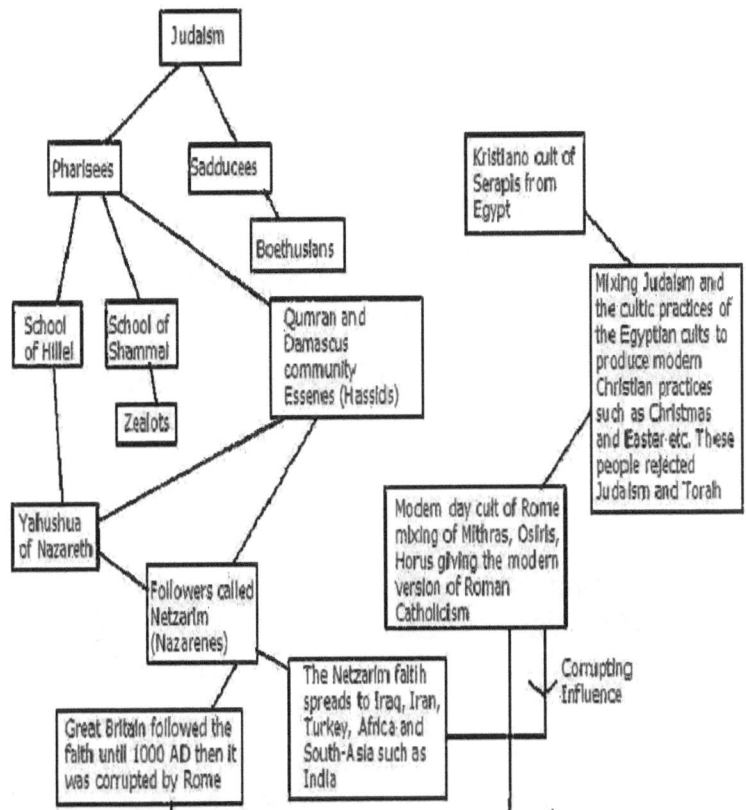

I have created a simplified diagram above to help you see this. Do we have evidence for this in the Covenant Covenant that the disciples of Yahushua were not called Christians? Yes indeed.

Ma'aseh Schilichim (Acts) 24:5 For we have found this man a troublemaker, and a stirrer of trouble among all the Yahudim (Hebrew people) throughout the Roman provinces, and a ringleader of the **sect of the Nazarenes.**

Rabbi Paul was called **RINGLEADER OF THE NETZARIM** and not the ringleader of Christians or as people saw Kristianos back then because this was a different group in fact pagan.

Before I show you the evidence it is important to understand that the true faith was taken to Great Britain, India, Iran, Iraq, Turkey and to other eastern nations in the early part of the first century.

Yosef of Arimathaea, Rabbi Paul, Nicodemus were the people who visited England to teach the true faith in the first century CE while Rabbi Paul also traveled to Rhegium in Italy mentioned in Acts 28:13 spending more than two years in Italy teaching the Netzarim faith as delivered by Yahushua and practiced by the disciples of the Master straight out of the Tanach (Hebrew Bible). He did not carry his <u>own</u> letters quoting from them as many people try to make new doctrines today unwisely from his letters rejecting key principles in the Tanach.

Ma'aseh Schilichim Acts 28:23 And when they had appointed him a day, there came many to him into his lodging; to whom <u>he expounded and testified the kingdom of</u> Elohim, <u>persuading them concerning</u> **Yahushua**, <u>both out of the</u> <u>Torah of Musa (Moses), and out of the prophets, from morning till evening</u>.

What do you think that the Jews in Italy would have been impressed by a book that had not yet been approved by the religious Jews in Y'sra'el? So we see Rabbi Sha'ul using the Tanach to witness to the people in Italy convincing them that the Messiah indeed was Yahushua the one people were hoping would come soon. Rabbi Sha'ul was an Egyptian dark skinned man and not the one branded about in the Churches.

The Tanach (Hebrew Bible) was the scripture for Rabbi Paul but for the Christians today the <u>letters of Rabbi Paul</u> take more precedence and have become Scripture instead of the Tanach which really for them has become abrogated. How ironic! Christians make vacuous claims of loving their Father in heaven while ignoring His commandments: they have actually made Rabbi Paul their father instead and quote him in everything, while what the

Father in heaven has demanded to be done which by for most Christians have become deaf to hear and understand.

How many times have you argued with Christians that the Sabbath is on Saturday, but they are adamant with "no, it's Sunday"? When you present scriptures to show them that they are wrong then they would use the resurrection as an excuse to justify Sunday worship but even the resurrection did not take place on Sunday, instead it occurred on Saturday before the close of Sabbath. See my book the feasts of YHWH the Elohim of Israel for clarification on this and the HTHS Bible which corrects the bad translation of the King James Version.

Then the first scripture they misquote is the letter of Rabbi Paul Colossians 2:16 to say it's no longer necessary for us to obey the Sabbath.

Colossians 2:16 Let no man therefore judge ye in meat, or in drink, or in respect of a set-apart day, or of the Rosh Kodesh (new moon), or of the Sabbath days:

So you can see Rabbi Paul indeed identified with the hope of Y'sra'el, the kingdom of Elohim and the scriptures of Y'sra'el. Did he say my letters are the hope of Y'sra'el?

Rabbi Paul and all the early disciples were part of Judaism, simply another branch with their similar way of worship. They did everything as most Jews did and did not subtract the Tanach as most Christians do today unwisely giving lip service to it. The main difference between the first century believers and all other Jews was that they believed Yahushua to be more than a prophet and not a mere man but the Son of Elohim and the divine Messiah. They saw in Him the fulfillment of Dani'el, Isaiah and Jeremiah plus numerous other prophets while everyone did not agree with all these things hence tensions arose at times.

Yaqub known as James in the Bible was not the only

man who became a High Priest but in fact another family member of Yahushua was Simeon ben Cleopas who also became a High Priest. Yaqub (James) was martyred by the house of Ananus in 62 CE when he was thrown down from the Temple into the Kidron valley.

[4] A Hebrew scholar David Flusser confirms the account;

> A similar clash between the Pharisees and Annas the Younger, probably the brother-in-law of Caiaphas, took place in the year 62 C.E. Annas the Younger "convened the Sanhedrin of judges and brought before them a man named James, the brother of Jesus who was called Christ, and certain others [probably Christians]. He accused them of having transgressed the Torah and delivered them to be stoned"

[4] http://www.jerusalemperspective.com

(Antiq. 20:200-203).

What David Flusser calls 'Christians' the comment inserted in the brackets above note early believers were <u>not</u> called Christians but were called Netzarim or known as the Nazarene followers of Yahushua.

It is reported that Yaqub (James) survived the fall miraculously but then was clubbed to death while on the ground by Ananus's supporters. While he was being beaten Simeon ben Cleopas his brother tried to protect him but none would heed his words. Yaqub (James) was entombed in Abshalom's tomb which you will find at the foot of the Mount of Olives in the Kidron Valley today in Y'sra'el.

Simeon ben Cleopas became the High Priest in the years 63 CE. Now let me tell you a well kept secret that even the Catholic Popes knew but they hid this report in order to deify Miriam. Note I called Simeon ben Cleopas the brother of Yaqub (James).

Hegesippus in Eusebius – "Some of these heretics

accused Symeon, the son of Clopus, of being descended from David and a Christian (note Nazarene), and so he suffered martyrdom at age 120, when Trajan was emperor and Atticus was consular governor." (Eusebius, Ecclesiastical History, 3:31)

So the three brothers Yahushua, Jacob (James) and Cleopas were all of the Dawudian lineage from the parents but were all Levites also since if Jacob (James) became the High Priest as did Cleopas then that can only happen if they were from the house of Tzadok which interestingly places Yahushua in the line of Tzadok firmly in order that He can enter the Holy of Holies in the heavens. Hallelu'yah.

How can Jacob (James) be the brother of Simeon ben Cleopas and at the same time he was alleged to be the brother of Yahushua?

We will find out soon keep reading.

Do you see that we do not hear much further news of the mother of Yahushua after Yahushua's death and resurrection? Most people assume that since Yahushua while being hung on the tree told Miriam his mother "behold your son" (John 19:26-27) about Yochanan the son of Zebedee and said to Yochanan (John) "behold your mother." That this was an order to take his mother and look after her.

However truth be told she was in the custody of Yosef of Arimathaea as her guardian or Gowra and this is why we read in Luke 3:23.

Luke 3:23 And when **Yahushua** himself began, he was about
thirty years of age, being (as was custom) the **son of Yosef**, which was the son of Eli.

Yosef of Arimathaea was the younger brother of Miriam. According to the Jerusalem Talmud Miriam was the daughter of Eli (Chaggigah 77:4). In Hebrew customs and law, a person's ancestry comes through the mother's side and tribal identity from the father.

The exception to this rule is mentioned in Numbers 36:6-7. In Hebrew law there is no difference between adopted and natural born sons. When a child is adopted they become that person's son in this case Yosef's adoption of Yahushua would place Yahushua in the line of Yahudah. Which Yosef? Yosef of Arimathaea!!!!

What do you suppose Yosef of Arimathaea did with Miriam the mother of Yahushua who was a widow since he was always traveling on business to England, Cyprus, India and other nations? He married her to Cleopas under the Levirate rules of marriage and that is how Miriam gave birth to her other sons like Jacob (James), Yosef, Thomas and Yahudah etc which are mentioned in Matt 13:55. This truth has been suppressed by the Catholic Church to glorify Miriam to a sinless status as a co-redemptrix.

We find even Epiphanius the Christian historian noted the difference in his writing about these disciples of the Master. One more observation is that Epiphanius called himself a Christian but he never called the disciples Christian. Now this is further proof that the first century disciples were not called Christians?

Epiphanius; Panarion 29; 4th Century

41

"They [the Nazarenes] have no different ideas, but confess everything exactly as the Law proclaims it and in the Hebrew fashion-- except for their belief in Messiah... but since they are still fettered by the Law -- circumcision, the Sabbath, and the rest-- they are not in accord with Christians."

Now my question, is today's Christianity behaving the way Epiphanius describes the first believers? No. So what happened? Many in Christendom today are behaving as Catholics who perverted the way of salvation and refused to obey the Torah of YHWH as eternal truth. Most Christians today follow after the ways of Rome.

So did the Creator change His words?

We look at this in the next chapter before we move on with Yahushua's family.

Chapter 3

Has YHWH changed the way of Salvation?

I am asking you today the readers and those thousands of ministries that send out newsletters, booklets and tracts each month and spend thousands of dollars each month "Does the Creator change His words?"

I am sure you will all start quoting what you call your scriptures for you the Christians will be the New Testament what it says and you would probably quote to me from the letter of Hebrews, once again Rabbi Paul will be your favourite as I stated earlier. Here is the standard Christian response.

Ibrim (Hebrews) 13:8 Yahushua (Yahushua) The Messiah the same yesterday, and today, and forever.

Is the Messiah everlasting? That is the only way He can be the same.

I then go to the Jews and ask them the same question "Does Elohim change His words or has He changed the way of Salvation?"

The Jews wholeheartedly quote from the Tanach the following:

Malaki 3:6 For I am **YHWH** (YHWH) I change not...

So far I seem to have a unanimous response from both the Christians and the Jews that they both agree that Elohim does not change His mind or His words. Now my second question is to both of them. How do I get saved?

The Christians – Believe in Jesus (note this name does not exist in the first century manuscripts for the bible).

Most Christians do not even know that this is not His Real Hebrew name because we all know names do not translate. My name is Simon and it means "the one who heard from Elohim." When you address me in Africa you do not translate my name and say "the one who heard from Elohim" please come here. Neither do people in Pakistan or

Y'sra'el call me "Go to the one who heard Elohim." My name across all continents stays the same then how much more the divine Messiah Yahushua?

The Jews say– Obey Elohim's voice His Torah and He will through His mercy give you salvation for accepting His provision.

Now back to the Christian camp.

Jesus is the only way…

Rabbi Simon -> But I thought you just said the Creator does not change?

The Christians -> Yes He does not change but He made Jesus our salvation so you must believe in Him only.

Rabbi Simon -> Show me this man with the name of "Jesus" in the pages of the book of Genesis where the Creator clearly and unambiguously states this fact. By the way the name "Jesus" is a name which is only five hundred years old. You have to show that this name is the only way to eternity for Adam, Able, Enoch, Noah, Abraham, Isaac and Jacob. Where do I find this conveyed to the Patriarchs and Matriarchs of Y'sra'el in the book of Genesis or the Torah with this name in it?

Do you see the problem in my question? If the name was invented only five hundred years ago, then how could there be the name "Jesus" in the first century? The name "Jesus" was non-existent in the first century: there was no J, and so this was actually known as Iesus in Latin and Iesous in Greek. While the Jews hated learning the languages of the oppressors such as Greek and Latin.

The historical evidence that we have clearly points to the name being Yahushua in the first century later shortened to its Aramaic form of Yeshua. The proof is

both in India and Pakistan where the name is used as Yesu and Yeshu with a variety of eeshu. These are Aramaic forms by the way and the terms were given to these nations from the Aramaic dialect of one which was arabised at least for Pakistan which largely speaks Urdu as its national language along with several others local languages and dialects. The Urdu
language is a dialect of the Aramaic which has many similar words to the Aramaic/Hebrew. Pakistan received its script from the Persian Empire when they conquered Northern India.

Clearly someone is misrepresenting truth because Adam had not heard that name. Noah did not hear it either. So who should I believe?

The standard parroted Christian responses now start to come back. "No, you have to believe in Jesus or you will go to hell." "All the Patriarchs also believed in Jesus." The Christian dilemma can now be observed: that in order to justify their new way of salvation defined by Rome and not Elohim, suddenly everything in the Tanach is "Jesus" even though the name is never found there in such a way of pronunciation.

They have to read all of the history of Y'sra'el as Christian history. The Muslims do the same thing because they read all the prophets of the Hebrew Bible as Muslim prophets to superimpose Islam upon the bible by saying that Abraham was a Muslim and Musa was a Muslim even though Abraham did not even know what the term *Muslim* meant in his day since it did not exist because Islam did not start as a religion until the 7th century CE in Saudi Arabia.

The irony is that Abraham never visited or lived in Saudi Arabia, he was born in South-Eastern Turkey though many people believe he was born in Iraq. Abraham had

African ancestors and family both in Iraq and Y'sra'el and from Turkey went to live in Y'sra'el followed with some stay in Egypt and then back to Y'sra'el where he eventually died. His mother came from Y'sra'el in Beersheba.

I find that the Christians have created an interesting dilemma for themselves. The Christians now read into all of Hebrew history and everyone turns out to be a <u>Christian</u> according to them. Yahushua is a Christian, Jacob (James) Yahushua's half brother is a Christian, Peter is a Christian but the reality is that none of them were Christians. They were Jews, Peter is really Kefa, James is really Jacob. John is really Yochanan also written as Yochanan. They all practiced Judaism. So just by giving them Western Christian names do you think they become Europan Christian?

If you read modern Christian authors they will write in this way: "Peter the Christian" or "James [sic] the Christian." One has to question their distorted logic calling these people *Christian* who never knew what the term *Christian* meant. The Term Christian is a 21st century terminology applied to the gentile followers of the Messiah yet the majority of the first century followers were Jews. The man Yahushua never followed a religion called Christianity. This was a non event for Him. He lived and died in Judaism and rose within Judaism.

Who are you trying to fool?

Many people who run to prove the word "Christian" exists in the bible lack knowledge of language to language customs and traditions to transfer. The term "Christianos" cited in Acts 11:26 reveals to the people knowledgeable in language to language translations that this term was taken from Latin and not Greek. You would now have to prove that Luke the Levite wrote in Latin and not Greek. It's in the Latin language that we find men's names or similar terms ending in the letters "*iani.*". Note the Greek text called the term "Christian" is Christianos therefore we see the connection with Latin. From this one can prove that the book of Acts was translated from the Hebrew into Latin then later into Greek.

Many cultures have different names for different groups of people i.e. in Pakistani culture Christians are called "***Esahi***" and not the English word "Christian." The same way we can conclude that the designation of calling the disciples "*Christianos*" came from the Romans who spoke Latin and not Greek and incorrectly assumed by many. The Jews at no point called themselves "*Christian.*"

Christians therefore are practicing teachings of such people as Ignatius and not Yahushua. In his letter to the Magnesians he wrote the following:

<u>Magnesians chapter 10</u> Let us not, therefore, be insensible to His kindness. For were He to reward us according to our works, we should cease to be. Therefore, having become His disciples, let us learn to live according to <u>the principles of Christianity</u>. For whosoever is called by any other name besides this, is not of God.

So there you have it that Christianity was begotten by Ignatius of Antioch who was anti-Torah or lawless and telling others to remove themselves from Judaism and her ways of Elohim. My opinion therefore is very clear that Christianity was begotten in opposition to the faith of the disciples which was and remains to be Netzarim Judaism.

Yet the disciples of Yahushua were Yahudim acting and behaving just as Yahudim do, by obeying Judaism obeying the Torah but them such as Jacob (James) and Peter believed in the Messiah as divine and zealously guarded and obeyed the Torah. Do Christians do that?

The Muslims on the other hand make all the Patriarchs Muslim: King Dawud (David) was a Muslim for them and Yahushua was also Muslim according to them. While according to the Christians they were all

Christians. Both camps are equally deceived and continue to parrot the deception yet this is what YHWH said:

Yeshayahu (Isaiah) 43:11 I, even I, am YHWH; and beside me there is no Saviour.

If Yahushua is YHWH revealed in a flesh body then yes it makes sense that He could be the saviour but it does not say that the name Jesus is the Saviour in the book of Isaiah. That is a gross contradiction and even removes what YHWH said in Isaiah 43:11 and changing His words is tantamount to blasphemy and sacrilege.

Rabbi Simon - > Not one shred of evidence is offered from the book of Genesis or any other book of the Tanach to say that this name and I mean the Romanized/Latin/Greek made up name "Jesus" is the only way for Adam, for Enoch and for Noah.

The Christians at this point really struggle to prove anything but continue to cast you down to hell. All these ministries and I mean start from A and end up in Z claim the same thing but the question was asked "Does Elohim change?" And it was answered unanimously with "No" and the text from the Scriptures both in Malachi 3:6 and Hebrews a letter alleged to be of Rabbi Paul verse 13:8 was quoted. The man (Rabbi Paul) who they have made their father actually said this:

Romans 4:3 For what said the scripture? Abraham believed Elohim, and it was counted to him for righteousness.

He did not raise his letters to scripture. Only fools raise the letter above the word of YHWH. This was Rome's guilt to remove the Torah by using Rabbi Paul as their head and so does today the rest of Christendom. Shame on them for twisting scripture in such a way to make a Rabbi's letter about the LAW of Elohim.

So what was Elohim's method of salvation if He does not change? The Yahudim agree with me that it was "**Torah His voice** and mercy granted by the Holy One" upon accepting His Covenants in the Torah, while the Christians are adamant that no it was "Jesus."

Here is what Elohim said to remind you again.

Hoshea 13:4 Yet I am **YHWH** your Elohim from the land of Mitzrayim (Egypt), and you shall know no Elohim but me: for <u>there is no saviour beside me</u>.

The point of doing this exercise was not to put the Christians down but for us to see how well they know the scriptures of the Yahudim and two to teach them the real way of salvation and to correct the bad teachings they have received.

One must ask the question that if the Christians cannot answer one question coherently then why are thousands of Christian ministries producing millions of newsletters, books and pamphlets at the expense of millions of dollars and I am going to be honest with you that most of that is total garbage because it is contradictory to the bible. If you are a Christian then You will be offended by my statement, I hope so because it offends me to see YHWH's words twisted and contradicted by false teachings that many of you have accepted as the written testimony of YHWH and it is not but which came out of Rome and not Jerusalem. If you look in the annals of history England followed the commandments in the Torah up to 1000 CE. Norfolk was the last place to fall with the Roman doctrine while Wales and Scotland even to this day hold to some teachings strictly that have been rooted in the Torah.

Breeding pigs in some areas of Scotland was banned by believers until the 19th century because they were seen as unclean beasts as stated in the book of Leviticus yet today many in Christendom happily munch on pork chops then wonder why they have high blood pressure and heart disease.

So in order to investigate further how were the Patriarchs saved?

Let's hear it from Elohim himself to Adam... Master of heaven and earth let Him speak!

Beresheeth (Genesis) 2:16 And YHWH Elohim commanded the man, saying, of every etz (tree) of the garden, that you may freely eat: **17** But of the etz (tree) of the knowledge of good and evil, you shall not eat of it...

Note Elohim strictly commanded. That means He gave an order not to do otherwise. He did not say its optional as most of you have taken it do it if you like or wait for Rabbi Paul to write his letters then you can interpret them wrong and do as you like. This is what I term stupid Christianity which does not know head or tail of scripture and interpretation.

Elohim said to obey His voice note this was the first instance of Oral Torah by the way which many Christians reject from the Master of heaven and earth by saying I do not accept oral Torah.

You can verify this by going and asking a Christian do you accept the oral Torah of the Yahudim they will say NO.

Since Adam did not receive a book in his hand to reference while Christendom rejects oral Torah but they are quite happy to keep pagan customs of Rome which are Rome's oral torah. Now you see why I said stupid Christianity! How can you tell the Muslims we reject your Hadith and Qur'an while you accept the teachings of Rome?

The actual bible never said to reject Torah yet most of Christendom has been interpreting it for 1600 years to reject Torah. Let us get the witness of Chava (Eve) Adam's wife just to be sure I am not making a mistake.

Beresheeth (Genesis) 3:2 And the woman said unto the serpent, We may eat of the fruit of the etzim (trees) of the garden: **3** But of the fruit of the etz (tree) which is in the middle of the garden, **Elohim has said**, You shall not eat of it, neither shall you touch it, lest you die.

The clear cut answer for Adam' salvation, **obey my voice** (Torah of YHWH) and Chava backs it up to say "Elohim has said." She did not say I have the book of Genesis Chapter three verse two so let me go and double check the reference because it says so and so…or let me quote you John 14:6. Or that Rabbi Paul said that the law is finished blah, blah, blah, typical Christianity.

Let Elohim speak for Noah

Beresheeth (Genesis) 8:8-9 But Noach found favour in the eyes of **YHWH**. **9** This is the genealogy of Noach: Noach **was a righteous man** perfect in his generations, **Noach walked with Elohim**.

Noah walked with Elohim which means He guarded and followed the commandments of YHWH given by voice which we read about in the first five books of Moses called the Torah. Did Adam have a book and pass it to Noah? No, it was oral Torah yet most of the Christians reject oral Torah. True Oral Torah later became the written Torah.

If we read the verse in Genesis 8:9, no "Jesus" and no "cross" yet Noah was completely saved and he was perfect which really is another way to say that he was blameless of any guilt and it says he walked with Elohim which is to keep and do Elohim's halacha (commandments) the Torah which was communicated with Noah orally and he knew the commandments what was right and what was not but most of all He had redemption for that all he had to do is to listen to Elohim. Noah's son Shem had a Yeshivah (A house of learning) and taught there. What do you suppose he taught? Christianity or Torah? In fact he received Torah instructions from his forefathers and from direct revelation of the holy One of Y'sra'el. (Enoch has been purported to have written many books many now lost but we have the book of Enoch today.)

Let Elohim speak for Abraham

> **Beresheeth (Genesis) 26:5** because Abraham obeyed **My voice and guarded My ordinance, My commandments, My statutes**, and **My Torot**.

Abraham **obeyed Elohim's voice** His Torah this means he kept the Sabbath and the feasts also which many today in Christendom reject since they walk after Rome's created religion and not the first century faith of the Messiah and His disciples. YHWH said Abraham kept two Torah's the oral Torah and the written Torah. The Hebrew word Torot is in the plural significant to show these people unlike today's Christians did not reject the two Torahs.

Again perfect example of "no cross of Rome" yet Abraham was **completely saved and redeemed**. There is no question about it? You probably have been fed the garbage that the Torah cannot save then how is it that Abraham through the same vehicle (Torah) was able to get from A to B? A is earth and B equals "redeemed" for heavenly things to go to the Kingdom of Elohim. This proves the Torah has the provisions for those who want to be saved by accepting the Covenants of YHWH which give you full redemption absolutely guaranteed.

If the Torah had no salvation then how can Yahushua the physical Torah (written Torah become alive) save us? This contradicts the very theology Christianity espouses.

I wanted to show you the contradiction in Christian theology. The only way the physical Torah Yahushua can save us if the Torah **had provisions in it for salvation** which I have proved to you that it does have.

The next question is were the people saved from keeping a list of do, and don'ts, or was it simply the fact that they were saved by simply saying "Yes" to Elohim's righteousness? The Torah makes it very clear that these men and women were the "Yes" men/women of Elohim. It does not say that they never got anything wrong but it does confirm their positive responses towards Elohim and even shows their sins where they got things wrong. While Christendom tries but fails to apply a false imperative on them to say they have to be perfect and makes a false claim that they are not perfect. I even discussed this with one sister and showed her people were perfect and shown to be so and once again we need not spread the lies of the church. She said to me only one man was perfect and I asked her how many perfect men do you want to see in the Bible I can show you numerous men and women and I quoted an example of two people which was enough to prove my point.

Beresheeth (Genesis) 6:9 This is the genealogy of Noach: Noach was a righteous man perfect in his generations^5, Noach walked with Elohim.

First Kings 15:14 But the high places were not removed: nevertheless Asa's heart was perfect with **YHWH** all his days.

So Christendom has been clearly misrepresenting Elohim and failed to understand Him by promoting a man-made religion completely different from the stated one in scripture.

So how does Yahushua fit in with the revelation of the Elohim of ancient Y'sra'el?

If we look at the gospel record of John the son of Zebedee he stated the following.

Yochanan (John) 17:1 These words spoke **Yahushua**, and lifted up his eyes to the shamayim (heavens), and said, Abbah, the hour has come; glorify your Son, that your Son may also glorify you:

You only glorify or exalt someone if that someone is higher than you or higher in stature or authority. Yahushua's authority was all derived from the Father and not from any particular church or denomination. Christianity has sold you counterfeit goods.

Yochanan (John) 17:2 As you have given him power over all flesh...

So our Abbah YHWH gave Him power over all flesh so that indicates our Father is higher in authority in order to grant that power to Yahushua. Yahushua cannot override His Father, although Christians think they have the authority to downgrade the

---

[5] This word 'walked', means obeyed YHWH's Torah.

Father's commandments by misrepresenting Rabbi Paul's writings (of which they have no real understanding).

Yochanan (John) 17:2 that he should **give eternal life to as many** as you have given him.

So Yahushua does have the authority to grant eternal life because He is not an ordinary human being but in the ancient past he was veiled but since two thousand years ago He has been revealed. The granting of eternal life is by the same method as was in the ancient past by **believing and hearing His voice which is the Torah of YHWH** and accepting the Covenants which are two way agreements that effect people and their lives to receive salvation. Yahushua did not contradict this.

Ibrim (Hebrews) 3:2 He has in these last days **spoken to us by his Son,** whom he has appointed heir of all things, by whom also he made the worlds;

He has in these last days SPOKEN (His Torah) to us through Yahushua.

The world was made by the Torah and the Torah here is the living Torah the Son Yahushua also quoted in John 1:14 when the "word was made flesh that existed with the Abbah in heaven."
This means that the Son who was brought out of Abbah YHWH has been manifested; but contrary to Christian theology, to have eternal life we must still continue to obey the voice of Elohim which is His Torah, since the Son CONFIRMS the same thing that Abbah YHWH does, not set a new way of salvation. Believing in a piece of wood no more saves you than putting your foot in a shark's mouth and hoping that it won't bite your foot and eat it. What are the chances of that? Go and ask all the people who have lost limbs both in American and Australian beaches. And the foolish people who get bitten by snakes who misrepresent the text in Mark chapter 16:18 have all died because there graves are with us. For your information Mark 16:18 is a later insertion and does not exist in the original copy of Mark's gospel.

John 17:5 And now, O Abbah, glorify me at your side with the glory which I had with you before the world was.

Clearly before the world began all we know is that Elohim was living in eternity we do not know who else was there before creation. Yahushua now tells us that He was there having fellowship with Abbah YHWH. This indicates a mystery: that if Yahushua was there, then he is also divine, meaning Elohim. So in this we find what many still refuse to believe: Akhad-- the Compound Unity of Elohim. In the wider world many do not yet understand this truth because we were never blatantly told such things, but for those of us who want to understand the plurality of YHWH, in Beresheeth (Genesis) we are given pictures, themes or hints.

How can YHWH be love if there is no one to love? So Yahushua was there, the visible manifestation of YHWH.

Yahushua **did not** bring a new way of salvation but emphasized the same way but Christians are too blind to see it because they would rather follow Roman Catholicism and their pagan Temple. While their money grabbing Pastors too often both in Nigeria, Pakistan, England and the UK chase after mammon and not truth.

If you ever go and visit Nigeria and see the big houses the Bishops live in with their three or four status cars. Ah that must be a blessing of Elohim right? Wrong. That is the greed that these people have shown by building up wealth instead of distributing it to their needful neighbours. In the same country of Nigeria where such Bishops live there are rural people who do not have clean water to drink and some starve with lack of food but the Bishops are happy with their fat stomachs which one day will not lack the fire of She'ol. Does Christendom not teach you to sacrifice your wealth for those more needful? I guess not although claims are made that it does but in reality I have not seen it on the ground. When I looked at Nigeria I knew Christianity was an utter failure and had no light but only reflected the light of Messianic Judaism from a distance.

And the same types of Bishops in Pakistan live in opulent homes with four wheel drive jeeps parked in their driveways and I guess their version of Christianity also does not condemn them but here is what Jacob the half brother of the Master said who was the first Nasi (leader) of the first assembly of Netzarim.

Jacob (James) 1:27 Pure religion and undefiled before Elohim and the Abbah is this, <u>to visit the orphans and widows in their affliction</u>, and <u>to guard oneself unspotted from the world</u>.

When was the last time you visited the widows and orphans to serve Elohim? The Netzarim are told to do this regularly and many do involve themselves in such work while the Christians in India have made a business out of the poor by setting up one home as an orphanage, collecting some homeless children from the street and then writing to all the big ministries abroad saying we are poor running orphanages please help us and help our children. This is big business in many parts of India and even Africa. There is no shame in these people how they use children to gather mammon for their unrighteous deeds.

Yeshayahu (Isaiah) 66:24 And they shall go forth, and look upon the <u>carcasses of the men that have transgressed against me:</u> for their worm shall not die, neither shall their fire be quenched; and they shall be an abhorring to all flesh.

Luke 16:23-25 And in She'ol he lift up his eyes, being in torments, and saw Abraham afar off, and Eli'ezer (Lazarus), in his bosom. **24** And he cried and said, abbah Abraham, have mercy on me, and send Eli'ezer (Lazarus), that he may dip the tip of his finger in mayim (water), and cool my tongue; for I am tormented in this flame. **25** But Abraham said, Son, remember that you in your lifetime received your good things, and likewise Eli'ezer (Lazarus), evil things: but now he is comforted, and you are tormented.

Who do you think are such people? Those I just described above, their end will be worse than their beginning and the wooden cross will not save them on that day that have rejected YHWH and chosen the things of this world to entertain themselves...

Jacob in his letter was doing a sum up of Torah like the prophets. One would only help the orphans and widows if they had mercy in their heart so he is really saying to be merciful is to keep Torah. We know some people are running orphanages to just make money this happens in the east especially a noted country is India as mentioned above but Some African Christians are also guilty of doing the same where many people only start orphanages to usurp money from the western congregations, be warned of such people and their practices. They who use children to do this will beseverely judged and put out of the kingdom and reserved for judgement. Ask yourself is it worth it to lose your eternity?

Christendom loves to pick one or two isolated scriptures and make new doctrines out of them. In order to make a doctrine it must exist in the Tanach and there has to be at least two to three witnesses in Scripture to justify any truth.

With this in mind let us examine John 14:6 which the Christians love to take out of Context.

Yochanan (John) 14:6 Yahushua (Yahushua) said to him, **am the way**, **the truth**, and **the life**: **no man** comes to the Abbah, but through me.

- The Way
- The Truth
- The Life
- Man – An idiomatic expression for gentiles or the lost sheep of the house of Y'sra'el.

The three words, the way, the truth and the life are idiomatic expression from the Torah. Yahushua also claimed to be the living Torah and that indeed He is, but will you believe Him to obey the Torah or continue to reject it out of ignorance?

So how is the world saved in Genesis? By being obedient to Elohim's voice (His Torah) . How is the world saved now? By being obedient to Elohim's voice meaning the Torah. The Torah is therefore <u>life</u> and not just a set of do and don'ts. **It represents life.** Yahushua confirms this truth in John 14:6 when He makes Himself to be the personification of that Torah. Let us examine these much abused four terms.

The Way

This term in the verse means living Torah pointing back to the written Torah in Gen 24:40, Psalm 1:6, 2:12 and Psalm 18:13. This shows Yahushua was declaring Himself to be the middle-pillar and the way to enter the kingdom.

The Truth

Idiomatic for Torah found in Psalm 119:142 and Psalm 40:10 among many references.

The Life

This term is also a reference to Torah keeping directly from Deut 30:19, Deut 32:47 and Proverbs 6:23.

The term "Man" or "Adam."

The term 'man' here is incorrectly applied to every man, woman and child in the whole world but this is not how the first century Hebrew people including the Messiah saw this statement. This is a loaded statement.

Whenever we apply scripture we need to be careful not to apply it incorrectly as many have erred over this one. We need to understand the terms because behind these terms are hidden expressions which many today do not realize nor understand because they are not living in the ancient rabbinical culture.

First of all: the term 'man' is a first century midrash term that the Rabbis understood <u>only</u> applicable to <u>goyim</u> (gentiles), therefore by definition this applied to the Ten northern tribes of Y'sra'el, who for all practical purposes had become many gentile nations.

The Hebrew Rabbis knew this fact very well and had communicated this truth orally until it was penned in the Gemara (Commentary on the Mishnah). So when the Messiah uses this term he is not saying that the Yahudim need to come through me because the fact of the matter is that they already have Him since they have the written Torah, which is the Messiah but they did not fully understand that truth, because He is the inner garment of the Torah being the Messiah while the Yahudim focused on the outer garment being the commandments.

Torah is the Messiah so if you have the written Torah and believe (believe means to obey) in it then by definition you have the inward Torah being the Messiah. This truth is not always evident and many today still do not understand this. Note the preceding three references in John 14:6 to 'the Way, the Truth and the Life' are all Torah references out of the Torah and for the House of Jacob, which the Yahudim have but they are all personified in the living Messiah.

The Yahudim are not meant to understand this truth yet because it is hidden for deliberate reasons to bring in the multitude of goyim (gentiles) from the nations. So by definition the Yahudim are saved through the same Messiah (one door) but He is not yet revealing this truth just as Yosef fed his brothers in Egypt and gave them the rich abundance of Egypt for his family to take home but did not reveal the truth to them. He made the truth known to them **<u>at the end</u>**.

This likewise is the same ancient pattern applied here.

However the Messiah himself tells us that Yahudah the elder brother is with Abbah YHWH in Luke 15:31.

Luke 15:31 And he said to him, Son, you are always with me, and all that I have is yours.

So those of you who say Judah is not saved seem to know more than Elohim? Be afraid and repent before He puts His wrath upon you and consume you in a moment.

Similarly, when we fail to understand terms as many out there do, we end up misapplying them to Yahudah but Yahudah has been placed as the lawgiver so why would YHWH make him (Judah) the lawgiver (Gen 49:10, Ps 60:7) but then subsequently be happy to send His appointed judges to the lake of fire? Does that make sense? Of course it does not as it is misapplied by many and that is only if you want to believe a two line gospel misapplied to Yahudah. The gospel is Torah and the Yahudim already have it. Yahudah is not meant to be evangelized. This is the veiled truth which is not evident to many. If we examine why the Catholics and Christians failed to bring many Yahudim into their church system for the last two thousand years of history bears this out. The divine providence of Elohim does not allow this to happen but I doubt many Catholics or Christians understand these reasons.

Judah has been placed to remain a <u>distinct</u> separate group as they were going to return and re-establish the land of Y'sra'el with Torah so the present establishment cannot be confused with a Torah government as one such does not exist yet. This is already given in the prophecies of Jeremiah. Do you think the Catholics were assigned to do this? Or were the Christians assigned to do this? The answer that YHWH gave for the question above was NO, clearly recorded in Psalm 78:67-68, where YHWH said He has chosen Judah but rejected Yosef, who personified the returning tribes as Christians untaught in Torah who will have to relearn everything.

Tehillim (Psalm) 78:67-68 Moreover **he refused the tabernacle of Yosef** and chose not the tribe of Ephraim **(Christendom): 68** But chose the tribe of Yahudah, the Mount Tsiyon which he loved.

This is why Yahushua returns only when Judah calls out in a national crisis mentioned in Matthew 23:39. He does not return as wrongly taught by or through worldwide evangelism.

The Messiah tells us that in Matthew 25 He judges goyim (gentiles nations) on account of 'these my brethren' (Judah) for being persecuted or killed in the nations for just being Hebrew but nevertheless they were and are judges appointed by Abbah YHWH.

How do we understand this fact of Judah being Judges? Think of it like this: if there was a policeman and he stops you for a crime but you beat that police man up yet he was installed by the state to control crime so how will the state rulers then react to this lawman being beaten up? Would they pat you on the back and say well done good citizen you did the right thing by beating that police man and committing a state. Or would they take a very harsh approach and instantly put you in prison and even throw away the key so others do not do the same?

Yahushua as the King takes this very harsh approach and is going to be throwing people in the lake of fire for this crime, read all of Matthew 25 and see our footnoted references in the HTHS Hebraic Study Bible on these verses. Also see this footnote in First John 4:15.
Yochanan (John) 17:6 I have made known your name to the men whom you gave me out of the world: they were yours, and you gave them to me; and **they have guarded your word**.

Note Yahushua confirms that all the disciples He has made are guarding YHWH's Torah. He did not say they are doing Hail Mary's a hundred times a day or praying to the saints or even venerating in front of a cross. Such types of idolatry should be avoided.

Does Yahushua put the pagan cross above His Father's voice? No. Does He say they are guarded because they looked at me being hung and dying? No. Does he say that they are saved because you raised me? No. He says they are His because **THEY GUARDED THE "WORD." The "WORD" is an idiomatic expression for Torah of Moses.**

Note the term 'the word' means Elohim's voice or the Father's voice. This is the Torah of YHWH or Moses' Torah. So this is clear cut proof that **the Yahudim are correct in that salvation is only through believing and putting your trust in Elohim's voice**. Granted that Yahushua is not seen by many Yahudim as divine but that mystery is not yet revealed to them see the chapter in this book "Is Yahushua the Messiah ."

This means either Christendom has been misrepresenting the truth for 2000 years or Elohim cannot be trusted. People were always only saved by keeping His voice and trusting His voice.

They were not looking up to any cross because the cross has no life in it, but the life is in the One who hung there and has the Father's authority. Wood cannot save anyone. Life is in the Son who hung upon the TREE because the Son carries the same Torah **Life** that He gives to others. Are you willing to listen to the Son who testified of His Father or will you go bow before a cross and a statue of the Roman 'Jesus" attached to it? This is both blasphemy and idolatry.

Debarim (Deuteronomy) 30:6 And **YHWH** your Elohim will circumcise your heart and the heart of your descendants, to love **YHWH** your Elohim with all your heart, and with all your soul, that You may live.

It is YHWH who gives the **COVENANT BIRTH** with what we term born again or born from above. It is not a new modern term but a very ancient term. While Christians today make it sound like a new buzz word, it is not new at all. When you walk with YHWH, you must come to Him with a repentant heart and He will circumcise it and give you the new birth. That happens via the Keter (crown), which is Yahushua the King, passing through the Middle-Pillar the Son Yahushua to His feet through Yesod (New Birth) to the Malchut, reaching into the (Kingdom) through the Holy Spirit. This is also what the Covenant Covenant terms, the narrow gate (Matthew 7:14). This is the path even Balaam's donkey saw where the Malakh YHWH was standing on the narrow path (Numbers 22:24), the middle path, not to the right or to the left.

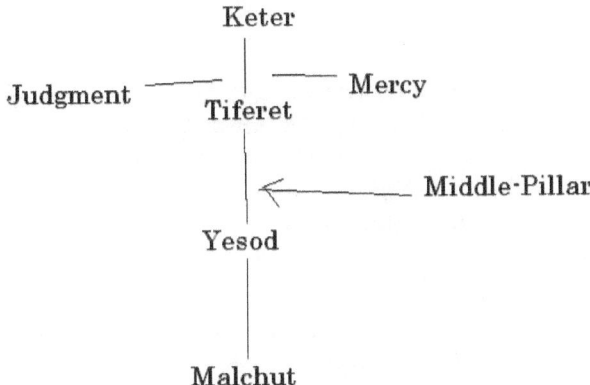

For a fuller explanation of the tree get the book Hebrew Wisdom
– Kabbalah by Rabbi Simon Altaf to be released in 2011.

One more thing, many in Y'sra'el in the future will accept Yahushua who is the majesty of YHWH to receive the new birth and in fact this will prove itself when it happens in the future. This is something very few people understand, it is not that they have to bow before a man but accept YHWH's authority. When the thief hung alongside Yahushua on the tree (Luke 23:40- 43), he did not have to grovel for forgiveness but only had to have the fear of Elohim and believed in what Yahushua could do by accepting His authority.

Luke 23:40-43 But the other answering rebuked him, saying, Do you not fear Elohim, seeing you are in the same condemnation? **41** And we indeed justly; for we receive the due reward of our deeds: but this man has done nothing wrong. And he said **Yahushua**, remember me when you come
into your kingdom. **43** And **Yahushua** said to him, truly I say to you, Today you will be with me in paradise.

That thief on the tree has shown more faith in believing Yahushua than I have seen in most people who are living today.

Paradise is down below and not up there in the skies, it still exists there and has not been taken anywhere please see our comments in Ezekiel 37 in the HTHS Complete Bible Edition. Yahushua granted mercy to the criminal without a repentance formula and without grovelling and reciting some church derived four spiritual laws or creed. Salvation is granted to the sons of Abraham, who come to the knowledge of the person of Yahushua because of the promise of the Covenant made in Deuteronomy 30:6 based on mercy and submission of the person to YHWH. When you submit to YHWH that automatically means turning around and repenting. It's not a four step process as Christendom touts presenting the four spiritual laws they have nothing to do with it. It's a one step process in which you accept the whole of the Torah with all of its covenants and take the yoke of heaven upon yourself and then sit under teachers/Rabbis or if you have the time and resources. to study by yourself to allow the Holy One to teach you His ways. In all cases unless you have help from heaven you will need teachers.

This is all part of the Covenant relationship of the Covenant Covenant revealed in the Brit Chadasha (New

Testament/New Covenant). The Covenant Covenant is simply Torah Covenant with a new attitude of the heart to accept what Elohim desires from us.

Note what Yahushua had said about the men "they are yours." These men could only belong to Elohim if they obeyed His voice His Torah and it was not a matter of getting the Ten Commandments
absolutely right but at least being obedient to them and saying yes I will do them. They were also 'Yes" men.

Yochanan (John) 17:15 I pray not that you should take them out of the world, but that you should guard them from evil.

Yahushua does not pray to the Abbah for a pre-tribulation rapture yet most Christians are stuck to this false doctrine. Yahushua simply **says to the Father to guard them which means to protect them from trouble.**

The only way one can be guarded is by being a "yes" man to Elohim and that means you have accepted the Covenant which ties everything including your salvation. To be safe, secure and prosper therefore it is absolutely essential to be Torah obedient.

Note the Torah contains many Covenants so it's a testimony of accepting the provisions of the Covenant. If a Covenant such as Abrahamic one requires you to circumcise if you are a male then you should be a "yes" man and if you are a "no" man then you have no blessings and no kingdom because you have rejected Elohim's voice as this Covenant also falls under His voice and this is the state of most of Christendom today because they have rejected the Father and **whoever rejects the Father also rejects the Son**. Such people will reap their own condemnation and it is by one's own mouth that one condemns self but for most of you it's yet time to change this status if you are in such a situation.

First John 2:29 If you know that he is righteous, you know that every one that does righteousness is born of him.

Note to be **righteous** is a term for being obedient to the Torah, in order to allow YHWH to clothe you one must be obedient to **HIS VOICE** see my comments above about Noah and Abraham therefore the method of salvation has not changed and is still to believe in Elohim's voice or His Torah. In order to do righteousness you have to be obedient to His or the Abbah's voice. If you are obedient to the Son's voice who is the living expression of the Abbah then for Torah which stands for "life" you must be a "yes" man or "yes" woman.

Even Yahushua confirmed this to the rich man yet many out there deny this and live in wilful disobedience.

Matthew 19:16-19 And, behold, one came and said to him, Rabbi, what Good mitzvoth (deeds) shall I do, that I may have eternal life? **17** And he said to him, Why ask me concerning the good? There is indeed one good, if you want to enter into Life, Guard and Do the commandments. **18** He said to him which ones? **Yahushua** said, you shall do no murder,
You shall not commit adultery, You shall not steal, You shall not bear false witness, **19** Honour your abbah and your eema (mother): and, You shall love your neighbour as yourself.

Now do you want to believe in your Pastor who probably knows nothing about the ancient Hebrew culture and Yahushua's words or do you want to believe Yahushua sent by the Father? Who has more authority?

If you reject the Torah as many in Christendom have and exalt the cross more than the voice of Elohim then you are veering towards destruction and Elohim will reject you for rejecting His voice.

Tehillim (Psalms) 52:3 -5 You love evil more than good;

and lying rather than to speak righteousness. Selah. **4** You love all devouring words, O you deceitful tongue. **5** El shall likewise destroy you forever, he shall take you away, and pluck you out of your dwelling place, and root you out of the land of the living. Selah.

The term "**Good**" is used here for Torah. If you love Evil more which is the term for any evil deed that means rejection of the Torah then you are heading towards destruction.

Yochanan (John) 3:16 For Elohim so loved the world, that he gave his only unique Son, **that whoever believes in him** should not be destroyed, but have everlasting life.

The Greek word Strong's G622 ap-ol'-loo -mee has a meaning of 'destruction' such as annihilation of the soul and not eternal conscious punishment. See HTHS Bible footnote Matthew 10:28 for further reading into this. This perfectly ties in with Psalm 52:3-5 above for those who love evil and reject Torah. The term "believes" is not used in an airy fairy way as Christians apply it but means to put Trust in the Torah that YHWH has sent. Yahushua is the personification of the inwards Torah which is in effect to believe in the Father. This applies to all gentiles for whom Yahushua came.

The death of Yahushua the Messiah is only one step to bringing the lost sheep of the House of Y'sra'el (Ten tribes) back home but it is not the means to an end but simply something in the scheme of things that have taken place according to the Covenant where Yahushua became the Lamb of Abbah YHWH. The death of Yahushua came as a result of the requirement of the Covenant and not vice versa that is because the House of Y'sra'el the ten tribes alone had broken Torah and did away with it going into idolatry.

The cross is not first but the Covenant is first while Christendom has and is still committing idolatry by putting the cart in front of the horse. We do not view the writings of Rabbi Paul to interpret the Torah but we look at the Torah to understand what Rabbi Paul was writing who was a Torah obedient Yahudee.

Christendom has committed grievous idolatry by raising Rabbi Paul above the Father in heaven and using him a mere man a mortal to annul and abrogate YHWH's holy words. All those that do this stand in for the great judgment to come.

Chapter 4

Who are all the Miriam's?

Yochanan (John) 19:25-27 Now there stood by the execution stake of **Yahushua** his mother, and his mother's sister, Miriam the wife of Qlopha, and Miriam of Magdala. **26** When **Yahushua** therefore saw his mother, and the disciple standing
by, whom he loved, he said to his mother, Woman, behold your son! **27** Then said he to the disciple, Behold your mother! And from that hour that disciple took her to his own home.

Most of you count and think there are four Miriam's in this text.

Some of you might see it as follows below;

1. His mother (one)
2. His mother's sister (two)
3. Miriam wife of Qlopha (three)
4. Miriam Magdala (four)

Here it appears we have four Miriam's. Let us look at another passage in the gospel of Matthew to see what he tells us.

Mattityahu (Matthew) 27:55-56 And many women were there beholding afar off, which followed **Yahushua** from Galil,
serving him: **56** Among which was Miriam of Magdala, and Miriam the mother of Yaqub and Yosef, and the mother of Zabdi's children.

Matthew lists the following:

1. Miriam Magdala

2. Miriam the mother of Jacob (James) and Yosef
3. An Unknown woman the mother of Zabdi's children

Mark tells us the following:

Mark 15:40-41 There were also women looking on afar off: among whom was Miriam of Magdala, and Miriam the mother of Yaqub the less and of Yosef, and Salome; **41** Who also, when he was in Galil, followed him, and served him; and many other women which came up with him to Yerushalim.

Note Mark names two Miriam's as well as Salome.

1. Miriam the mother of Jacob (James), Yosef and Salome.
2. Miriam Magdala

Yochanan (John) 19:25-27 Now there stood by the execution stake of **Yahushua** his mother, and his mother's sister,

Who is Salome? She is the wife of Zebedee and the mother of John the son of Zebedee and Jacob (James Junior). She is also from the line of Levi and it is she who is mentioned in John 19:25 as the sister of Miriam the mother of Yahushua. She is a cousin to Miriam the virgin.

Now we seek to answer the question whether John lists four Miriam's or is this a mistake in reading the text while both Matthew and Mark list only two names of such women.

The gospel splits as follows. Here it is one Miriam and another woman mentioned as sister.

The second portion of John

Miriam the wife of Qlopha, and Miriam Magdala.

Miriam the wife of Cleopas (Qlopha) is the same

Miriam who is the mother of Yahushua and the second Miriam is Magdala. There is a sister mentioned here so who is this sister? Jacob the father of Yosef did have another daughter whose name was Miriam and she was the sister to Miriam the virgin in a cousin/sister relationship.

The rest of the text is only to emphasize the same point and reveal the different relationships.

The three Miriam's mentioned in the above scripture are then as follows.
1. Miriam the mother of Yahushua.
2. Miriam Magdala.
3. The daughter of Jacob also called Miriam.

The forefather was Eli'ezer whose son Matthan fathered these sons:

Fig1

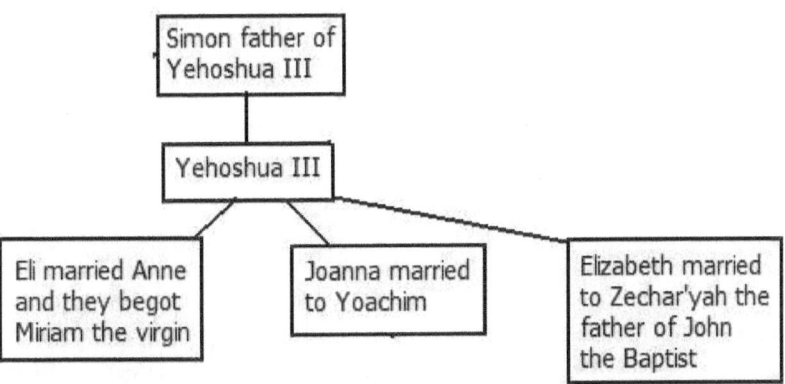

Yahushua III a relative of Yahushua became the High Priest in 36 BC and just one year before he became the High Priest the Great Sanhedrin had decided to include the children of Abiyah and Rhesa to be High Priests and rightful heirs of Y'sra'el as Kings on the throne. Previously these two lines were not included due to various disputed marriages in the lines but here then the Sanhedrin resolved these disputes. The Abiyan line came from

Zerubbabel's first wife Amytis a Babylonian princess and the Rhesan line came from Zerubbabel's second wife from Persia the sister of King Cyrus the son of Esther.

The kingly/priestly lines were having major problems with lack of sons and these kingly/priestly families having only daughters causing great issues for concern of who will succeed the throne. The kingly lines were becoming virtually extinct in which the purposes of YHWH were to narrow down the kingship to a few families only. Yahushua III was the father to three daughters Anne, Elizabeth the mother of Zechariah and Hannah. These would now be royal princesses after the decree of the Great Sanhedrin and their children would then be entitled to the throne or priesthood. Therefore Miriam the virgin was a princess of a royal line and so was her husband.

Yoachim married Hannah and begot Elizabeth which married Zechariah begetting John the immerser popularly known in the west as John the Baptist.

Next we document Mathan's children for you to understand who they were. Yahushua's family was one big family connected both to Jerusalem in the south and to the Galilee in the North where most of the resistance took place and many Yahudim were murdered by the Herodians because they were threatened that someone will come up and take back the throne.

The ruler classes basically lived in the North/South axis as kings had lived with two wives one controlling the southern territories and one controlling the northern territories. This pattern was the same for even Abraham with one wife in the North (Sarah) and the other wife Keturah in the South axis. See the HTHS Complete Bible for further information on this pattern for ruling chiefs. This is the pattern that Matthan had with his three wives too.

Nathani'el in the gospel account of John said "can anything good come out of Nazareth. This is because this area was the hotbed of political activity: there were a lot of radical zealots trying to overthrow the illegal Roman government which was occupying Y'sra'el. Many righteous people did not feel it was right to go and remove the government forcefully such as Nathani'el hence why his comments. They felt this was part of the divine punishment upon the nation and that in due time the Messiah would remove the Yoke and it would not be removed by personal zealot force. We can see Yahushua also likewise refused to join such zealot ideas.

This area was the hotbed of political activity and with various people trying to overthrow the illegal government in place in Y'sra'el there were a lot of radical zealots trying to overthrow the Roman government. This area was considered a danger zone by the Edomite rulers in the south.

Judah the Galilean was a well known name there in the North who was the son of Matthan and also related to Yahushua.

Yochanan (John) 1:45 -46 Philip finds Nethani'el, and said to him, We have found him, of whom Musa (Moses) in the Torah, and the prophets, did write, **Yahushua** of Netzer'eth, the son of Yosef. **46** And Nethani'el said to him, Can there any Good thing come out of Netzer'eth? Philip said to him, Come and see.

Phillip was not referring to Yahushua's step-father Yosef, the husband of Miriam; but many in Judaism at that time had a belief that the coming of the Messiah would be as the suffering servant Yosef (Prefiguring Yosef in Egypt as a slave) if the nation was unrighteous, and as the reigning king Dawud if the nation was righteous.

This is how Nathani'el references the prophecy of Zechariah 9. And he calls him Yahushua the son of Yosef (The son of Jacob in Genesis) the suffering servant Messiah ben Yosef (Messiah the Son of Yosef), who was the foreshadowing of Messiah to come for the lost sheep of the house of Y'sra'el.

Matthan had three wives through whom he fathered different

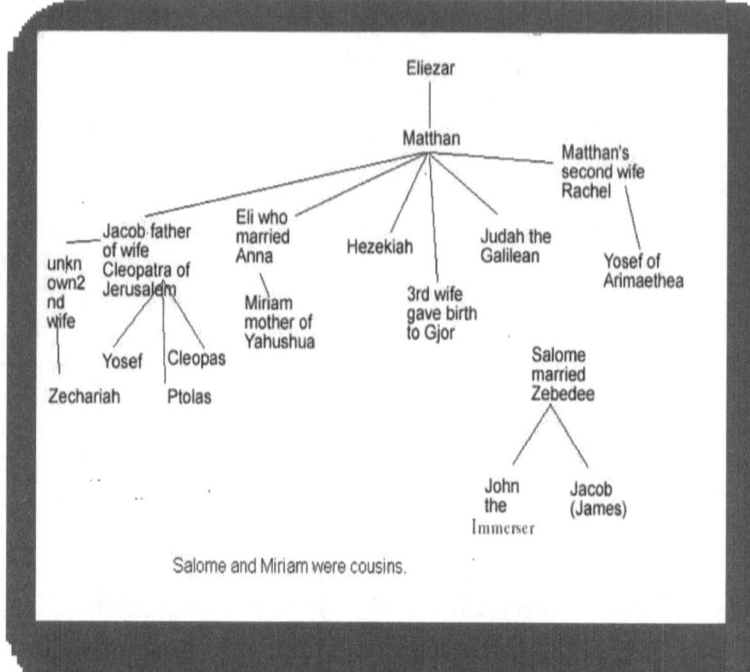

children because he is the common ancestor of Yahushua. Note in the King James Version Bible he is called Matthat. In the north/south axis for Matthan his wife Rachel was in the north and his wife Salome was in the

...d have been likely the daughter
...er's side and Salome would
...mother's side as the pattern was
...archs.

A: Yosef of Arimathaea

Yosef of Arimathaea was the wealthiest man in Jerusalem being the son of Eli and the younger brother of Miriam and he also held a very important seat in the Sanhedrin for the House of Dawud. After the death of Miriam's husband Yosef elder he became the gowra (guardian) of Miriam.

Luke is very clear about this connection and we cannot mistake this.

Luke 3: 23-24 And when **Yahushua** himself began, he was

about thirty years of age, being (as was custom) the son of <u>Yosef, which was the son of Eli,</u> **24** Which was the son of Mattityahu, which was the son of Lewi, which was the son of Melchi, which was the son of Yanna, which was the son of Yosef,

The man Yosef the son of Eli is no other than Yosef of Arimathaea. He would not give his brand new expensive tomb to Yahushua for
no reason because he is related and the guardian. With this adoption comes responsibility.

Note "as was custom" means that according to Torah and rabbinic law Yahushua was adopted as a son by Yosef of Arimathaea after his father died so therefore any rights that belonged to Yosef of Arimathaea were now conferred to Yahushua to be a legal king.

This is the reason why Yosef of Arimathaea would place Yahushua in his own tomb which was unused and brand new considering the life span of people during that time was short and we can see that no one was buried in the tomb where Yahushua was put in. This brings to a fulfillment a prophecy in Isaiah 53.

Yeshayahu (Isaiah) 53:9 And he made his grave with the

wicked, and <u>with the rich in his death</u>; because he had done no violence, neither was any deceit in his mouth.

He went to be laid in a rich man's tomb that happened to be his own uncle and adopted father.

We know that Miriam became a Temple virgin and we can see the reasons why because her brother Yosef was young and he could not look after her when both of their parents died and therefore she ended up in the Temple while as he grew up he went into the business of metal merchant and would travel a lot. It was during this time on one of his travels that Yahushua was convicted but he was not around to take part in his trial and to assist him but he did whatever else he could. The High Priest Caiaphas would have taken a proxy vote both for Yosef of Arimathaea and Nicodemus because both were out of the city at the time of the trial. The proxy vote would have been taken because they held important seats in the Temple.

Since Yosef of Arimathaea traveled extensively we do know that Miriam became a Temple virgin in the custody of the Temple priests until her marriage at around the age of thirteen which was the onset of puberty and this would have also forbidden her from touching the sacred things in the Temple during the times of her menstruation.

Yosef owned properties in many areas including in Arimathaea which was an area in modern day Ramallah today. Anciently known
as Ramla today this city is part of modern day Palestine. This is also the birthplace of Samuel the prophet.

Yosef of Arimathaea was a wealthy merchant tradesman and traveled extensively to Great Britain and other countries even as far away as India. Nicodemus accompanied him to some of these journeys alongside Yahushua when he was young when Yosef died and then by law and custom Miriam returned to her father's house.

Then Yosef of Arimathaea became the adopted guardian of Miriam and Yahushua and would be known as the gowra of Miriam just as Luke described.

It is speculated that Yahushua had traveled to the UK and India when he was young and had many conversations with the Buddhists in India who derived some principles of their religion out of these conversations with Yahushua which they still follow today.

Fig 3

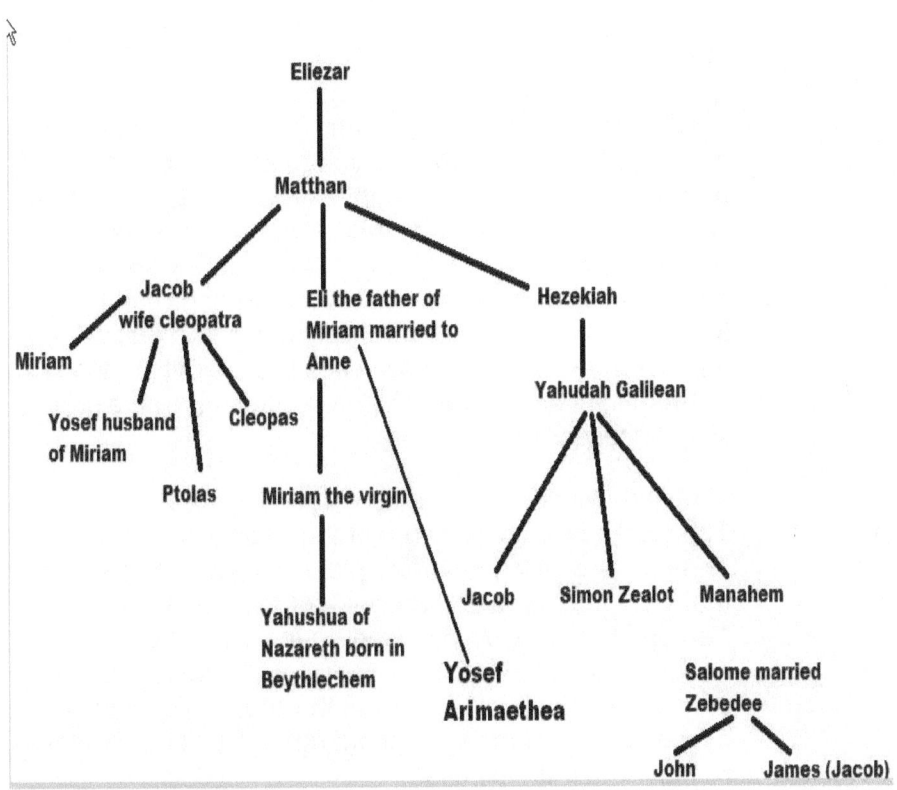

Note in the diagram above the name Anne. Do not confuse this name with Joanna she is a different woman and many commentators have confused her name with Anne for this see the diagram below because she is the wife of Yoachim.

Yahushua was not a poor peasant without a home as many have been taught but he had some very wealthy and powerful connected family. His grandfather Jacob from Yosef's side the husband of Miriam was the Patriarch and Nasi of Jerusalem who was killed in political rivalry by Herod. The same fate befell to Eli the father of Miriam the grandfather of Yahushua from the mother's side he was also killed because of political rivalry with Herod. Eli was most likely the wealthiest man in Y'sra'el so Miriam was from this wealthiest background and not a poor Bedouin girl as depicted in pictures and stories.

After her father's death shortly there after her mother Anne died and Miriam was given to the Temple to be brought up as a Temple virgin. She was fluent in all three languages, Hebrew, Greek and Aramaic. The main language spoken in the Temple was Hebrew and all ecclesiastical business that included writings scrolls for the Tenach (Hebrew Bible) or any other religious writing was always done in Hebrew while the majority of the Targumim (Commentaries) were written in Aramaic for student teachings.

Miriam would have seen the daily services in the Temple and was well aware of the wrangling of the Temple as a child in the Temple. Also note any gentile that went into the area reserved for the gentiles in the Temple had to be circumcised. In fact Aristobulus I upon conquering Galilee made a decree with the people that only those people could stay in the area which people chose to be circumcised according to the Torah of Moses or they would be expelled.

This explains why circumcision played an important part in Rabbi Paul's theology in the first century. The issue of gentile salvation was hotly contested in the first century between the two main schools the school of Shammai and the school of Hillel.

Rabbi Paul never taught to do away with it but Christendom with its incorrect understanding of rabbinic customs/traditions and by extension the bad translations and anti-Judaic commentaries of the Covenant Covenant confused the subject altogether. We have some extremely bad scholarship from the many Christian converts in Christendom which are of Hebrew background which then go on to rubber- stamp circumcision as not needed at all. If the Sanhedrin sat today and made a decree the first thing the Sanhedrin would do is to strip away such scholars of any self acclaimed authority of becoming judges and jury to decide on the everlasting law of Elohim that is still mandatory and alive in the kingdom of Elohim.

Please note the royal family of Miriam was from the House of Tzadok from which Yahushua gets his blood line connected to the House of Tzadok. This was important because he could not be the High Priest without having this connection hence why He could enter the holy of Holies once and forever. This indicates why then he would be the rightful heir to the throne as King and High Priest.

Ibrim (Hebrews) 9:12 Neither by the blood of goats and bulls, but by **his own blood** he entered in once into the set-apart place having obtained eternal redemption for us.

Yahushua III son of Shimon Fig 4:

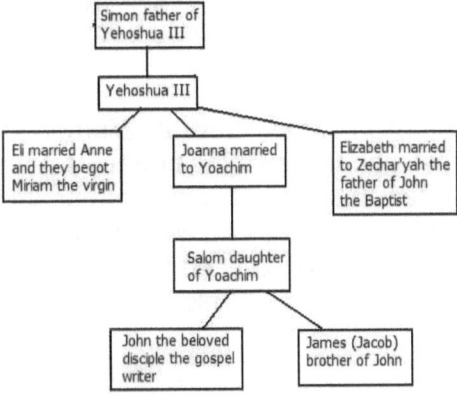

Let me show you how this fits. Yosef of Arimathaea would become the adoptive father of Miriam's son (Yahushua), which was the case according to the Yahudit law and custom. Her brother would have to take custody of her since she had no father because she would have gone back to her father's family with her dowry. Yosef would not accept Yahushua if he had reason to believe that He was illegitimate but he knew that Yahushua was by the divine will of the Father in heaven born to Miriam who was pure and undefiled. For Yosef to accept Miriam if she was with an illegitimate son of a Roman as false rumors had spread would mean the ruin of Yosef and expulsion from the Temple of his rights, his Davidic Royal seat and he would be thrown out of the Roman government where he had an important position of power.

There stood by the execution stake his mother and his mother's sister. Then the gospel mentions Miriam the wife of Cleopas. In actual fact the wife of Cleopas is the same woman that is the mother of Yahushua because she had married Cleopas after the death of Yosef. Cleopas was the younger brother of Yosef the first husband of Miriam and after being a widow as was again custom and law Miriam was married to Cleopas in a Levirate marriage Technically Yosef the elder had no son so his brother would have to raise seed for him in accordance with Torah see below Deuteronomy 25:5.

Debarim (Deuteronomy) 25:5 If brethren dwell together, and one of them die, and his wife had no child, from the dead brother, she shall not marry outside to a foreigner: her husband's brother shall go in unto her, and take her to him to be his wife, and perform the duty of a husband's brother unto her.

This is called 'Levirate Marriage.' This is commanded polygamy even if the brother is married and has children. Then YHWH orders the brother who is alive to take his brother's wife as an <u>additional</u> wife. The reason was to give sons to the dead brother by marrying his sister in law who has no son. This way the children could get the dead brother's name and the dead man's progeny may continue in Y'sra'el.

So John is actually giving us the same woman but in different relationships one relationship of Miriam is to her Son Yahushua and the other is to Cleopas as his wife so the two women are one and the same and cannot be counted twice. Therefore Miriam that is mentioned as the wife of Cleopas is the same Miriam. There is some confusion at the way many people look at the text and the Catholic Church wanted to maintain the incorrect teaching that Miriam had no other children basically creating the confusion which many have been following. The sister of Miriam was the daughter of Jacob and her name was also Miriam she is mentioned as standing there.

The gospel actually fits with both Mark and Matthew who also mention the same.

Everyone assumes that Miriam the mother of Yahushua went with John the son of Zebedee to Ephesus but she actually stayed in Jerusalem married to Cleopas after Yosef's death and died naturally. John was her natural nephew and in the absence of Yahushua he would become the son so to speak but he would not break the Torah/Law of Moses and take her with him since Yosef of Arimathaea would marry her to Cleopas. We know this indeed happened and Miriam had many more children which are mentioned in the gospels.

Fig5:

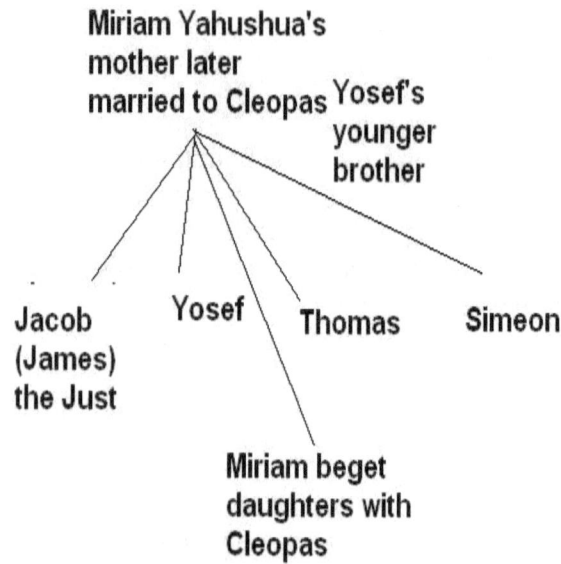

She had many other children with Cleopas mentioned in the diagram above. Simeon the son of Cleopas was born to Cleopas before this wedding in a previous marriage. Note Salome was the cousin of Miriam and John the son of Zebedee was the cousin of Yahushua. The rich man Yosef of Arimathaea was Yahushua's uncle, a man with a lot of influence and authority, alongside Nicodemus the chief teacher over the Yahudim, whose other name was Shimon or Simon.

This is why we see Yahushua being put in a prime location in a new tomb that was owned and never used by Yosef of Arimathaea. This is not the present day Garden Tomb where Christians flock to see in Y'sra'el and it's neither the Church of the holy Sepulcher. This tomb was located on the Mount of Olives at the present site of Dominus Flevit where a Roman Catholic Church stands today.

While it may not be apparent that even Kefa (Peter's) grave was found in Jerusalem around 1960 and not in Rome and many Christian scholars in error attribute his death in Rome where he never went. His Ossuary was found at the Church on the Mount of Olives known as Dominus Flevit too. The inscription found there on the Ossuary read Simon bar Yonah from the Aramaic inscription. This was also ground zero for many other disciples of Yahushua and I believe that Yahushua himself was interred in there but his body is not there since He indeed is risen and ascended to the Father YHWH in heaven to return again soon. This is also where Yahushua wept (John 11:35). [2]

The Catholic high clergy have known this truth for a long time that this is the original site of the burial since 1952 but do not divulge this information so as not to rock the boat and disturb the peace keeping people in the dark.

Some people propose another site for the tomb to be in

---

[2] http://www.hol.com/~mikesch/peters-jerusalem-tomb.htm

the church called Paternoster which is on the top of Mount of Olives where it is believed that He taught the disciples the famous prayer called the Lord's prayer but actually it is the disciple's prayer as taught similar to other Rabbis to their disciples (Matthew 6:9-15) and Paternoster is considered the place of His ascension also. Paternoster is only about five to ten minutes walk away from
Dominus Flevit, they are both close to each other on the Mount of Olives.

Coming back to the deceased body of Yahushua in order to acquire the dead body of a deceased relative you have to have a relationship such as the next of kin who have the rights over the body. Since Yosef of Arimathaea was then the technical guardian and caretaker for Yahushua he had the right to go and ask for the body. We note that Nicodemus was with him because he was also related to Yahushua. He brought in the spices to embalm the body another important task that only family members got involved in being the father of Miriam of Magdala who was the wife of Yosef of Arimathaea. He also accompanied with Yosef to Pilate to acquire the body.

Yochanan (John) 19:38-40 And after this Yosef of Ramathayim (Arimathaea), being a disciple of **Yahushua**, but secretly for fear of the Yahudim (Hebrew people), besought Pelatoos that he might take away the body of **Yahushua**: and Pelatoos gave him leave. He came therefore, and took the body of **Yahushua**.**39** And there came also Nakdimon Nicodemus), which at the first came to **Yahushua** by night, and brought a mixture of myrrh and aloes, about a hundred pound weight.**40** Then took they the body of **Yahushua**, and bound it in linen clothes with the spices, as the manner of the Yahudim (Hebrew people) is to bury.

You could not just be any outsider or non relation to just go to Pontius Pelatoos, the governor of Judea, and demand the body of the dead. In order to do so, you would have to be the legal guardian, and Yosef of Arimathaea was indeed the legal guardian of Yahushua.

Some people today have run off with the idea that Yahushua was perhaps married to Miriam of Magdala but this is in complete error. Miriam was technically **His aunt**, since she was the wife of Yosef of Arimathaea. And so together alongside her husband, she was Yahushua's disciple. It would not be difficult normally for Yahushua to get married as a Rabbi but in His case since he had the curse of Yekoniah upon His family then that would make Him a least favorite candidate for marriage. Marriages were not a love affair matter as in the West but you would have to satisfy the strict conditions of the father of the bride in order to marry someone which means no curses in the line.

B: Does not a Rabbi need to be married?

We know Yahushua did not get married yet people ask, "why not?" and, "How can he be a Rabbi and not be married as that was one of the requirements?" The reasons are simple he did not need to since He knew He would die for His mission to restore the lost sheep and be raised so why would he leave a widow behind secondly His mission did not call for marriage and thirdly no man wanted to give him his daughter because they knew about the curse (Jer 22:24- 30). We find Jacob (James the just) took an oath not to marry and he also had similar problems because no one would want to give him their daughter either because everyone knew about the curse. Jacob (James) the just for various reasons decided to take the oath but the bigger reason behind it likely to be this curse. The other thing is that he became the High Priest for one year and that indicates that He did not shun marriage but He also knew his time was short on this earth and he therefore decided to follow what mission Elohim gave him in the time he had.

In the Eastern culture people look at your background,

your family before they are willing to give you a daughter for marriage and the curse played an important role for most people to be wary of not giving their daughter for marriages. This was and still is the way typically middle-eastern families behave. We know after His miraculous healings and dynamic personality any woman would have married him but this was not part of his calling hence He never married. There were some ancient Rabbis that did not marry though few and far but the reason they gave was that they have to serve Elohim and did not have time for a family.

We can see that Yahushua had a very rich and varied family and all the people who followed Yahushua did not just wake up one day and decide to leave business and family to follow Him but many were direct family members and they trusted Yahushua as a Rabbi and great teacher who they later came to realize through the Ruach ha Kodesh (Holy Spirit) was/is also the divine Messiah. Many of these people would put modern men to shame because they left wives and families to go after the kingdom of Elohim and did not value their earthily businesses and families at the same level as the
calling of YHWH. While today many people shamefully chase ministry work for money gains only and only a few sincere ones who do it for Elohim.

In my twelve years in ministry I have worked a fulltime professional job and served Elohim all other hours of the day and I have not looked at handouts from Churches this is the way most ancient Rabbis worked in Y'sra'el as they had to balance a job with their ministry work. I have still managed to travel at least three times a year to teach abroad so I have done very well in service to the Holy One while it is good to be in a full-time job so I can teach my children how to do likewise and not depend on donations. Any donation that comes in then can be used in the work. When you serve Elohim with your own money things are very different and your work is of lasting value.

While I have personally witnessed that many people

who are in fulltime ministry are more interested in how many houses they can purchase and how many cars are parked on their driveways hence in Christendom the gospel for many is simply a business to get rich. Such people will be judged in the coming world with a severe judgment and will regret their actions but then it will be too late for them.

So hopefully this addresses the question of Rabbis, work and marriage for Yahushua.

Now coming back to Miriam's remarriage which has been hidden by the Catholics and the popular error is believed by the Anglicans also but according to the Torah law and local customs Miriam the mother of Yahushua was remarried in a Levirate marriage to Cleopas. Simeon ben Cleopas was likely an earlier son because we are not told of what happened to his biological mother though likely to be deceased at the time Cleopas married Miriam the widow of Yosef as we do not hear of him having any other wives at that particular time. In ancient Y'sra'el there was no social security system for divorced women or widows but generally when a woman was divorced or widowed she would return back to her father's house for support.

The Temple helped widows normally but on a day to day basis they needed to be married if young and if old then other ways were sought to assist them but the system of Levirate marriage was an effective system to deal with this type of issue even Rabbi Paul mentions to put this into affect for those who do not have husbands he asks people to take them on as wives in a similar way to levirate marriage what would be called polygamy. This was very common in the early assemblies and throughout ancient Y'sra'el's history.

First Timotheous 5:9-11, 14 Let not a widow be taken into the number under sixty years old, having been the wife of one man, **10** Well reported of for good works; if she has brought up children, if she have lodged strangers, if she has washed the *Y'sraelite* kedoshim (set-apart saints)' feet, if she has relieved the afflicted, if she has diligently followed every good work.**11** But refuse the younger widows: for their passions will lead them away from the Messiah, and they will desire to marry;

14 I will resolve that the younger widows marry, bear children, and guide the Beyth (house), give none occasion to the adversary to speak reproachfully.

There was a list of widows that the early believers were helping. While those of young age were supposed to marry next of kin or someone else hence why they could not be taken in that list and there was nothing wrong with them remarrying. Normally widows were added on as second or third wives because most young men wanted to marry virgin girls as was and still is custom in the east.

In fact Rabbi Paul commanded them to be married in a levirate model where a man who is already married may take a widow as an additional wife. The church fathers deliberately hid this truth and distorted it because of their cultic ascetic lifestyle and hatred of biblical polygamy and monogamy.

Rabbi Paul is very clear that the widows should be married to the men in the assemblies and he is not talking to single men but to those men who are already married and perhaps have children so they bear children for the widows that they may have an inheritance in Y'sra'el. He invokes the Levirate law (Deuteronomy 25:5-10) where a next of kin of someone other could step in to marry a widow and raise children for the dead husband of the widow. This was seen as personal charity and is one of the most commendable things to do for people in the east. He is not talking about giving $ 10 monthly charity to the widows this is of no use to them in the long term and in the scheme of things. Today $10 will get you a burger
meal with a drink but cannot run the house of a widow who needs the love and care of a husband and there are no age restrictions while in the east usually older widows did marry men younger than them in age or even it

worked the other way where a younger widow married an older man. The story of Ruth and Boaz is all about this the older man Boaz marrying the younger widow Ruth.

In the West women think they are so independent but they fail to understand how Middle-Eastern cultures worked to this day and many women were especially vulnerable like the divorced and widows had to have secure shelter and that could only be under a family roof and certainly not a woman by herself living on social security who could easily be abused or attacked by another individual. Even in the western model no matter how independent women are they still need the love and protection of a loving husband because our society still carries many ills due to the sin nature in man and the woman is the weaker vessel and needs to be protected.

The Muslim culture is both eastern and patriarchal, taking its things from the Torah of Moses, while also in Netzarim households polygamy is common and accepted. The levirate law is mentioned in Deuteronomy 25:5. 'If brothers dwell together, and one of them dies and has no son, the widow of the dead man shall not be married to a stranger outside the family; her husband's brother shall go in to her, take her as his wife, and perform the duty of a husband's brother to her.

This is comprehensive commanded polygamy both in the Tanach and the Covenant Covenant (NT) Matthew 22:24 -30. We can see that a man other than a brother could also marry the widow as is shown in Ruth's story in the Bible with Boaz.

In Miriam's case if her father was alive he would support her and if he had died then the brother would have to step in and offer support and if there was no one else then another family member close to the father would have to step in. In Miriam's case her brother Yosef was very well known and had no problem supporting his sister. Subsequent to death of the husband a widowed woman would be married to one of the brothers of the deceased husband and we do see this here with Cleopas the younger brother of Yosef taking on Miriam as wife.

So who is standing at the hung body of Yahushua beside the tree of Yahushua?

Yochanan (John) 19:25 Now there stood by the execution stake of **Yahushua** his mother, and his mother's sister, Miriam the wife of Qlopha, and Miriam of Magdala.

Many people confuse this statement for four Miriam's but there were only actually three.

- His mother Miriam is number 1.
- His mother's sister who was also called Miriam is number 2.
- The wife of Qlopha is the same Miriam mother of Yahushua so cannot be counted twice. Note there is no conjugation or hook in the text to make this a separate Miriam.
- Miriam of Magdala is technically step mum to Yahushua or more correctly an aunt who was the wife of Yosef of Arimathaea making her number 3.

So when we finish the count Miriam of Magdala is unique, Miriam the sister of Miriam his mother so we end up with three Miriam's and not four.

We find John has given us the above statement trying to clarify the two relationships that Miriam had one to Yahushua her son and the other to Cleopas her second husband.

This in the gospels shows the clear switch of relationships.

This is not a second Miriam though sometimes confusing translations makes it appear like that but this is the same Miriam though now described as the wife of Cleopas the father of Simon the high priest and Jacob

(James) the Nasi of Jerusalem.

The widow being remarried also took care of the tribal inheritance because people did not like their inheritance passing to outsiders. YHWH has also forbid this from happening as He did not want a widow who nobody would marry to end up outside Y'sra'el losing her inheritance to a stranger.

YHWH did not want Y'sraelites to marry foreigners and give the land promised to the Y'sraelites to someone else and therefore transfer land rights. Living in Y'sra'el and marrying in families with your cousins was and is still legal according to Torah which also meant that you would retain your land. Even if you leased your land to someone it would mean at the jubilee cycle the land will revert back to you so the land could never be sold permanently.

This even happens today in Pakistan and in Arab nations with marriages the same clans are sought and usually most marriages are made within families to cousins or distant cousins so that the inheritance can stay in the family and not be passed to a third party or some new person from outside who cannot be trusted and may decide to sell the family inheritance or dispose off it unwisely.

Simeon the son of Cleopas was from the House of Tzadok and his father Cleopas who is referred to in Luke 24:18 talking to Yahushua when they did not recognize Yahushua in His resurrected state. Note Cleopas had actually married his mother Miriam but since Yahushua was not fathered by Yosef the son of Jacob therefore there was no real blood relationship but the sons born to Miriam and Cleopas count as his half brothers from the mother's side such as Yosef, Judah, Thomas and James (Jacob).

Simon or Simeon was born to Cleopas before he married Miriam and Jacob (James) the just was also the son of Cleopas too but half brother of Yahushua who is mentioned numerous times in the gospels as the person presiding over the Netzarim council.

Luke 6:15 Mattityahu and Toma (Thomas), **Yaqub the son of Alphaeus**, and Shimon called Zelotes,

Alphaeus is the same person as Cleopas because his name is mentioned in Greek and Hebrew as you read Alphaeus and Cleopas two names and he is mentioned as the son of Jacob (James).

Matthew the Levite the gospel writer

Matthew was born to Alphaeus through another wife and was the one picked to write the gospel of Matthew. He was known as the tax collector. Bad Christian theology has made him a bad man who was a sinner and later came to faith. Such error can only arise from the western seminaries and churches. Here is who Matthew was. He was a righteous Levite. He was placed to collect taxes of grains and other crops by the Temple authorities who were closely linked to his grandfather Jacob. He was picked by Elohim to write the gospel since he was of Levite stock which carries the eternal priesthood. He was not a sinner as poorly described. The monies that he would have collected from the Yahudim would have gone back to the Temple authorities who would have handed it to the Roman authorities. There was a process and everything worked according to that. The Roman's would not directly collect crop taxes so the Temple authorities were responsible for these things.

Jacob (James) the just the half brother of Yahushua was also of Levite stock and this is one of the reasons why he became the Nasi of Jerusalem. In order to be the Nasi you have to have some qualifying attribute since this position was not sought out by a university degree but by what pedigree you were born from. We are not told of any elections so this place was pretty much given on pedigree to Yahushua's half brother without a fight because he was also eligible to be a High Priest being the son of Tzadok son of Aharon.

It may not be a well know fact but Jacob (James) the just also became the High Priest just before he was killed in the Temple. He even entered the holy of holies to atone for the sins of the people in Y'sra'el as was Torah law however Yahushua's death did not deter him from offering the sacrifices as prescribed by the Torah as they were and still are an everlasting ordinance even when Yahushua returns they will continue. To understand this concept you have to read the last four chapters of Ezekiel's book.

Luke 24:18-21 And one of them, whose name was **Cleopas, answering said to him, Are you the only foreigner in Yerushalim**, and have not known the things which have come to pass there in these days? **19** And he said to them, what things? And they said to him, Concerning **Yahushua** of Netzer'eth, which was a prophet mighty in deed and word before Elohim and all the people: **20** And how the chief kohenim (priests) and our rulers delivered him to be condemned to death, and had him impaled. **21** But we trusted that it had been he which should have redeemed Y'sra'el: and beside all this, today is the third day since these things were done.

Note Yahushua pretends to know nothing as a stranger and tests them. Cleopas was Yahushua's uncle and after marriage to His mother step-dad and the other man mentioned with him in verse 13 is Simeon his son who later became the overseer or Bishop in Jerusalem of the first Netzarim congregation, which is confirmed by Hegesippus Eusebius, Ecclesiastical History 3.11.1 and later followed to become the High Priest in 63 to 65 CE.

C: Cleopas the brother of Yosef the elder

Cleopas was the younger brother of Yosef the husband of Miriam. It is pretty certain that Jacob (James) the just was born in this wedlock of Miriam the mother of Yahushua to

Cleopas while some other children are also mentioned that most likely were born to Cleopas with Miriam and not Yosef the elder. Miriam also gave birth to daughters and I would suggest possibly three in her two marriages. One of these daughters was married and this is the wedding that Yahushua attended in Cana where he did his first miracle of turning water into wine. She was married to Simon the Zealot (Luke 6:15, Matt 10:4) who was also related to Yahushua.

Yochanan (John) 2:1-4 And the third day there was a marriage in Cana of Galil; and the mother of **Yahushua** was there: **2** And both **Yahushua** was called, and his disciples, to the marriage. **3** And when they wanted wine, the mother of **Yahushua** said to him, They have no wine.

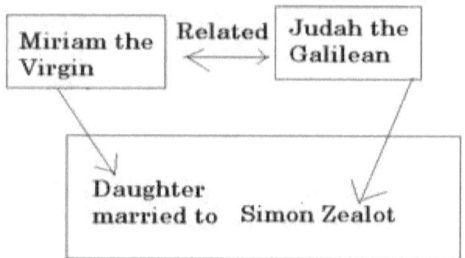

The only reason Miriam is able to ask Yahushua her son about the wine is because this marriage is of his own sister though we are not given the name of the sister. The reason why Yahushua is there with his twelve disciples is because many of these had direct relations to his family.

The half brothers of Yahushua are referred to in Matthew 13:55. Note in middle-eastern cultures half brothers and cousins are
referred to as brothers. Even in modern Chinese culture today cousins are referred to just as brothers and sisters. It is certain that there were daughters born to Miriam the mother of Yahushua and it is possible that Cleopas may have had daughters from a previous marriage too.

The doctrine of the perpetual virginity of Miriam

was formulated by Aurelius Ambrosius of Milan in the 4th century CE who was made Bishop overnight in a dispute in the Catholic Church. The perpetual virginity of Miriam has been perpetuated by Roman Catholic Church to this day while Miriam was married twice and had several children and died a happy mother, wife and daughter the blessed amongst women chosen by Elohim but Rome chooses to ignore this important Torah fact and calls her a perpetual virgin and sinless both of which are gross errors.

A woman who begets at least seven children in two marriages does not remain a virgin and she cannot be perpetually sinless because she was also redeemed like all of us through the blood of Yahushua the one and only sacrifice.

Mattityahu (Matthew) 13:55 Is not this the carpenter's son? Is not his mother called Miriam? And his brothers Yaqub and Yosef, and Shimon and Yahudah? 56 **And his sisters are they not all with us**? Where then did this man get all these things?

Also in Matthew 10:3 James (Jacob) the martyr is referred to as the son of Cleopas. If his legal father was Yosef the elder then the gospel narrative would not put here the son of Cleopas but would have called him the son of Yosef therefore this confirms he was the legal son of Cleopas and born to Miriam the mother of Yahushua in her second marriage. This then technically was the Levirate son raised as seed for Yosef the elder but since Jacob (James) did not marry and have children therefore Yosef elder's seed becomes extinct at the death of Jacob (James).

Mattityahu (Matthew) 10:3 Philip, and Bartholomi; Toma, and Mattityahu the tax collector; Yaqub the son of Alphaeus, and Lebai, whose surname was Theddai;

We need to identify two other characters one which was the

direct disciple of Yahushua and the other Mark called Markus John.

So who was Mattityahu (Matthew) the gospel writer?

Mark 2:14 And as he passed by, he saw Lewi the **son of Alphaeus** sitting at the tax booth, and said to him, Follow me. And he arose and followed him.

Now we know who Mattityahu is, he is the son of Cleopas as well. We are not told about his mother and he is never mentioned as the son of Miriam so it's highly likely that he was born to Cleopas prior to the marriage with Miriam the daughter of Eli.

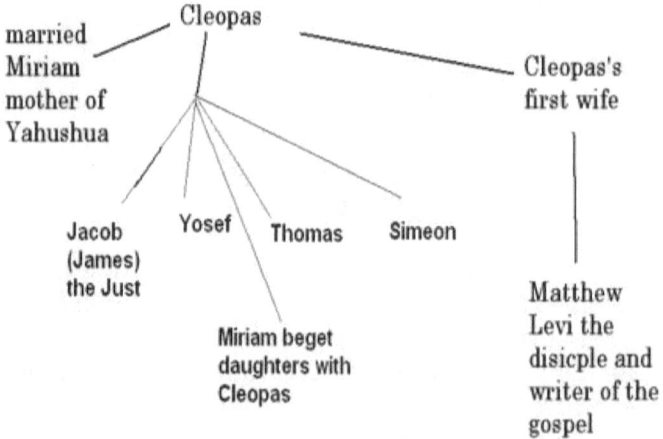

Therefore one can clearly see that Yahushua's many disciples were family members usually cousins and distant cousins and half brothers such as Jacob (James). And even John the son of Zebedee the gospel writer and Yaqub (James) his brother the son of Zebedee were also His cousins. Peter and Andrew both were the sons of His aunt Salome.

Note all the people mentioned as James in the Covenant Covenant have the real name as <u>Yaqub</u> in Hebrew or the later anglicised form Jacob and James is the English conversion while if you went looking for him under the name of the English 'James' in the first century Y'sra'el you will not find him.

One can now begin to understand why Yahushua would ask them to follow Him and they would gladly trust one of their own family members well known in the family circles as a miracle worker and also talked about as the anointed one to come as the Messiah. Who would not want to follow a leader sent by YHWH?

What about Markus (Mark) the gospel writer, who was he?

Ma'aseh Schilichim (Acts) 12:12 And when he had considered the thing, he came to the Beyth (house) of Miriam the mother of Yochanan (John) whose surname was Mark; where many were gathered together praying.

Why would Peter (Kefa) go to the house of Miriam the mother of Mark John? Yes this is another Miriam. So Mark is the son of Miriam but which Miriam?

When Peter escaped prison with divine help he came to the house of Mark and he happens to know his mother Miriam. Mark is mentioned as a relative to Bar'nabah also. Note if a person escaped prison in any circumstance he would seek help either from his relatives or friends and in this case Peter went to his direct relatives and not strangers so Mark John is connected to Peter. Let us see the connections of this mysterious relationship.

Colossians 4:10 Aristarchos my fellow prisoner greets ye, and Musa-Marcus (Moses Mark), my sister's son to Bar'nabah, (concerning whom you received instructions: if he comes to ye, receive him;)

Rabbi Paul (Sha'ul) calls Bar'nabah my sister's son so this gives us another clue that Bar'nabah who lives in Cyprus the Hebrew scholar is related to Markus who actually lived in Jerusalem with his family. Bar'nabah was the cousin of Markus both of Levite stock. This tribal identity is a big clue for us.

There were two families mentioned clearly of Levite origin in the Covenant Covenant and that was of Miriam the mother of Yahushua alongside Elizabeth her cousin. The other members of this family were Yosef of Arimathaea the brother of Miriam the virgin and uncle of Yahushua with mixed Judah/Levite both from Father Eli from the tribe of Judah and his wife Anne she was Levite from the House of Tzadok.

The fixation of Rome to pervert the gospels and its desire to make it appear using Roman names such as Markus instead of his Hebrew name Yochanan (John) makes it appear to be a Roman writer who wrote in Greek. Eusebius is quoted as saying that Mark had picked up the sayings of Peter and wrote them down according to another earlier historian called Papias while both Clement in 212 and Irenaeus who died in 202 CE supported Mark of a Roman origin. I am afraid all these people missed the fundamental clue that Markus or Yochanan is of Levite origin and certainly not of Roman descent.

As I said the western world with its idolatries is fixated in attributing anything written in Y'sra'el with Rome and Greek. This is not so. Markus was simply the Roman name or second name of the man called Yochanan Moshe (John Moses) yet this person was also connected to the family of Yosef of Arimathaea.

We are not exactly given his parentage but we are given two clues one that he is from a priestly stock and two that he lived in Jerusalem. Therefore it is highly likely that he belonged to both of the Levite families mentioned in the gospels. We know that he is not the son of Miriam the virgin so there is only one other family left and that of Yosef of Arimathaea who also had a large house in Jerusalem. Yosef of Arimathaea's son was Josephus hence the Josephus mentioned as a priest is the same one who wrote the histories and was a commander in the Roman forces and was also a secret Netzarim believer of Yahushua. He was in an important Roman position similar to his father.

Yosef of Arimathaea's first wife was Mary of Magdala and the word Magdala is from the Hebrew word Migdol which means tower or pillar. She was the daughter of the very important influential man called Nicodemus whose other name was Shimon or Simon in English. He was from the tribe of Benjamin who were keepers of the Temple records.

It is highly likely that Markus was the second son of Yosef of Arimathaea. Rabbi Paul of the thirteen letters of the Covenant Covenant calls him <u>my sister's son</u> so Rabbi Paul was a member of the family of Nicodemus. We know Nicodemus was of Benjamin
stock and so was Rabbi Paul. Rabbi Paul was therefore related to Nicodemus.

We are not told in the Covenant Covenant what relationship Rabbi Paul had with Nicodemus but it is highly likely that since he is calling <u>Miriam</u> his sister (Col 4:10) that would be a cousin/sister and I would suggest that Rabbi Paul would be the nephew of Nicodemus. We are given another clue that Bar'nabah was in Cyprus and of Levite stock. Well what was Bar'nabah doing in Cyprus? Cyprus would be an important place for the trade of Tin and metal and we know that Yosef of Arimathaea was trading in that field both in the UK and probably sailing to Cyprus and Turkey also which was the closest location for trading of these metals.

Using the rules of kinship analysis (For these rules see Lewis Morgan, Bronislaw Malinowski and Ernest L. Schusky) of ruling tribes of Africa and Israelites which connect back to their African ancestors such as Enoch known as Nok in that land and Noah (Bor-Nu the land of Noah in Africa) whose ark floated around Lake Chad bordering Nigeria landing upon Mount Meru (see for more

Dr. David M. Westley on his African studies) (Meni in the Bible) note it used to be a sea. We find that using the rules of kinship pattern like his forefathers Yosef of Arimathaea would have more than one wife as was custom in the ruling classes. Nicodemus also in the same pattern would have had two wives in the north and south axis. How do we know this? This is because Nicodemus's wife named her eldest son the name Eli'ezer and that was a grandfather in the line of Nicodemus's wife.

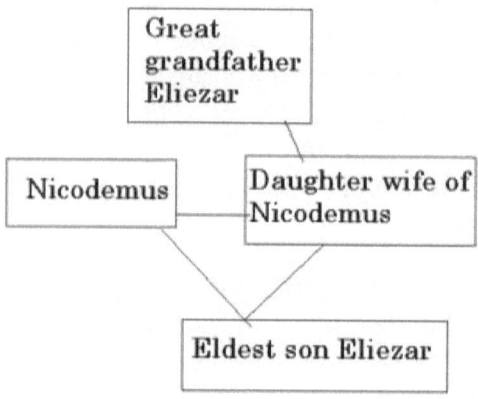

The name of the grandfather indicates to us that this is the same ruler pattern we find in Genesis with three sons and two wives. This pattern can be noted in Genesis 4, 5 and further on.

The kinship pattern is first clearly revealed by Lamech but followed on all the future generations later.

Genesis 4:19 And Lamech took unto him two wives: the name of the one was Adah, and the name of the other Zillah. **22** And Zillah, she also bare TubalQayin, an instructor in every instrument of brass and iron: and the sister of TubalQayin was Naamah.

The fact that Zillah has given the name TubalQayin to her son is evident that the pattern is running in these families of the North and South Axis. TubalQayin's name is identical to his father while the name means metal worker we can see that Zillah was Lemech's wife from the Father's side so she names her firstborn after the grandfather. The Torah says that Qayin went to the land of the Nod that is the land of Nok or Enoch in Africa where he started his family.

Genesis 4 pattern

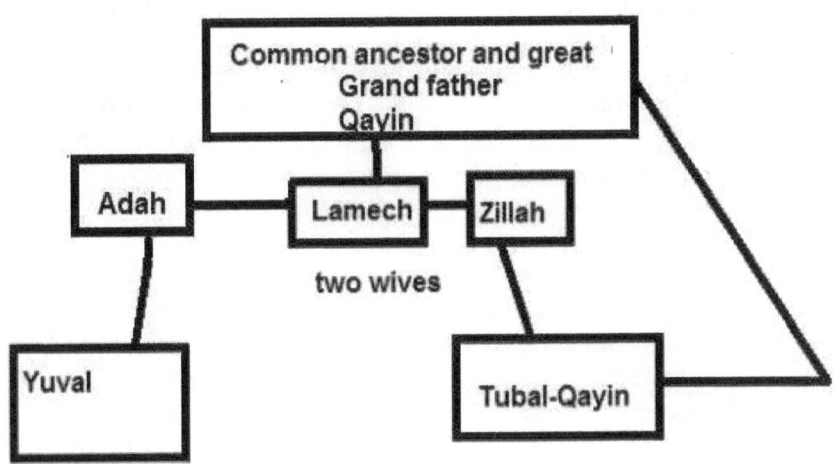

This means that Nicodemus also married this wife from his matrilineal line from the mother's side who would have had Levite blood and he likely married his cousin/sister. This also tells us that his first wife would have come from his patrilineal line or father's
side which we are not revealed in the text but we get a very good idea from this short analysis that I did.

The North is quite important in Kabbalah the mystical study of Elohim and the Torah. The number for the North is the numeric one which applies to the Hebrew letter Alef the source of all things living and the place of Elohim while the Bible tells us that the heaven is in the North (Job 26:7 and Ps 48:2). The ancient ancestors of Y'sra'el had fallen into idolatry worshipping the sun so they did not keep their wives in the East and west locations as these were considered by the ancestors to be the setting and rising of Elohim e.g. the place of the sun.

The ruling and priestly classes always had at least two wives in the north and south axis. Therefore it is my opinion that Bar'nabah was living with his mother the second wife of Yosef of Arimathaea in Cyprus who would be controlling his northern territory while Yosef's first wife Miriam Magdala would have been controlling the southern territory in Jerusalem. Bar'nabah having land which he sold (Acts 4:37) to give the money to the Netzarim leadership. How did he acquire this land? Some automatically assume this land is in Israel but the text says no such thing and even if it was the Levites were not supposed to sell it for gain (Lev 25:34). This was by Yosef of Arimathaea and his purchases in Cyprus, he would not have been given free land in Cyprus.

We have found that Josephus the historian and Mark John were the two sons in the south belonging to Miriam Magdala and we had to locate the third secret son which we have located through kinship pattern and the help of the text in the New Covenant (NT) to be Yosef who became known as Bar'nabah.

For more on this see the HTHS Hebraic Study bible on Abraham and his wives. This would make Mark (John Moshe Mark) the brother of Bar'nabah.

This also explains why Bar'nabah wanted to take his brother with him when Rabbi Paul who was their uncle refused to take his nephew the son of Miriam Magdala.

Acts 15:37 And Bar'nabah determined to take with them Yochanan (John), whose surname was Mark. **38** But Rabbi Paul (Sha'ul) insisted not to take with them this one because he departed from them in Pamphylia, and had not gone with them in the work.

How do we know that he was the son of Yosef of Arimathaea?

Bar'nabah's name has been mentioned as <u>Yosef (Acts 4:36)</u> and that is our clue to connecting with the kinship analysis because it was custom to name the first born son in the name of one of the grandfather's.

Luke gives us the name of this grandfather in Luke 3:24.

Luke 3:24 Which was the son of Mattityahu, which was the son of Lewi, which was the son of Melchi, which was the son of Yanna, **which was the son of Yosef**,

This woman in Cyprus who was the Northern wife of Yosef of Arimathaea would have been likely to be the daughter down the lineage of Yanna who was the son of Yosef.

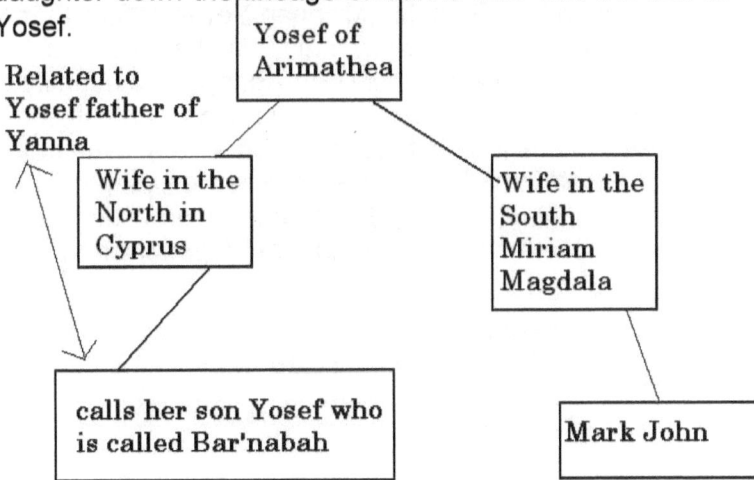

The Northern territory wife as was custom in ruling classes living in Cyprus daughter of grandfather Yosef married Yosef of Arimathaea and then called her firstborn son Bar'nabah by the name of his great grandfather.

Mark John was the son of Miriam from Magdala of the Levite stock (from father's side as tribes were counted from the father and being Hebrew from the mother) living on the Mount of Olives. Her sister Martha who was widowed had a son who worked as a priest in the Temple who was mentioned in the Babylonian Talmud Sukkah 52a. After her first husband died she would have returned to her father's house which we find her living with her brother Lazarus and later she has been attested to have married a high priest by the name of Yehoshua who is mentioned in the Talmud. This is probably one of the few marriages where a High Priest married a widow which was not common practice but on special circumstances was allowed.

[3]After her first husband died, she became engaged to Joshua ben Gamala. (Mishnah Yevamot 6:4; Talmud Yevamot 61a.) Rav Assi said that she paid King Jannai (whom scholars identify with Agrippa II) a quantity of money equal in size to 72 eggs to nominate Joshua to become high priest (Talmud Yoma 18a), even though the Sanhedrin had not elected him to the post. (Talmud Yevamot 61a.) Even though the general rule was that a high priest should not marry a widow (Mishnah Yevamot

---

[3] http://en.wikipedia.org/wiki/Martha_daughter_of_Boethus

6:4), the couple went on to marry, and the Mishnah cites the event for the proposition that a priest who betroths a widow and subsequently becomes high priest may consummate the marriage. (Mishnah Yevamot 6:4; Talmud Yevamot 61a.)

It was said of Martha's son, who was a priest that he was so strong that he could carry up two sides of a huge ox to the altar without any lack of decorum. (Talmud Sukkah 52b.)

See below the chart for Yosef of Arimathaea's family.

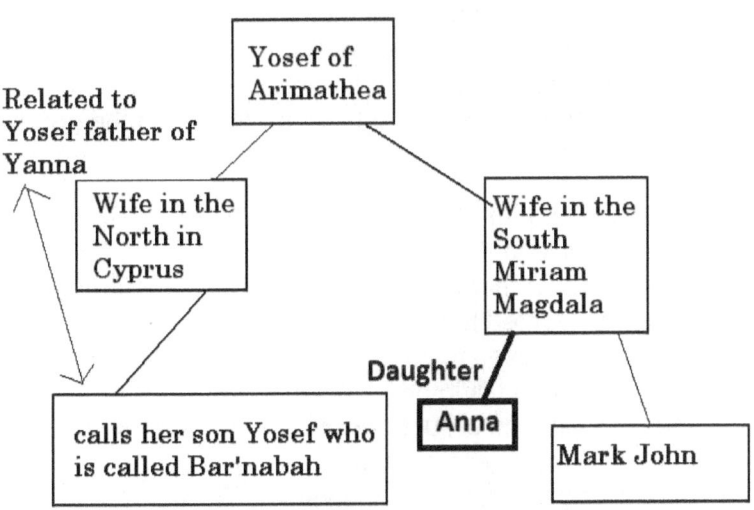

The Talmud recounts the story of Martha's last days during the Roman siege of Jerusalem. (Talmud Gittin 56a.) At that time, Martha sent her manservant out to bring her some fine flour, but it had sold out. He told her that there was no fine flour, but there was white flour. She then sent him to bring her some white flour. By the time he went, the white flour had sold out. He told her that there was no white flour, but there was dark flour. She sent him to bring her some dark flour. By the time he went, the dark flour had sold out. He told her that there was no dark flour, but there was barley flour. She sent him to bring her some barley flour.

By the time he went, the barley flour had also sold out. In desperation, without even putting on her shoes, she went out to see if she could find anything to eat. She stepped in some dung and died of shock. Rabban Johanan ben Zakkai thus applied to her the Biblical verse, "The tender and delicate woman among you who would not adventure to set the sole of her foot upon the ground." (Deut. 28:56.)

Some report that she ate a fig left by Rabbi Zadok, and became sick, and died. Rabbi Zadok observed fasts for 40 years in order that Jerusalem might not be destroyed. When he wanted to restore himself, they used to bring him a fig, and he used to suck the juice and throw the rest away. (Talmud Gittin 56a.) When Martha was about to die, she brought out all her gold and silver and threw it in the street, saying, "What is the good of this to me," thus giving effect to the verse, "They shall cast their silver in the streets." (Ezek. 7:19.) (Talmud Gittin 56a.)

Note in traditions it has been said that Anna the daughter of Yosef was married to the martyr Stephen (Tzephan'yah) who is mentioned in the book of Acts (Acts 7:59). Also the marriage at Cana (John 2:1) was the wedding of one of Yahushua's sisters with Simon the zealot. Note Simon the zealot was a direct disciple of Yahushua in fact his brother in law by relation and he was the son of Judah the Galilean who was murdered by Pilate (Luke 13:1).

Fig7:

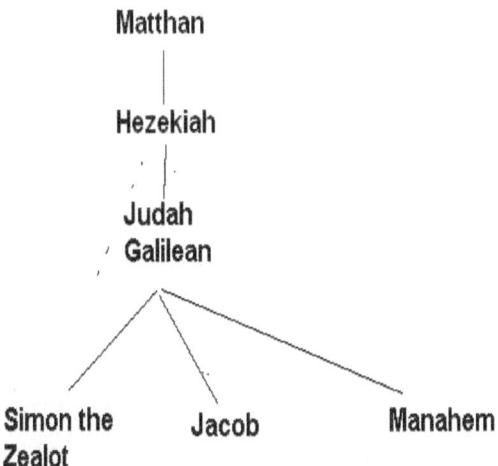

The other family that was related to Yahushua were the zealots in Galilee one important figure which is shown in the diagram above is Hezekiah who beget Judah the famous zealot called Judah of Galil who had three sons. This is the Judah who fought an active gorilla war with the Herodians and many people were killed in Galilean under the direct orders of Pontius Pelatoos.

Luke 13:1 There were present at that season some that told him of the Galileans, whose **blood Pelatoos had mingled** with their sacrifices.

Ma'aseh Shlichim (Acts) 5:37 After this man rose up

Yahudah of Galil in the days of registration, and drew away many people after him: he also perished; and all, as many as obeyed him, were dispersed.

There was an incident where people were unsure of who Yahushua was and whether He was the prophet, the Messiah. Some were afraid to grab him when he was speaking otherwise they wanted to get hold of him and beat Him up. Some argued about his prophethood being of Galil and not the status of Messiahship of Beythlechem. Here is the incident.

John 7:40- 44 Of that of the crowd of people therefore, when they heard this saying, said, of a truth this is the Prophet. **41** Others said, This is the Messiah. But some said, **Shall Messiah come out of Galil? 42** Has not the scripture said, That Messiah comes of the seed of Dawud, and out of the town of Beyth Lechem (House of bread and House of meat), where Dawud was? **43** So there was a division among the people because of him. **44 And some of them would have taken him; but no man laid hands on him**.

As can be noted that they did not know that He was born in Beythlechem so they were confused how can the Messiah come out of Galil. They also made a certain sarcastic quote that 'Shall the Messiah come out of Galil".

The reason why they spoke sharply against Galil was not just because that was an unknown northerly backward region but because the region of Galil was full of freedom fighters and the most well known family was of Yahushua called Yahudah the Galilean. So these people reasoned how can Elohim send the Messiah from the hotbed of political activity and people who wanted to overthrow the government because some of these people standing had aligned themselves with the Herodians while others knew that the anointed one or the Messiah has to be born in Beythlechem. In John 7:44 we are told in no uncertain terms that some people would have seized him and given him a bit of thrashing but were afraid to touch Yahushua. The Question is why were they afraid of an innocent unarmed man?

Most people are quite happy at this stage to assume that because he was the Messiah that is why they could not touch Him but this was not the case since we know that later He was seized

upon and taken to the tree and hung till dead. The reason why the people were afraid at this particular time was because of Yahushua's freedom fighting relatives one being Yahudah the Galilean. He was a fierce fighter and his reputation was well known across all of Y'sra'el. Many people feared him so they thought if we would touch Yahushua what if his uncle finds out hence why they were afraid to seize Him and this was by divine intervention that Yahushua had such formidable family. Sometimes YHWH places you in a family that is well known, the reason is to protect you so its not by coincidence because we know that Musa was also placed in the protection of Pharaoh of all people who did not even believe in YHWH the Elohim of Y'sra'el as the supreme deity.

However note after his uncle's death they were quite happy to arrest him and take him to the Romans without fear.

Josephus the historian ben Yosef of Arimathaea notes an event where many Galileans were murdered by Pilate. This man Judah of Galilee, who tried to draw away some of the Hebrew people from the Roman government, and told them it was not lawful to give taxes to Caesar; at which Pilate being enraged, sent a band of soldiers, and murdered them all. This man was a relation of Yahushua hence why many people in the government viewed Yahushua with nervousness because they thought He was perhaps another revolutionary and may draw away crowds to act against Rome. However Yahushua stated very clearly at their puzzlement that He did not come to fight the Romans and His kingdom was not of this world. In the very next verse in Luke 13:2 Yahushua makes an astounding statement.

Luke 13:2-3 And **Yahushua** answering said to them, do you suppose that these Galileans were worse sinners than all the other Galileans, because they suffered such things? **3** I tell you, No: but, except you repent, you shall all likewise perish.

In those days people thought that if someone was killed or acquired a sudden disease then it must be because he or she had committed many sins but Yahushua corrects the perception that just because these people were fighting the Roman occupation of Y'sra'el that they were not sinners for doing so.

Some historians try to humanize the gospels taking Yahushua's special status away by making him out to be a zealot and freedom fighter.

One important thing to note is that all the present theologians completely ignore the model that YHWH does not allow a gentile to write His revelations given to Y'sra'el for Y'sra'el. Even Rabbi Paul said the following which is often ignored.

Romiyah 3:1-2 What advantage then has the Yahudi (Hebrew)? Or what profit is there of brit-milah (circumcision)? **2** Much every way: chiefly, because that to them were committed the oracles of Elohim.

So even Rabbi Paul confirms that the oracles of Elohim to date were given to the Yahudim alone. No not one gentile can write any revelation from the Holy One of Y'sra'el unless he is a Hebrew and of the stock of Y'sra'el. Otherwise we make not only Rabbi Paul a liar but also falsify Elohim by dictating our terms upon Him. If a gentile left the world idolatries and entered the Covenants of Y'sra'el then he can no longer be called a gentile but a Hebrew and an Israelite.

We also note that the name Mark or Markus was given because he had a Roman name and a Hebrew name. His Hebrew name was John Moses. Likewise Luke was not a Greek writer but a Yahudee who knew the intricate details of the Temple that no gentile would have known since they were not allowed beyond the wall of separation.

Ma'aseh Shlichim (Acts) 13:5 And when they were at Salamis, they preached the word of Elohim in the synagogues of the Yahudim (Hebrew people): and they had also Yochanan (John) as an attendant.

Our second witness from Luke also confirms what I said earlier. Mark is ministering to the Yahudim in a synagogue. No Yahudee in his right mind will allow a gentile to minister to them. The only person they would be happy to minister to them would be a Levite a priest as can be seen in Acts 13:5. They would be happy to see a teacher from Judah or Benjamin but will be most happy with a Levite because these were the legal Torah experts in the Temple.

The other fallacy that the western scholarship pertains to is that the gospels were written in Greek while it is certain that no Levite would dare write in Greek but only Hebrew and I can tell you categorically and reject all Western love affairs of a Greek Covenant Covenant (NT) as utterly false. The writings of the Netzarim were written in Hebrew and Hebrew alone while later translated into many other languages starting with both Aramaic and Greek. All historians usually write by saying "first century Christians" while there was no such people of belief.

This is an oxymoron. There was no Christian in the fist century because all the Yahudim disciples of Yahushua referred to themselves as just Yahudim and Netzarim and nothing more. The people who called themselves Christians were Romans and gentile who started to pervert the truth and adopt and mingle their idolatrous pagan feasts in with the truth to make it look like they were practicing the truth and this is true to this day where you find paganism in the churches such as Christmas and Easter which is clear testimony that they do not practice truth.

The religion of Christianity did not get a stamp of approval from Elohim but the king Constantine in the 4th century CE while the Netzarim faith was sealed by YHWH himself because at least two people in that assembly became High Priests that is Jacob the just and Simeon ben Cleopas.

It makes clear sense that Yosef the dad of Mark would give him a second Roman name alongside his Hebrew name of John Moses so that his son would carry on the family trade from where Yosef left trading metals and exporting them from the United Kingdom and Turkey.

Now Taking this into consideration looking at Acts 12:12 the only other Miriam that I have not looked at is Miriam of Bethany who was the wife of Yosef of Arimathaea therefore this Miriam I would suggest to be the wife of Yosef who was very wealthy, the brother of Miriam the mother of Yahushua. And that Markus belongs to this family. This Mark is therefore the relative and cousin of Yahushua and the only person who has plenty wealth to support the disciples appears to be this Miriam, we shall refer to her in this book as Mark's mother from here on.

Ma'aseh Shlichim (Acts) 15:37-39 And Bar'nabah determined to take with them Yochanan (John), whose surname was Mark. **38** But Rabbi Paul (Sha'ul) insisted not to take with them this one because he departed from them in Pamphylia, and had not gone with them in the work. **39** And the contention was so sharp between them, that they parted company one from the other: and so Bar'nabah took Mark, and sailed to Cyprus;

There seems to be a serious dispute between Rabbi Paul and Bar'nabah about taking Mark with them while Rabbi Paul was still respectful of the two men unlike many in Christendom today slandering each other on little things, these men continued to teach the words of YHWH. It's clear that Bar'nabah wanted to take his relative with him while Rabbi Paul did not think it conducive but I would suggest Bar'nabah was correct in that a Levite which Mark John Moses was would be a big asset and to use him to reach to the various lost sheep of the House of Y'sra'el. This showed a maturity in Bar'nabah whose name was Yosef.

Note Bar'nabah was also a Levite (Acts 4:36) since he is related to the family in Jerusalem who were Levites. He had a field which means he was a wealthy person. He sold the land and gave the money for the work of YHWH, a true Levite would do that. This is corroborating evidence that he was related to Yosef of Arimathaea and to Mark John Musa (Moses) the son of Yosef.

Even Rabbi Paul later commended Mark in his epistles therefore proving Mark was a worthy man.

Second Timotheus 4:11 Only Luka (Luke) is with me. Take Musa Mark, and bring him with you: for he is profitable to me for the service.

Note Rabbi Paul never holds any grudge and asks to bring Mark along too.

Colossians 4:10 Aristarchos my fellow prisoner greets ye, and Musa-Marcus (Moses Mark), my sister's son to Bar'nabah, (concerning whom you received instructions: if he comes to ye, receive him; Mark whose dad held seats on the Sanhedrin and had authority on the board of the 70 elders was preaching and teaching

Mark 14:51-52 And there followed him a certain young man, having a linen cloth cast about his naked body; and the soldiers tried to arrest him: **52** And he left the linen cloth, and fled from them naked.

This is certainly to be Mark and it is quite likely that he

had heard about Yahushua's fame because he was also a family member and therefore he kept watch at a distance perhaps because he was a young man and not ready to join their movement. He was wearing a linen cloth; this indicates if this is Mark as I believe that he was of the priestly order of Levite and likely the House of Tzadok also, he would not be completely naked because people wore breeches underneath so saying naked means he wore something underneath.

YHWH has never qualified anyone other than the Levites to write scriptures so we can clearly identify Mark in this passage as a Levite.

Note the gospel of Mark in chapter 14 starts talking about a person called Simon the leper which is an inaccurate translation for the translation actually says Simon the jar merchant. This jar merchant is living in Bethany very close to the Temple. I would posit that this man is Nicodemus ruler and teacher of the Temple Pharisees. Nicodemus means "innocent of blood" however Simon or Shimon means the one who heard Elohim. So was Nicodemus a jar merchant and or trader of grains? In fact he was doing both.

As a businessman as most businessmen today do they usually trade in several businesses and not just one business and I would therefore posit that it was just one of the offshoots of his business most likely connected to the grain trade. Wheat was not always transported in sacks as today but in ancient times sent in large jars for long and arduous journeys and also kept in jars for long term protection and to protect from damp and water this is why this would be connected. Note when a distant relative Yosef made wheat silos in Egypt he made silos specially to hold wheat for years so that the wheat and corn would not become damp and they were specially coated inside with special materials to prevent dampness.

Wheat is never just left in sacks because if anyone has ever kept wheat and corn as my forefathers who were farmers did the wheat left on its own with dampness would breed worms in the rooms where wheat is kept unless you remove all possibility of disease as I have seen this phenomena with my own eyes as a child.

What do we know about Simon the Pharisee?

Mark 14:3 And being in Beyth-Anya (Bethany) in the Beyth (house) of Shimon the jar merchant as he sat at the meal, there came a woman having an alabaster box of ointment of spikenard very precious; and she broke the box, and poured it on his head.

Simon had a very large house in a rich sought after prime location and only a rich and wealthy man in fact the second richest man in Jerusalem could afford to live in such a location. Note do not be surprised that Nicodemus has two names because in Y'sra'el some people even had three names such as those who had returned from the exile in Iran/Iraq had three names one being Persian. Therefore Nicodemus and Simon is the same person.

The name mentioned as the son of Alpheus which is actually the same as Cleopas so Jacob (James) most definitely was the son of Alpheus who is the same man. Cleopas is the Hebrew name while Alpheus is the Latin and Qlopas is the Aramaic versions of the same name.

According to the Torah when a woman's husband died then she would be married to the next brother in line even if the brother is already married this is what I term commanded polygamy in the Scriptures. Moses wrote about his in Deuteronomy 25:5.

There are two other children of Miriam mentioned one is Joses which is Hebrew for Yosef and one is Judas or Yahudah.

When Miriam married Cleopas he already had a son by the name of Simeon who later became the High Priest in the years 63, 64 and 65. Note only one from the House of Tzadok could be the High Priest. So who is Miriam? She was from the House of Tzadok being a Levite because her father was Eli who is referred to in the Jerusalem Talmud as Miriam's father he was married to Hannah from the tribe of Levi so Yahushua is from the House of Tzadok from His maternal lineage and related to Simon the just or Simon from the House of Tzadok the son of Onias.

Simon I ha Tzadik the son of Onias I was the High Priest and relative of Yahushua from the line of the House of Tzadok. He presided over the last of the great Synagogues. To him is prescribed the famous saying: the world stands on three pillars -the Torah, worship and the showing of kindness."

So now we can answer the question of Yahushua being able to enter the Holy of Holies in heaven because He is from the line of Tzadok maternally and House of Yahudah but how does He bypass the curse of Yekoniah?

D: So who was Dr Luke a Yahudi or Gentile?

There has been much speculation and love affair to make Luke seem to be a gentile but this is only because the Christian world which has lived in much ignorance over 2000 years of Yahudim customs continues to view many things in Scripture from a modern 21st century perspective ignoring the milieu it was written in and the message that it carries onto all generation of Y'sra'el.

Here I am going to give you straight forward opinion and proofs why Luke can never be a gentile but he was of Yahudee stock and He was from the House of Levi.

Evidences:

Luke is the only writer who knows of the order of the service of the Temple the priestly order because he lists the division of Abia in Luke 1:5.

Luke 1:5 There was in the days of Herodes, the king of Yahudah, a certain Kohen (Priest) named Zechar'yah, of the **course of Abi'yah**: and his wife was of the daughters of Aharon,

Luke in fact Himself was the order of Kohenim. This is why he knows the divisions of the priests. This does not mean the other writers did not know about these divisions but it is clear that Luke was a Levite for several reasons. As a physician which was his profession he would only have to attend the Temple three times
annually on three feats the other times he was free to conduct his business as he wished which of course he did.

The entire gospel of Luke is addressed to the Sadducees. The person mentioned as Theophilus was the High Priest (Sadducean) who served between 37-41CE according to Josephus, Antiquity of the Jews.

Shimon the son of Boethus was the High Priest after Theophilus. His two other relatives were Ananus (His abbah) and Caiaphas (His brother-in-law), listed in Luke 3:2. Theophilus would certainly not have been the Hebrew name of the said person as it is stated in Greek and wrongly translated instead of transliterating. No Greek person would have ever been allowed to be the High Priest in the Temple no matter how much money he would give. His name in Greek means 'The one who loves Elohim.' Luke also could not be a gentile doctor as most assert, he was a Yahudee and of Levite origin, one well versed with the Temple services. And was witnessing events to the High Priest and showing him that the truth would benefit many in the aristocracy class occupied by the Sadducees.

This is point blank proof that if I was a High Priest I would only accept a letter of proof from another person who belonged to the same group of people or class i.e. a priest or a son of Tzadok. Bear with me as we further uncover the identity of Luke. I am not going to waste your time with names of Yahudim that looked like and felt like gentile in Colossians 4:10 but I will and have presented irrefutable evidence that Luke was a Levite and from the House of Tzadok.

Rabbi Paul tells us in the letter to Rome.

Romiyah 3:2 Much every way: chiefly, because that to them were committed the oracles of Elohim.

This proves YHWH is not a liar but reliable that all scriptures were only given to the Yahudim. I myself am of the Yahudim stock and the House of Levi this is the reason why these revelations have been opened to me the one who was brought up in a Muslim household very similar to Musa brought up in the House of the King of Egypt. Myself of the priestly stock and kingly stock because in 1998 Yahushua called me out and in 2004 YHWH told me I am of
the House of Musa and will be used likewise with the sceptre given by YHWH to disseminate truth to the world from country to country.

A man does not tell you of certainly of something unless he has the credentials to prove it. Well to most in the west Luke as a doctor seems to be good credentials but this is not so. His credentials were that he was from the House of Tzadok. You do not need better credentials than that.

Luke 1:4 That you might know the certainty of those things, wherein you have been instructed.

The Covenant Covenant writings were committed to those in Y'sra'el and they were from the stock or tribes of Y'sra'el. The most important people in this group were those who were of the priestly tribes such as we revealed the identity of Mark who was a Levite the son of Miriam of Magdala. Matthew was also a Levite the son of Cleopas and his first wife because as was custom of ruler class kinship he was named Levi which was the name of Matthew's Great grandfather.

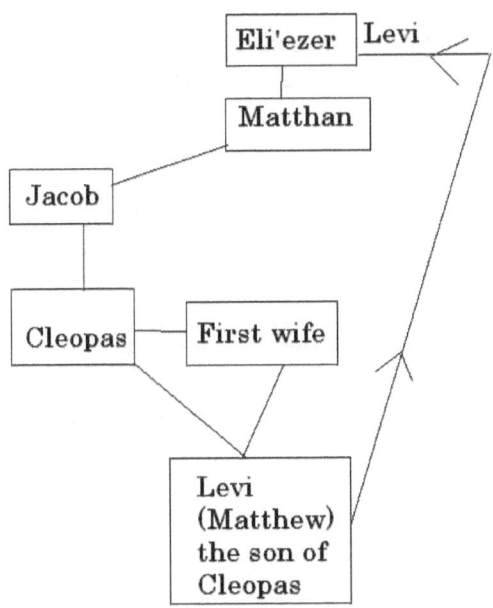

Using the kinship analysis pattern we can see Cleopas had two wives and his first wife was Patrilineal means from his father's side who gave birth to Matthew who was named Levi so that was his firstborn and as was custom he was given the names of both his grandfather and great grandfather. Cleopas's second wife Miriam the mother of Yahushua came with the Levirate rule when he married her after his elder brother Yosef's death.

We have already proved Matthew, Mark and even John the son of Zabdi were Levites. We have ample evidence to prove that Luke had Levite blood but I will also prove his father and his real name. This is an important fact that all four main gospel writers had Levitical bloodlines. This gives the writers the credentials from Elohim and is an important signature for the revealing of the Messiah.

People who decided to make Luke a gentile will be disappointed but he was not your traditional Christian though he was a follower of the way and a Hebrew Netzarim the follower of Yahushua and Judaism. A lie told many times does not make it true. It is time for Christendom to correct its errors and stop the lies.

More Evidence

Luke 1:6 And they were both **righteous** before Elohim, **walking in all the commandments** and ordinances of **YHWH** and blameless.

Luke also seems to know that both Zechariah and Elizabeth were righteous. How does he know this detail did he conduct an interview? Did he ask Elizabeth are you righteous and is your husband righteous?

Even if he did conduct an interview that seems rather impossible and it has nothing to do with him being Elizabeth's personal doctor.

To westerners maybe these were his patients however the reality is that the only way a first century person would pronounce someone righteous is, if he would see their state of good or evil by being a member of the Temple and would have seen these people there on a regular occurrence and of course determined by their actions that these were righteous Torah obedient believers because he mentioned they were "walking in Commandments", which means keeping the halacha (agreed Torah customs) of the Pharisees. He was not talking about the modern twist that Christianity is performing today disobeying the commandments. If you asked Luke to give you a paraphrase of what Christianity should be termed then by observation he could tell you they are anti-Torah and not walking blamelessly therefore they are unrighteous. I would apply the same principle that Luke applies. However I have generalized to show you there are only a few ways to arrive at the truth. The priests function in the Temple was not just to do sacrifices but they also prayed for people, took their tithes and pronounced their sins forgiven upon a confession which is how a priest could determine someone's standing in Elohim. They were not psychic and did not play mind games. When they were not sure of something they would enquire of Elohim and the Ummim and Thummim would be used to determine a yes or no answer.

Was Luke from Antioch?

There is not enough proof to make this conclusion, just because he met Rabbi Paul in Antioch or accompanied him on a journey does not automatically make him a native of Antioch. Unfortunately the Western scholarship has run away with many ideas and majority of which are proving to be false. Trinity is another one of them.

Luke is mentioned three times twice directly in the following three places and none of them mention him living in Antioch yet most of Christendom has already concluded he is a resident of Antioch. Colossians 4:14; Philemon 24; and 2 Timothy 4:11. If I go on a journey to the USA and meet my friends there and we travel from there to the East then would you conclude that I lived in the USA because I started my journey with some friends there? This type of scholarship is not only foolish but leads one to make conclusions that would not be tenable in the Netzarim writings.

Luke 1: 1-2 Forasmuch as many have taken in hand to set forth in order a declaration of those things which are most surely believed among **us**, **2** Even as **they** delivered them to **us**, which from the beginning were eyewitnesses, and servants of the word;

Who is the 'they' and who is the 'us?' What are the "believed things amongst us" which includes Pharisees and Sadducees.

The 'they' are prophets of the Bible sent to Y'sra'el and the 'us' is Kul Y'sra'el, the twelve tribes of Y'sra'el and its not talking about the
three gospels and Rabbi Paul's letters but talking about truths penned down many centuries ago that were coming

true at this time written in the Tanach about the coming days and Jerusalem. This would declare things of the arrival of the anointed one (The Messiah) and what was to take place. This tells you that Luke has identified Himself with kol Y'sra'el and not with gentile Church. He was not a gentile because this is fundamental proof of how he proves the accuracy of the Hebrew Bible. Also his writing to the High Priest reveals that he had a relationship with him therefore was a member of the Levite tribe in the Temple and was a frequent traveller. NO he did not collect air miles like Europeans and Americans so we cannot conclude how often he travelled and how many air miles he collected but he did travel, served as a Physician and also as a Levite in the Temple.

Who was he and where did he live?

He lived in Jerusalem during the times of the feasts where all the priests officiated but otherwise would have been a resident of Galilee. We are given his Roman name but his Hebrew name was likely to be Hezekiah or Mattityahu. How do we know this? I will show you how by using the rules of kinship analysis we can determine his father, his mother including his missing name. As I illustrated in this book there were two main Levite families one of Miriam and one of Yosef of Arimathaea. We have evidence that Luke had a cordial relationship with the High Priest and knew many inner Temple processes which only a Temple priest would know. We also see that when Rabbi Paul is being arrested in the Temple he is there but not arrested as a gentile when Rabbi Paul was charged with bringing a gentile into the Temple. If Luke happens to be also gentile then why did they not arrest him also? This is because he was one of the officials of the Temple there. His father was a key figure why he had access to the Temple areas as a priest.

It was an offence to bring a gentile to the Temple and especially if he was uncircumcised it was prohibited strictly and one of the charges that they applied to Rabbi Paul was that he was teaching uncircumcision which was

seen as an act of rebellion against the covenant and considered ritual impurity to be within the precinct of the Temple in such a state. Today Christians are quite proud to be without physical circumcision forgetting that this breaks the Covenant that YHWH gave to Abraham and puts Christianity
squarely in the bracket of rebelliousness and unclean. In the ancient land of Egypt the Egyptian priests had to be circumcised and they would not take wives who were uncircumcised. Even today in Africa when people get married there are mass circumcisions prior to marriage. It is well known and reported that in Africa the disease of aids is worst in Christian areas of no circumcisions and the least worst in Muslim areas where they are circumcised. Circumcision has proved to be of benefit against many diseases though it is still scientifically unclear how the benefits come about however since YHWH made this a strict covenant command there is no getting out of it. Christians who do not perform this act are simply plain disobedient and have no part in the abrahamic-covenant which requires the act.

Even in the Temple the court of the gentiles where the gentiles were allowed to enter in legally the gentiles had to be physically circumcised without which they were not allowed to enter. It was possible that someone could potentially take another gentile in the Temple premises who perhaps was not circumcised as a favour through a person who had access to the premises. Rabbi Paul had access to the premises and knowledge of some key officials so the charge against him was the more serious though he was not guilty.

Acts 21:29- 30 (For they had seen before with him in the city **Trophimos an Ephesian**, whom they supposed that Rabbi Paul (Sha'ul) had brought into the Beyth HaMikdash (Temple).) **30** And all the city was stirred up, and the people ran together: and they took Rabbi Paul (Sha'ul), and dragged him out of the Beyth HaMikdash (Temple) courts and shut the doors.

This clearly shows us Luke is the writer and onlooker, since he is not even spoken against this indicates that Luke was a Temple official watching the whole episode so he was an eye witness account. About his father this is what another relative Josephus had to say:

> Flavius Josephus tells us in his works
> Now there was one of these Essenes, whose name was Manahem, who had this testimony, that he not only conducted his life after an excellent manner, but had the foreknowledge of future events given to him by God also.

This brings us one step closer to the identity of Luke. I will set forth this opinion that Luke was the son of Manahem the Av Beth Din or the Vice President of the Temple courts. Manahem was the son of Hezekiah the son of Mattityahu who in the gospels is known as Mattat or Matthan/Matthias these are all variants names of the same person. Therefore being of the Levite clan Luke would have been likewise been Levite working in the Temple but also a willing traveller just like his father. His Hebrew name would have been Mattityahu named after his great grandfather since it was the custom for ruler classes to name their first born son with the name of the father/grand father. We know that Manahem left the Temple courts to travel abroad because he took with him 160 Rabbis eighty of them from the school of Hillel and went to the Diaspora to teach the Torah. It was known that he went to serve the King i.e. YHWH.

The Talmud tells us the following:

Hillel the Elder had 80 disciples, 30 of whom were worthy of the Divine Spirit resting upon them…30 of whom were worthy that the sun should stand still for them…the greatest of them was Jonathan ben Uzziel, the smallest of them was Yohanan be Zakkai… Talmud Sukkah 28A

So Manahem took with him 80 pairs meaning 160 famed Rabbis of which eighty were the disciples of Elder

Rabbi Hillel and eighty the disciples of Rabbi Manahem to go teach the Torah to the nations. This occurrence is recorded in the Talmud Hagigah 16b that around 20 CE he took off with the eighty pairs of men.

According to Rabbi Harvey Falk he stated it as follows:

Rava the Hasid stated that Menahem the Essene "went forth to the King's (God's) service, along with 80 pairs of disciples dressed in silk." (Rabbi Harvey Falk, "Jesus the Pharisee, A New Look at the Jewishness of Jesus", Paulist Press, 997 Macarthur Boulevard, Mahwah, N.J. 07430, 1985, page 49-50)

    It is highly likely he knew about the tribes being in the Diaspora and decided to reach out to them for restoration. They were in neighbouring Africa, Mesopotamia where the Ethiopians had a dynasty and in far away places as India. These were Black Hebrews. There is no question about it that as was custom
Manahem would have had two wives one in the south in Jerusalem and one in the north at the north/south axis and he would have had children from both. I do not think Luke lived in Antioch but was a resident and son of the Northern wife of Manahem who lived in Nazareth. I will present corroborating evidence later.

    The people of Y'sra'el could easily travel between Turkey and Y'sra'el as they had relative and friends there and it was easy to travel there by ship see Yonah who travelled to Tarshish from Modern Jaffa (Jon 1:3), which was one of the seaports not far from Nazareth. Turkey was a place where there was a large population of Yahudim and gentiles this is why we see Rabbi Paul heading off to Turkey on his journeys to reach the lost tribes.

    This makes Luke also a relative to Yahushua in fact the son of an uncle. Also this is obvious that Luke was appealing to the Saducean High Priest in his gospel account which is critical evidence to show us that his father had relations with these people and so did Luke.

Manahem actually had very good relations with both the Pharisees and Sadducees and he had very good relations with the Hassids (Essenes) in Qumran because he was also a Hasid and he is the best candidate to be Luke's father given the evidences that I possess of first century Judaism and the Temple.

When the school of Shammai took prominence it was then that Manahem was forced to resign from his post and his position was taken over by the school of Shammai as these Pharisees hated the gentiles and did not want to teach them the Torah while the Pharisees aligned with the school of Hillel wanted to teach the gentiles Torah and reach them in love including Manahem.

This is one of the sayings of Elder Rabbi Hillel recorded:

That which is hateful to you, do not do to your neighbor. That is the whole Torah; the rest (is commentary, the explanation); go and study it.

Shammaites objected to this idea and saw them as people who did not merit salvation since they were also occupying them while the Hillelites did not see it this way and saw it fit and proper to reach them with the message of the Torah.

The day Shammai came to power in the Temple the Talmud records it was as if Y'sra'el had built the Golden Calf (Shabbat 17A) this is because Shammai had put in eighteen new measures which caused bitter fighting and several of the school of Hillel followers were murdered. These measures were in essence from Shammai's point of view to protect Judaism from the gentiles, the Hellenists who were trying to conform Judaism to be like the rest of the world.

We also see the big debate in Matthew Chapter 23 between Yahushua and the Pharisees who were from the school of Shammai.

Matthew 23:13 But woe to you, scribes and Pharisees, hypocrites! **For you shut up the kingdom of shamayim (heaven) against men** for you neither go in yourselves, neither you permit those that are entering to go in.

The course of discussion in Matthew 23 with the Shammaites clearly sees Yahushua said 'For you shut up the kingdom of shamayim against men'. The term 'men' here only applies to the gentiles. See the Talmud Shabbat 31a and Sanhedrin 105A as per R Eli'ezer for more details.

So here is our chart for Luke's family.

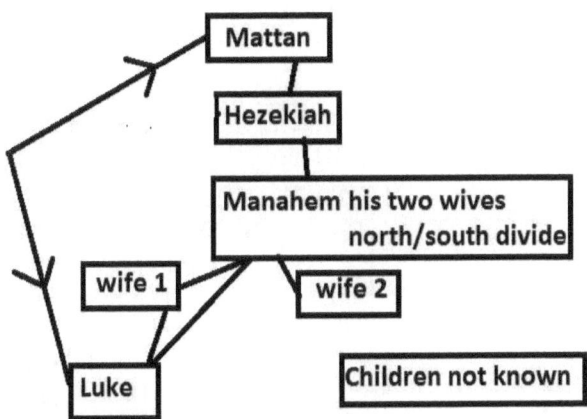

Luke's Hebrew name would be Mattityahu

Manahem was a famous person who also received divine revelations and it was said about him by Josephus the historian the son of Yosef of Arimathaea who was also related to him.

Flavius Josephus, Antiquities, XV, x, vi
We have thought it proper to relate these facts to our readers, how strange so ever they be, and to declare what hath happened among us, because many of these Essenes have, by their excellent virtue, been thought worthy of this knowledge of divine revelations."

There is another key figure a person by the name of Hananiah and we have often talked about the North/South wife pattern in the ruling classed and princes. We find the same is true in all the relations coming down from Abraham's ancestors' majority of who were of African decent.

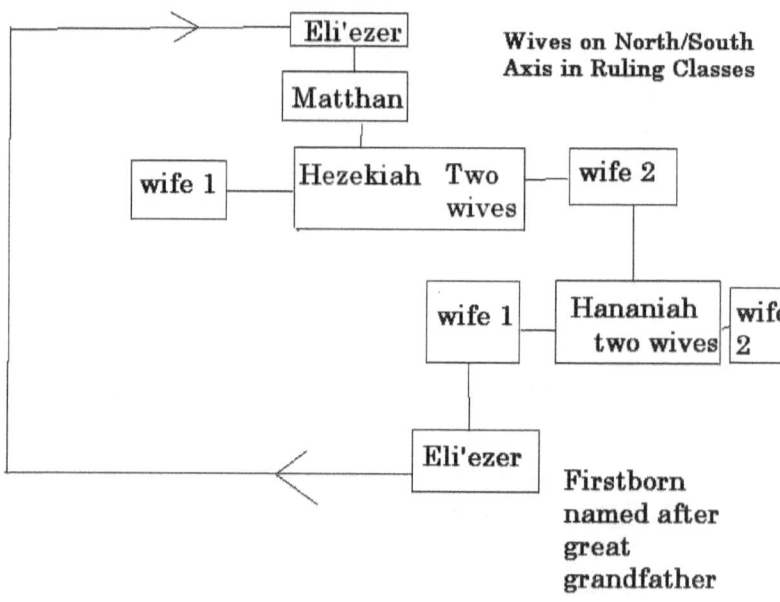

As can be seen in the diagram both the wife of Hezekiah the son of Matthan and the wife of his son Hananiah name their first born sons after the name of the Patriarch Eli'ezer. This as I have stated was normal custom with two wives based on the North/South Axis. To understand this more you will have to purchase the HTHS

Hebraic Study bible and read it. Who was Hananiah? This was the person who sat in arbitration between the two dominant schools in Jerusalem (Shabbat 13B) the school of Shammai, and the school of Hillel. It was in his house that discussions took place to resolve disputed matters so as to provide a mutual ground for talks. He is the compiler of Megillat Ta'anit the official scroll on the Jews fasting days. The debates that took place between Elder Hillel and Elder Shammai are recorded in the Talmud (Shabbat 17A and Tosefta Shabbat 1:8).

Corroborating evidence in support of Luke being a Levite

1. Intricate knowledge of the Temple only available to the priests.
2. Knowledge of the cycles of the priesthood only mentioned by Luke because he was trying to tell us that he also was a priest.
3. The priestly city location was in Nazareth where Luke also lived another factor behind his priesthood. There is no reference in any of the epistle that he lived in Antioch this is only based on conjecture and speculation.
4. He had intimate knowledge of Miriam's family this would only be because he was one of their family members and physician to the family living close to them in Nazareth.
5. He had detailed knowledge of Hebraisms used in his gospel because he was a Hebrew speaking man who could converse in more than one language and also wrote his gospel in Hebrew which was later translated into Greek and Aramaic.
6. He knew the High Priest and was frequently in the Temple otherwise how would he know where the altar of incense was (Luke 1:9)?
7. He knew about the Torah and Haftorah reading cycles in the synagogues (Luke 4:16-17, Acts 13:15) which many Christians even to this day do not know anything about yet this man writes about it and this was because he was a Levite and a genetic Jew.
8. He has extensive knowledge of Nazareth and Galil only one who lived there would have that kind of knowledge

(Luke 4:29-31).

How did he know that Sabbath healing was forbidden (Luke 13:14) when in fact this information was what Beyth Shammai believed and not Hillel. This was a Temple ruling by Shammai and he can only know this if he was there in the Temple and also the fact that he understood the disputed teachings and discussions that had taken place between the two major schools. Gentiles rarely show interest in Hebrew things but the Rabbis and priests show interest in these types of debates which we see Luke presenting this type of information.

I have absolutely no doubt in my mind that Luke was a Hebrew of Levite stock and that he wrote his book in the language of Hebrew. All the evidence that I have examined points us to these undeniable facts and that he was a resident of Nazareth close to the family of Yahushua.

E: The curse of Konyahu (Jehoiachin)

Jehoiachin is also known as Konyahu (Coniah) in the Bible, he was the second last king of Y'sra'el before Zedekiah. The big problem with him was as with many ancient kings in Y'sra'el that he was not obedient to Elohim and sinned on many occasions. This resulted in the extreme displeasure of YHWH to punish him and his descendants by putting a curse upon him. Some Scholars see three important elements of this curse which I will also examine. However I see at least seven elements to it which many fail to take into consideration.

We shall examine the two main solutions given by traditional Christendom and then I will present the third solution since I feel the first two solutions are not adequate and do not render the solution however I am certain that any of the two solutions would be suffice for any seminary to pass the student in a given test but in my case I would contend that neither meets the criteria set by Elohim as I will demonstrate here.

The Curse:

Yirmeyah (Jeremiah) 22:24-30 As I live, says YHWH, though Konyahu the son of Yahuyakim (Jehoiakim) king of Yahudah were the signet upon my right hand, yet would I pluck you there; **25** And I will give you into the hand of them that seek your life, and into the hand of them whose face you fear, even into the hand of Nebukadretzar king of Babylon, and into the hand of the Chaldeans. **26** And I will cast you out, and your mother that bare you, into another country, where you were not born; and there shall you die. **27** But to the land whereunto they desire to return, there shall they not return. **28** Is this man Konyahu a despised broken idol? Is he a vessel wherein is no pleasure? Therefore are they cast out, he and his seed, and are cast into a land which they know not? **29** O earth, earth, earth, hear the word of **YHWH**. **30 Thus says YHWH, Write this man childless**, a **man that shall not prosper in his days**; **for no man of his seed shall prosper, sitting upon the throne of Dawud**, and **ruling any more in Yahudah**.

The three elements of the curse seen by many scholars
1. The man shall be childless
2. The man shall not prosper in his days
3. His descendants cannot sit on the throne of Judah.

Many people believe that since Jehoiachin had children in exile later the first part of the curse was lifted quoting the following.

Dibre Hayamim alef (First Chronicles) 3:17-18 And the sons of Yekon'yah (Jehoiachin); Assir, Shealti'el his son, **18** Malchiram also, and Pedi'yah, and Shenazar, Yecamiyah, Hoshama, and Nedabiah.

Malekhim Bet (Second Kings) 25:27-29 And it came to

pass in the thirtieth- seven year of the captivity of Yaukin (Jehoiachin) king of Yahudah, in the twelfth month, on the twentieth-seventh day of the month, that Evil -merodach king of Babylon in the year that he began to reign did lift up the head of Yaukin (Jehoiachin) king of Yahudah out of prison; **28** And he spoke kindly to him, and set his throne above the throne of the kings that were with him in Babylon; **29** And changed his prison garments: and he did eat lechem (bread) continually before him all the days of his life.

Solution 1:

Using the above verse it is stipulated using the Talmud to back the assertion that the curse was lifted noting that Jehoiachin had children and did sit comfortably upon the table. Using the thesis above it is then assumed that the line of curse was fully erased and thus any descendant could now sit on the throne.

It is also noted in the following Talmudic passages that the conditions of the curse was lifted according to Hebrew authorities citing the Talmud or opinion of some of the Rabbis.

Pesikta Rabbati, Piska 47, translated by William G. Braude, Yale University Press, pg. 797-798
"R. Joshua ben Levi, however, argued as follows: Repentance sets aside the entire decree, and prayer half the decree. You find that it was so with Jehoiachin, king of Judah. For the Holy One, blessed be He, swore in His anger, As I live, saith the Lord, though Coniah the son of Jehoiakhim king of Judah were the signet on a hand, yet by My right - note, as R. Meir said, that is was by His right hand that God swore - I would pluck thee hence (Jer. 22:24). And what was decreed against Jehoiachin? That he die childless. As is said Write ye this man childless (Jer. 22:40). But as soon as he avowed penitence, the Holy One, blessed be He, set aside the decree, as is

shown by Scripture's reference to The sons of Jehoiachin - the same is Assir - Shealtiel his son, etc. (1 Chron 3:17). And Scripture says further: In that day . . . will I take thee, O Zerubbabel . . . the son of Shealtiel . . . and will make thee as a signet (Haggai 2:23). Behold, then, how penitence can set aside the entire decree!

Is it not ironic that Christendom is quite happy to use the Talmud to prove that the curse was lifted in order they can convert the Yahudim to their way of lifestyle and bring them into idolatry since they reject the laws in the Torah paying only lip service to them but when the Talmud is used to show that the Torah law is valid then Christendom has a problem accepting the decrees set therein. I find this is a double standard often employed by Christendom.

Now I will show the second answer of Christians that they use to prove the curse does not apply any longer.

Solution 2:

They contend that since Yahushua was born through a virgin birth therefore this renders the curse useless because He did not biologically belong to Yosef the husband of Miriam.

This is indication to me that Christendom has little understanding of scriptural curses and Hebrew law.

One then must ask the question that if his supernatural birth avoids the curse then how is Yahushua any longer heir to the throne which He was acquiring through Yosef Miriam's husband?

Hebrew law is very clear on the rules of adoption that whether one believes in the virgin birth or not that if a child say of Miriam was adopted by Yosef as son therefore all his property rights and kingship belong to him irrelevant of the virgin birth. He could have been a child left in a basket on the doorstep and Yosef merely picked him up and made him a son still holds true to Hebrew law that his property rights and kingship rights belong to the baby picked up from the basket.

In fact this did happen to Moses who was picked out of a basket. Let me show you.

Dibre Hayamim alef (First Chronicles) 4:18 And his wife Yahudi'yah bare Yared the father of Gedor, and Cheber the father of Socho, and Yekuthi'el the father of Zenowah. And these are the sons of Bith'yah[9] the daughter of Pharaoh, which Mered took.

Musa (Moses) had several names (see the HTHS Hebraic Study Bible) and one of the names was Yared and please note that in the above Scripture in First Chronicles 4:18 he is called the son of Yahudi'yah.

Shemoth (Exodus) 6:20 And Amram took for himself Yeh'kobad, the daughter of his father's brother as wife; and **she bore him Aharon and Musa** (Moses):

How could this be since he was actually born to Yeh'kobad.

This is the case of a birth and adoption. When Musa (Moses) was born he was born through Yeh'kobad but his life was under threat from Pharaoh and his men so his mother cast him into the water. He was subsequently picked up by Pharaoh's daughter who had converted into Judaism. She was going down to the river to take a bath to remove uncleanness from her because she had cast off all idolatry according to the Talmud. Her original name was Bith'yah but after conversion her name became Yahudi'yah.

When the book of Chronicles speaks about Musa it simply says Yahudi'yah bare him because according to the rules of adoption whether he was born from one woman (Yeh'kobad) and brought up
in the house of another (Yahudi'yah) it sees no difference between the two. Musa was the son of both and legally he could have been the next Pharaoh as a prince but we know that he did not aspire to the throne and joined his people to be persecuted for righteousness sake. See diagram below.

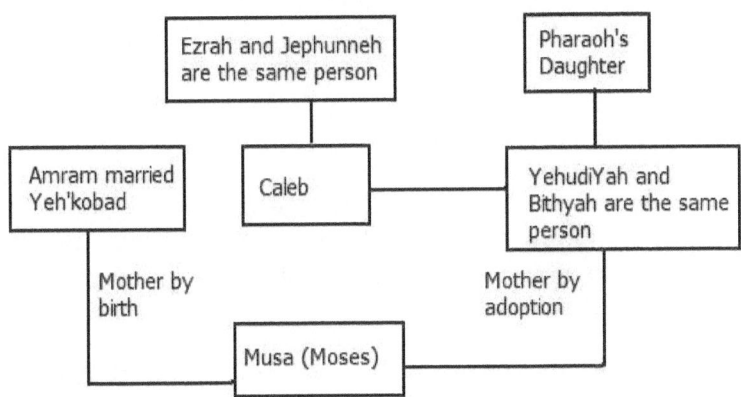

In the diagram above Mered is the same person known to us as Caleb and his father was known as Jephunneh who after conversion into Judaism became known as Ezrah. So what does this teach us? Upon conversion the person is no longer seen as a gentile and he or she should take a New Hebrew name of suitable meaning.

So from the above example we can see that Yahushua had the legal right to the royal throne both with the birth through Miriam and even with the adoption did not need to be physically born to Yosef the son of Jacob.

What we also need to remember, when King Dawud was king the rightful heir to his throne was Amnon the firstborn but YHWH told King Dawud that King Solomon would inherit the throne. There was a switch for various reasons too numerous to discuss in this book so likewise

Yahushua would become king as He was also designated by the Father in heaven (Ps 2:6).

Now we will look at the issues surrounding the curse being lifted although many Christians use the argument that the virgin birth bypasses the curse or the lineage to Miriam to go around the curse but I contend that I will set this premise that YHWH's curses unless conditional do not lift unless He said so which He did not. Why are we then trying to circumvent what was not circumvented?

His blessings also unless lifted by His words are forever. We have to be careful that in Scripture YHWH is not light-minded about putting a curse upon someone unless the situation really called for it and was extremely bad. He is not human like us so does not jump to conclusions nor has irrational jealousies, fears or tantrums because He is abundantly merciful, above measure righteous and very long suffering while we humans have a low suffering ratio, can get irate easily, tend to get sidetracked easily.

Most of us live with a problem of getting angry quickly when someone does not agree with us. I know I used to have this problem until YHWH changed my nature to look upon Him and learn to be more patient.

I do not believe that this curse is conditional because YHWH had set no conditions upon it and therefore this cannot be lifted in the life of Jehoiachin and nor from his descendants. There is a solution but first I must show you the problems in what is termed lifting of the curse. The first problem that I see with most people who believe in this view simply do not understand what is at stake and why the curse was put there in the first place.

It is very unwise to make light a curse that was invoked by the creator Himself.

Furthermore, just because the king had children or sat at the Babylonian King's table who freed him from jail does not annul the decree set by the King of Kings from above. Why do I say that? YHWH does in his curse allow mercy so any mercy that is seen should not be seen as an annulment of the curse. I will set forth two clear examples one that the curse upon Chava (Eve) that was put upon her for bearing children in pain never lifted even to this day because a woman still has children in pain and the second curse on Ahdahm was never lifted either because man still toils in labour with sorrow. Don't we all want to be rich and not have to do a day's work? We all wish we have loads of cash and we can just do what we want.

Haggai 2:23 (KJV) In that day, saith the LORD of hosts, will I take thee, O Zerubbabel, my servant, the son of Shealtiel, saith the LORD, and will make thee as a signet: for I have chosen thee, saith the LORD of hosts.

Christians also claim that this prophecy in Haggai shows that the curse had been lifted. This is not true as I will demonstrate.

When YHWH says the following:

Yirme'yah (Jeremiah) 22:24 As I live, says YHWH, though Konyahu the son of Yahuyakim (Jehoiakim) king of Yahudah were the signet upon my right hand, yet would I pluck you there;

   Christians try to use the signet ring that YHWH will give to Zerubbab'el to say that this curse had lifted. This is not true. The prophecy of Zerubbab'el is yet future and has nothing to do with the past. In the future YHWH will overthrow the radical Islamic Empire that is what this prophecy relates to. Note Haggai 2:22 is yet to take place. Zerubbab'el will return in the future as one of the witnesses to rebuild the future 3rd Temple.

Haggai 2:21-24 Speak to Zerubbab'el, governor of Yahudah, saying; I will shake the heavens and the earth; 22 And I will overthrow the throne of kingdoms, and I will destroy the strength of the kingdoms of the nations; and I will overthrow the chariots, and those that ride in them; and the horses and their riders shall come down, every one by the sword of his brother. 23 In that day, says YHWH of hosts, will I take you, O Zerubbab'el, my servant, the son of Shealti'el, says YHWH, and will make you as a signet: for I have chosen you, says YHWH of hosts

Points to note from Haggai the prophet:

…And the horses and their riders shall come down, every one by the sword of his brother – **This means radical Muslims will kill other Muslims in a future war involving Y'sra'el.**

Kingdoms of the heathens or nations surrounding Y'sra'el. Only applied to Muslims who go up to fight.

World War III - Unmasking the End -Times Beast page 347 this is amazing! Haggai is told that the Master will destroy the "throne [Turkey/Pergamos/Beth Togarmah] of these kingdoms." They are the Islamic confederacy with 10 heads/kings as seen in Psalm 83, Ezekiel 38, Zechariah chapters 12 and 14. This is the prophesied Islamic coalition, of surrounding heathens. They are killed by confusion and by their own brothers. The reference to "in that day," is none other than the "Day of the Master" yet future. The Master reveals HE HAS CHOSEN Zerubbabel for a divine mission and given him a special ring as a sign that he has been selected to fulfill YHWH's future purpose.

The curse is not made up of three parts as some have suggested but I propose that it is made up of seven parts. You could count it as seven mini curses as follows:

1. **Plucked out of the land of Y'sra'el**
2. **Given to the Chaldeans and to Babylon.**
3. **He will die there in exile.**
4. **He cannot return back to Y'sra'el in his lifetime.**
5. **He is despised in the eyes of YHWH.**

6. He will be childless in Y'sra'el.
7. No descendant of his will rule in Y'sra'el as a king.

In Jeremiah chapter 22 from verse 24 to verse 30 this is all connected and not separated at all.

Let us examine the steps.

1. **Was he plucked out of the land?** – Yes he was removed from Y'sra'el so the curse was fulfilled and remained there included in the curse was his mother Nahushta who went with him.

2. **Was he given to the Chaldeans and to Nebuchadnezzar?** Yes.

3. **Did he die in exile or return to Y'sra'el?** He died in exile and never returned to Y'sra'el neither did his mother so the curse fulfilled its purpose.

4. **He will be childless in Y'sra'el this has nothing to do with having children in captivity** because if he had children in Y'sra'el then he would have left an heir to the throne but YHWH strictly said "in his days" so what days is Elohim connecting him with? Many scholars take this for his entire life but **I would suggest this term "in his days" is only connected with his reign in Y'sra'el which was about to come to an abrupt end** and that he would not bear children in Y'sra'el. So the curse fulfilled. He then having children in Babylon is of no consequence either since they could not sit on the throne either.

In Hebrew it says B'Yemi V' Ki Lo Yizlakh m'zara'v'aish Yshav. This means **his days in Y'sra'el** sitting upon the throne followed by the hook, the Vav, which connects this with "In his days AND for no man of his seed shall prosper or sit upon the throne. Well the throne was in Y'sra'el and not in Babylon so the term "in his days" is only connected to his tenure in Y'sra'el and not in Babylon.

The children that he was to have as King would no

longer be born upon the land of Y'sra'el from where he was going to be expelled. This cannot be applied to the children of captivity because they no longer had relevance to the kingship status. We note that scholars use the argument that Zerubbab'el was governor because the curse had lifted but what they do not reveal to the layman that there is a marked difference between a governor and a king. He was not going to be the king and that is all the curse said and required. The curse did not stipulate that a son could not become a governor so we cannot use this to annul the curse.

In the above passage here is what is not mentioned by the people who espouse the lifting of the curse: The implications of the curse were until his death and his descendant's death that is when the curse will finish and not a moment before. Note death is the ultimate punishment of a sovereign or otherwise.

If we examine the curse of Adam, we know that both Adam and Chava were fully redeemed even though they physically died but their curse did not lift. Their curse will also be lifted by Yahushua when He returns but it will only effect the faithful in Y'sra'el and will not be a worldwide lifting.

Yeshayahu (Isaiah) 65:23 They shall not labour in vain, nor bring forth for trouble; for they are the seed of the blessed of
YHWH, and their offspring with them.

They shall not labour in vain is also the curse that was put upon man to toil in hardship will be fully lifted in the coming kingdom. Also women in the kingdom will give birth to children and there will be marriages but they in the kingdom will not have a painful labour.

The curse on Jehoiachin did not mean that he could not be redeemed of course repentance would have allowed him full redemption and a relaxing of the curse as we see mentioned in the two Scriptures I presented above but this does not remove the cursed line since YHWH did not stipulate a condition to remove the curse. When YHWH does not stipulate a condition that means it will remain until the condition is met which was both Jehoiachin's death and his descendant's death.

We should not be treating the curse of the Most High like sweets and toffees then what point would there be in putting on such a curse if it had no bad implications?

So how do we get around the curse? A few important points first that tribal affiliations were determined from the father that is which tribe you are from.

Bmidbar (Numbers) 1:18 And they assembled all the congregation together on the first day of the second month, and they declared their pedigrees after their mishpachot (families), **by the Beyth (house) of their ahvot (fathers)**, according to the number of the names, from twenty years old and upward, by their censes.

Furthermore, whether you are a Yahudim or not came to be determined by the mother which was taken at the time of Nehemiah how he separated the people from their foreign wives.

Nechem'yah 13:23-30 In those days I also saw Yahudim (Hebrew people) that had married wives of Ashdod, of Ammon, and of Moab: **24** And their children spoke half in the speech of Ashdod, and could not speak in the language of Yahudah, but according to the language of each people. **25** And I contended with them, and called a curse upon them, and smote certain of them, and plucked off their hair, and made them swear by Elohim, saying, You shall not give your daughters to their sons, nor take their daughters to your sons, or for yourselves. **26** Did not Sulahmon king of Y'sra'el sin by these things? Yet among many nations was there no king like him, who was beloved of his Elohim, and Elohim made him king over all Y'sra'el: nevertheless his foreign wives made him sin. **27**

Shall we then hearken to you to do all this great evil, to transgress against our Elohim in marrying foreign wives? **28** And one of the sons of Yoyada, the son of Eliashib the Kohen ha Gadol (High Priest), was son in law to Sanballat the Horonite: therefore I chased him from me. **29** Remember them, O my Elohim, because they have defiled the priesthood, and the covenant of the priesthood, and of the Lewites. **30** Thus I cleansed them from all foreigners, and appointed the wards of the kohenim (priests) and the Lewites, every one in his business;

Whether we take Yahushua's genealogy from Matthew or Luke he is the son of Yosef and his ancestry connects back to Dawud. Note that the Yosef that is mentioned in Luke 3:23 is in fact Yosef of Arimathaea and not the husband of Miriam. After Miriam's husband's death she went home to the father who had also died and then Yahushua technically became adopted by Yosef of Arimathaea. Since Yosef was from Yahudah and held the seat of the House of King Dawud from the Temple Yahushua could rightly be passed the kingly line.

This means that Yahushua has a royal lineage from both sides that Matthew and Luke mentioned.

Luke 3: 27 Which was the son of Yahanna, which was the son of Refa'yah, which was the son of Zerubbab'el, which was the son of Shealti'el, which was the son of Neri,

Mattityahu (Matthew) 1:13 And Zerubbab'el begat Abihud; and Abihud begat Eliakim; and Eliakim begat Azor;

Zerubbab'el was married to three wives and different children are mentioned for genealogical royal lineage. Zerubbab'el's wives were Amytis a Babylonian princess who was the mother of his firstborn Shazrezzar. His second wife was Rhodah a Persian princess who was the mother of his second son Reza, and the third wife was Eshthra the mother of Meshullam, who was a Hebrew princess.

It was decided by the Great Sanhedrin prior to the birth of Yahushua in 37 BC that they were going to incorporate the two lineages the lineage of Abihud and the other of Refa'yah to inherit the throne of Dawud which before was forbidden to these lines because of uncertainly of Babylonian women being married to Hebrew men.

The decision to allow the lineages came because the lineages of the royal throne were running out of male heirs for the kingly lines. This means in their eyes they had decided that the curse had lifted also and decided to enthrone the male heirs of these tribes.

However we have not fully dealt with the curse yet which we will deal with now.

Solution 3 Proposed by Rabbi Simon Altaf

First a question why is it necessary for Yahushua to bypass the curse on His first coming?

My solution is probably going to be revolutionary to this question because if you take the view of the Talmud then the curse had already lifted in which case Yahushua is legal heir but do we agree that YHWH is eternal and his curse and blessings cannot be revoked unless He Himself mentions them as conditional. We note Jehoiachin's curse is not conditional.

The reason why I asked the question above is why does Yahushua at His first coming has to bypass the curse? It was yesterday when I was travelling on the train and asking the question to the Master that this answer was handed to me straight and I thank the Holy One that I can write this now. Christians do not have to do gymnastics to prove the curse is lifted. Let us accept the curse is until the death of Jehoiachin and to the death of his descendants and Yahushua is a descendant so He would also have to die before the curse can be lifted.

I will answer my own question above now that Yahushua did not at His first coming invoke kingship because not only was He from the cursed kingly line but He took the curse of the Ten tribes of breaking the Torah upon himself also so that they could be reconciled back. Let me show you even Rabbi Paul saw this and wrote about it in his letters.

Galutyah (Galatians) 3:13 Messiah has redeemed us from the curse of the human law, being made a curse for us: for it is written, Cursed is every one that hangs on an etz (tree):

Note this translation is from the HTHS Bible and most bibles get this translation very wrong because no man who obeys Torah is under a curse but those who do not obey Torah are still today under a curse so which LAW was Rabbi Sha'ul writing about? Human law which has no power to save us. While if we believe in the Law of Elohim that indeed brings us to all the Covenants and to grace and we indeed are saved through accepting the provisions of the Covenants. If you accept Torah then you accept ALL the Covenants in turn you accept the death and resurrection of the Messiah as tied to these in a mysterious hidden ways.

Since the Messiah was hung on a tree (Acts 5:30), it is clear Rabbi Paul makes a point using the tree from the Torah. Anyone who broke the Torah such as the Ten tribes of Y'sra'el or anyone who does it today remain under an active curse which is invoked by us by saying I do not believe in YHWH or His law and will not do it. These words of abrogation of the Torah invoke the curse in your life.

The Messiah not only came to break the Torah curses but also after His death what was important in declaring the end of the curse of Jehoiachin was His resurrection. His resurrection signalled an end to the curse of Jehoiachin since all his descendants had died but only one had the power to be raised back to life through the Father.

When He died He said "It is Finished." What is finished? Most Christians unfortunately simply this by just attaching it to their salvation but he was not talking about the finishing of salvation but actually was saying the curses have finished and no longer have any further effect upon Him and the children of the Most High.

So is Jehoiachin's curse finished after His death? Yes. There was no need for the curse of Jehoiachin to be lifted at the first coming while He was alive because Yahushua needed no earthly
throne. Note the Torah itself tells us that anyone not obeying Torah is under a curse.

Debarim (Deuteronomy) 27:26 Cursed be he that does not continue in all the words of this Torah to do them. And all the people shall say, Amen.

Rabbi Paul mentioned this in Galatians 3:10. Anyone even claiming to be a believer one who does not continue in all the words is still under a curse even if he claims to be in the Messiah. The Messiah only removed the curse of sin and the second death. There are many curses written in the Torah and there are also many blessings, in order to reap these you have to 'hear and do,' the words of this Torah. These curses are separate from the Messiah of Y'sra'el, which people usually mix up with blessings and curses.

The solution to the curse of Jehoiachin was so obvious but we have all been so busy trying to go around the curse that we forgot to look at the obvious, the death and Resurrection of the Messiah. If you go searching on the internet then you find every Pastor, theologian and scholar in Christendom stuck with the three standard answers but today I have given you the answer as seen fit by the divine HOLY blessed YHWH Himself delivered to me through prayer.

Yahushua came to suffer in His first coming through death for the sins of the House of Y'sra'el so at this moment He did not proclaim kingship. He was in the role of the suffering servant the son of Yosef as the Rabbis wrote two reports about such events though they appear to conflict.

They said that a Messiah the son of Yosef will come and will die in battle and then the Messiah Son of Dawud will come and resurrect him. Many Rabbis ascribed the death of this particular messiah to Simon bar Kosiva. Such a teaching can be found in Sukkah 52b. This is ascribed to Zechariah 12:10.

Sukkah 52b
This is a minority opinion that Zachariah 12:!0, speaking of a fallen servant, refers to a Mashiach son of Yosef, and that like the Yetzer haRa, his misleading nature and his death at the hands of Elohim will be required to Ussher in a period of
redemption and righteousness so that the righteous Mashiach, son of Dawud, can fulfill what has been written about him.

So we can understand that Yahushua's coming was the divine providence for the healing of Ephraim.

The rules are that any Covenant or any oaths including curses are only binding until a person's death unless otherwise stated. This curse that was put on Jehoiachin was not everlasting but only until the death of Jehoiachin and his descendants technically the curse could extend all the way to the millennium because all his descendants could live until then before the final one dies.

Note Yahushua did die as a descendant and thereby breaking the curse of Jehoiachin of it's time stipulation and also breaking all the Torah curses through His righteous sacred blood that were upon the House of Y'sra'el and rose again.

Therefore when He returns at His second coming He is then no longer under any curse since the curse that was put upon Jehoiachin would no longer be effective because of its stipulation to the death of the descendants and cannot be activated after the death of the descendants. YHWH will not punish for the same sin twice. Even no courts of law upon the earth does that as it is called double jeopardy while YHWH's court is the highest court in the Universe and not a human court.

Note Yahushua did not claim any kingship while on the earth so the curse of Jehoiachin does not affect His first coming at all as a son of Yosef. Upon his second coming the curse is no longer binding therefore he can claim His rightful kingship as the Son of Dawud. Hallelu'yah only Yahushua could do this through the death and resurrection. What the death and resurrection also offered us beside the removing of our Torah based curses was a rightful king upon Y'sra'el's throne that is one of the mysteries of the resurrection.

Now the question of the lineages of Luke 3:23 and Matthew 1:16 of conflicting father's names for Yosef. Some people have answered this by stating that the two father's name being different one being Eli (Luke 3:23) and one being Jacob (Matthew 1:16) could be because after Jacob's death his wife was perhaps married to Eli and therefore he is mentioned as the father of Yosef the husband of Miriam. There was actually no legal precedence for such a marriage to take place because Jacob already had a son so his wife would not need to reproduce seed for her household where the Levirate marriage would be invoked with the brother.

In fact if you look at the diagrams I have given above in Chapter 4 you can see and trace the sons of Matthan. In fact we know that Jacob's wife was not married to Eli the father of Miriam. If the genealogies are correct as given by David Hughes then Jacob the father of Yosef was killed by Herod the Great for sedition and his wife was married to the then High Priest Simon Ben Boethus who after the High Priest subsequently remarried in her 3rd marriage to Herod the Great. Herod the Great did this to acquire Boethus's daughter Mariamne in marriage.

If the timelines are correct Herod the Great took Cleopatra of Jerusalem the widow of Jacob the father of Yosef as his 5th wife around the year 21 BCE.

Note Boethusians were also Sadducees who did not believe in the afterlife or any type of resurrection.

There was extreme rivalry of the Herodians with the tribe of Judah and with those who could inherit the throne that they had all people killed who could inherit the throne or even their children were sought to be killed as Yahushua was a baby when Herod the Great sent his troops to murder (Matthew 2:18) Him but the Father in heaven saved Him. Note that Eli the father of Miriam was also similarly killed for sedition and probably was seen a threat to the throne.

Yahushua came under his headship when he was adopted as the son of Yosef of Arimathaea. Even the Great Sanhedrin had already decided that the offspring of these people could sit upon the throne or become High Priests but as I have suggested that Yahushua did not come to sit on the earthly throne and the curse was really irrelevant in the scheme of things while He was alive but after His death He has the legal title to the throne without the curse.

F: Which Zechariah?

According to Rabbi Shmuel Safrai who is one of the founders of the Jerusalem School of Synoptic Research states the following in his article: "Apparently the priestly division of Abijah was named after one of the priests who returned to the land of Y'sra'el with Zerubbabel and Jeshua (Nehemiah 12:4).

Another Abijah, mentioned in Nehemiah 10:7, was one of the signatories of the covenant during the time of Nehemiah, a number of generations after Zerubbabel and the first wave of returnees to Y'sra'el.

This Abijah probably was a descendant of the Abijah after whom the division was named. Other priests of the Second Temple period were named Zechariah. Rabbinic works mention two such priests from the last generation before the temple was destroyed: Rabbi Zechariah ben Auvkulos (Lamentations Rabbah 4:3) and Rabbi Zechariah ha-Katsav (Mishnah, Ketubot 2:9)."[1]

I am going to suggest that neither of the above two Zechariah's mentioned by Rabbi Shmuel is likely to be the one that was the husband of Elizabeth. This particular Zechariah was a relative of Yahushua and both the fathers of the Zechariah mentioned above have no relation to Yahushua's family therefore neither is the one. I know who this Zechariah could be so I present the following evidence collected by me so far.

I am going to suggest unless further evidence emerges that Zechariah the husband of Elizabeth was a close relative of the family of Yahushua. He was likely the direct relative of Judah the Galilean who was the son of Zedekiah. According to Hebrew tradition Zechariah was killed by Herod for not divulging the information of the whereabouts of the baby Yahushua the Messiah.

Why would Herod go to him unless Herod knew that because of being a close family member Zechariah will have information of the whereabouts of the baby Yahushua so that Herod could kill the baby because Herod was threatened by any person who could inherit the royal throne?

I believe this would only happen because Judah the Galilean was also active and that would worry Herod and since he knew that Zechariah was a relation to him that is why he would have assumed that Yahushua would be hidden by Judah the Galilean or his close family who were all Zealots against the Herodian stronghold. They wanted to oust the Roman occupation and put their own royal princes as the kings upon the throne. Yahushua was one such royal prince as shown in this book. However Yahushua had no aspirations to the throne since his first mission was to redeemed the house of Y'sra'el.

Zechariah not disclosing this information cost him his life.

Chapter 5

Is Yahushua the Messiah?

One of the themes that have always been difficult for those who believe in the Messiah of Y'sra'el being the person of Yahushua is how to address the challenges that come from Orthodox Rabbis in Judaism who say He is not the Messiah.

When I get asked the question "Is Yahushua the Messiah I ask who wants to know?"

The Orthodox Rabbis believe that when the Messiah turns up there will be world peace and that the land of Y'sra'el will be handed to them and the Messiah will deal with all their problems and fix them since this did not happen with Yahushua at least in His first appearance therefore they have rejected the Messiahship of Yahushua at least for themselves for now. The also state that there will be universal knowledge of the Elohim of Y'sra'el at that time and no longer will people fight wars and the world will be in peace.

Let us examine these statements in light of scripture.

Here are some challenging questions to reconsider;

1. Why is it felt necessary that the Yahudim need to accept Yahushua at the first coming which clearly did not bring world peace?

2. What did the ancient Rabbis and present Rabbis think of this prophecy?

3. Why should the Yahudim leave Torah and become let us assume Christian which is a religion that has no respect for the law of Elohim the Torah given to Moses?

4. The Messiah came for the lost sheep. Can we say the Yahudim who kept the Torah were those lost sheep?

5. Does the Tanach back up a second return of Messiah?

The confusion comes when people do not realise that the Messiah was meant to be veiled or hidden for the Yahudim upon his first coming this shall be demonstrated in this article completely and accurately. The bible has themes or patterns and one theme that we find that sticks in our memory from the book of Genesis is the theme of Yosef who became number two or prime-minister of Egypt a very important position in the scheme of things and while the family of Yosef living in Y'sra'el ran short of food because of a famine sent by YHWH the severity of the famine caused them to seek food from Egypt. Note YHWH already had a person there to take care of the bad times.

When his brothers went searching for food to Egypt and spoke to Yosef they did not recognise him at all but he recognised them and gave them food. In this is a very important statement that many do not consider today and just gloss over it and think they must take the Messiah back to the Yahudim in Y'sra'el and convert them. Nothing could be further from the truth and we shall examine this closely today.

Christians and the Netzarim brethren obviously are not learning the lessons taught here in the very first book of Genesis about thematic analysis. First Yosef became a type of Messiah for the Y'sraelites and was put in an important place of authority and second there was a period of time before which he could not reveal himself and it is this period of time that we are in today thematically speaking. While the Messiah cannot reveal himself to his brothers the Yahudim but they nevertheless are provided sustenance from YHWH.

Yosef was thirty years old when he was made chief overseer. This by the way is the starting age for a priest of the most High hence why it is assumed Yahushua started his ministry at 30
though we cannot be conclusive about this because we

lack important data.

Beresheeth (Genesis) 41:46 Yosef was thirty years old...

Yosef was sold when he was 17. He was in Potipherah's house about 11 years and just under two years in prison. He was overseer for about 9 years so he would be close to 39 before his brothers reach out to him for food. The total period of plenty and the famine is 14 years that is 7+7

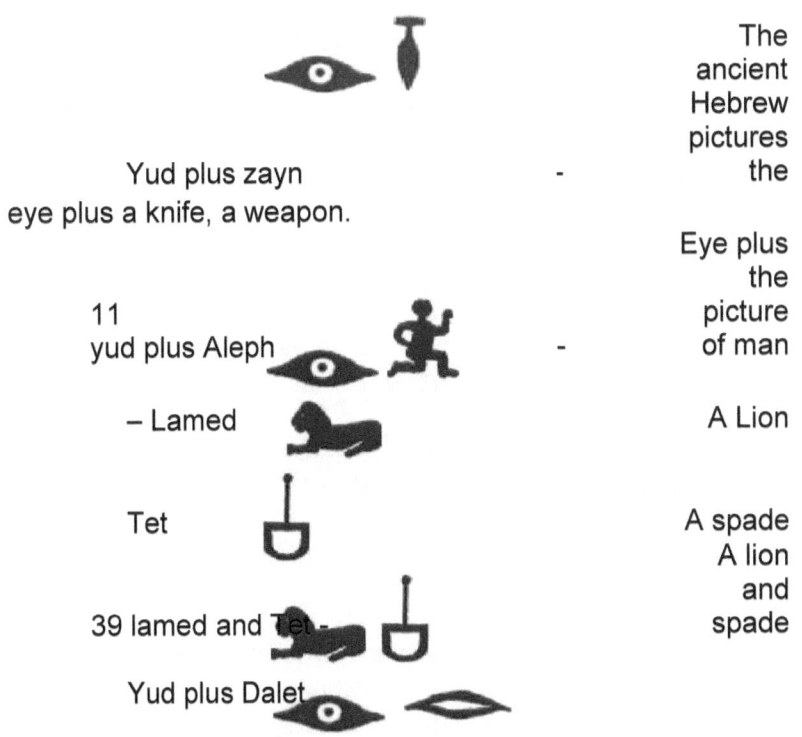

Yud plus zayn
eye plus a knife, a weapon.

11
yud plus Aleph

– Lamed

Tet

39 lamed and Tet

Yud plus Dalet

The ancient Hebrew pictures the

Eye plus the picture of man

A Lion

A spade
A lion and spade

Mystical analysis
The number 17 – Yosef was sold and his life was in danger hence the knife.

The number 11 – Yosef lived under the watchful eye and authority of poti-pherah.

The number 30 – Yosef now had the authority that YHWH had reserved for him, Lion is the king of the jungle so Yosef was now in an authority structure.

The number 9 – A spade, Yosef could easily use the spade as a weapon for his brothers or send them back empty handed if he
wanted to take vengeance but he uses the spade to expand his mercy the principle of love your enemies is proven by Yosef.

The number 39 – A kingly reign in the hands of Yosef depicting the lion of Judah for the Messiah and a spade depicting fullness or expansion that will come from the Messiah to all of Y'sra'el in this case Yosef's biological family.

The number 14 – The only eye of YHWH and mouth of the Holy one for entry back into Y'sra'el into the Kingdom of Elohim is through the Messiah as our blessed Rabbis predicted. If we obey Torah we get restored to the Covenants and if we don't we remain separated.

- What lessons do we learn from this thematic view when applied to Yahushua compared to Yosef?

- Yosef was loved by his father Jacob. Yahushua is loved by His Father in heaven.

- Yosef was hated by his brothers who plotted to kill him. In like manner some Sadducean/Shammites Pharisees Yahudim from the first century hated Yahushua and plotted to kill him.

- Yosef was exiled from his country and became an important figure for Egypt to the gentiles like a deity to the dying people in hunger and need.

- Yahushua is currently also exiled from his nation unrecognised by his brethren while he is gathering the outcast and is the Almighty Elohim himself who is yet veiled from many of his people.

- Yosef was called Zaphnath-Paaneah which means "One who reveals the hidden things/secrets." Yahushua is also the one who reveals the hidden things/secrets because only Elohim can reveal these things.

- Yosef started his important function at the age of 30, Yahushua was assumed to be 30 in His ministry. Yosef was in an important place of authority to do the needful. Scripture tells us Yahushua is at the right hand (Matt 26:64) of the Father meaning in a place of authority to judge and enact important decisions.

When we understand the picture of the theme of Yosef we then understand Yahushua a bit more. Yosef did not go advertising himself to his brethren in Y'sra'el they in fact came to him. Likewise one day when Y'sra'el is at a crossroad of destruction the Yahudim will seek their Messiah and come to the realization of who he is and until then they will live as if he never came.

We must understand a few things why the problem comes up with the Hebrew people because no where in the Hebrew Bible the term Messiah is used exclusively for a single person but has been applied to kings, priests and prophets generally. We are given hidden clues for the identity of the Messiah through thematic pictures one which I described earlier.

Sometimes we are given clear information for his identity and at other times much of the information is veiled for deliberate reasons because this information is not necessary for the Yahudim who want to live through the Torah they should live it and they do not have to be converted into any other faith other than Judaism.

The coming of the Messiah was and remains to be only for the ten northern tribes who departed both from the Torah and then later were expelled from the land by the hand of Elohim for Torah disobedience. One of the major roles of the Messiah is to bring these back from the exile to Torah and to the land those who accept the yoke of heaven (Torah) and those who do not will never be allowed to return.

What makes Christians think that Elohim will allow the people of the ten tribes to return without repentance demonstrated in being Torah obedient?

Furthermore we will examine a little detail of what the Rabbis thought of the Messianic figure and did they apply it to any one person. There are numerous discussions on this in the Talmud and other Hebrew writings we will only cover a few pieces here.

Question 1) Let us address question one first "why is it felt necessary that the Yahudim need to accept Yahushua at the first
coming which clearly did not bring world peace and was not meant to do so?"

Many faithful followers of the Messiah are clearly not reading scripture and if they are reading scripture they are failing to understand it and at best not accepting its statements in full or either not even understanding what has been said through perhaps what I can term pastoral ignorance and lack of a broad vision. Let us examine this.

Yeshayahu (Isaiah) 53:1 Who has believed our report? And to whom is the arm of **YHWH** revealed?

The prophet Isaiah started his ministry around 740 BC that means at least 740 years before the birth of the Messiah so he basically asks two questions which I believe Christians and the Netzarim need to answer as they have also rejected his statement in ignorance.

Question 1) Who has believed our report?
Question 2) To who is the arm of YHWH been revealed?

Since Isaiah is writing prophetically to Y'sra'el for Y'sra'el and its setting is really for the future rather than the present he is clearly asking a question of "who (Y'sra'el) has believed our report," which means Y'sra'el or the ruling parties there who were the tribe of Judah had rejected the prophecy of Messiah of the suffering servant to which these prophesies are connected. It does not matter what the ancient Rabbis say or the modern Rabbis in Judaism (Edomite converts from Sephardism or Ashkenazi converts not the genetic seed of Israel) say but what matters is the prophet is adamant and implies no one has believed his report this means essentially both. The "who" is always applied to the majority not to the minority of Y'sra'el.

This was mentioned both in Isaiah 52:13 and connected with Isaiah 42. It would be good for you to glance over Isaiah 42.

Yeshayahu (Isaiah) 42:1-4 Behold my servant, whom I uphold; my elect, in whom my soul delights; I have put my Ruach (Spirit) upon him: he shall bring forth right-ruling to the nations. 2 He shall not cry, nor lift up, nor cause his voice to be heard in the street. 3 A bruised reed shall he not break, and the smoking flax shall he not quench: he shall bring forth right-ruling according to truth. 4 He shall not fail nor be discouraged, till he have set right-ruling in the earth: and the isles shall wait for his Torah.

If I apply the servant to Y'sra'el as many ancient and modern Rabbis have applied then let those Rabbis answer when did Y'sra'el bring right-ruling to the nations?

Let us examine this through a historical timeline. We examine the kings of Judah from the time of Isaiah forward because the prophecy of Isaiah is not to the kings of Northern Y'sra'el who were about to be disbanded.

741-726 BC Ahaz, very unrighteous king 728–699 BC Hezekiah - very righteous king 699–643 BC Manasseh – very evil king 642–640 BC Amon - very evil king 640–609 BC Josiah - very righteous king 609 - BC Jehoahaz - Bad king
609–598 BC Jehoiakim - evil king 597 BC Jehoiachin – bad king 597–587 BC Zedekiah – bad king

----

Leading to the fall of Jerusalem

Was the Messiah revealed to any of these kings? The words Arm of YHWH reveal a living and personal "word" which applies to a real living being and not to a static word on paper. The naked arm of YHWH is His Messiah which is open to revelation but only to those who have the spiritual eyes to see and receive Him.

Can we apply the servant prophecy of Isaiah 42 or Isaiah 53 to any of these? No, none of these kings can be considered the servant in the way Isaiah described. Because none of them brought justice to the nations they mainly ruled in Y'sra'el but the servant is a far wider role of an individual who was in yet future times from Isaiah going to bring forth justice to the nations. Can the servant of Isaiah apply to Y'sra'el? Literally no but loosely it can apply to anyone who serves in a capacity to exalt YHWH. Did Y'sra'el exalt YHWH to the nations? No never in the history from Isaiah to the present time has Y'sra'el exalted YHWH to a level where many nations will go up to Jerusalem to visit the Elohim of Abraham, Isaac and Jacob. There have been revivals in Y'sra'el from a downward spiral but they have all been short lived.

People forget that Y'sra'el was never totally righteous not even from Moses's time while only a few individuals in Y'sra'el have ever been righteous. Let us examine this a bit more closely. If you do not believe this then look at the Egyptian exile from which only two from the first generation that is Yahushua (Joshua) and Caleb made it into the land while the rest were all second generation Y'sraelites.

Yeshayahu (Isaiah) 42:6 I YHWH have called you in righteousness, and will hold your hand, and will guard you, and **give you for a covenant** of the people, for a **light to the Gentiles**;

Note the Y'sraelites a nation of priests had pretty much failed their task hence why a special servant was needed to complete the task. People misapply the covenants and start to exalt Y'sra'el the land and the people but Y'sra'el is not **The covenant** that YHWH was going to give the gentiles but Y'sra'el had the covenants so Isaiah 42 says **I will give you for a Covenant** to the peoples meaning gentiles.

The Hebrew word and will hold your hand and will guard you the Hebrew word for "guard" is Netzar. This is a hidden Hebrew clue that the Netzar רצנ is the **Branch** which also has the similar word and is applied to the Messiah, see the Branch reference in Isaiah 11:1.

Was the Messiah a Covenant for anyone? Yes, he was the fulfilment of the New Covenant known as the Sinai Covenant Covenant. He himself tells us this in Luke 22 that he is the Covenant given to the gentiles. We also know that the "Word" that was with Elohim and Was Elohim in John 1:1 is at times personified and reveals deeper truths of the Messiah who would in fact become personal to us or at least in the form we may come to know him.

The Hebrew language does not have capitals and small letters to illustrate a point but in the Tanach we do have lowered and raised Hebrew letters given to describe or emphasize certain spiritual truths. You can see all the raised and lowered letters in the HTHS Hebraic Study Scriptures that can be purchased from www.forever-israel.com.

Luke 22:19-20 And he took lechem (bread), and gave thanks, and broke it, and gave to them, saying, this is **my body** which is given for you: this do in remembrance of me. 20 Likewise also the **cup after supper**, saying, This cup is the **Covenant Covenant** in my blood, which is shed for you.

Where does it say this whole thing applies to the gentiles?

Luke 22: 30 That you may eat and drink at my table in my kingdom, and sit on **thrones judging the twelve tribes of Y'sra'el**.

The ones who are sitting on the table are the twelve disciples and elders of Y'sra'el who are shown to have spiritual and physical authority so the reference "my table" is to his Kingly table where only the elders can sit and is not to all the rest of Y'sra'el.

Note the ten tribes of Y'sra'el are goy or gentiles today who are slowly and surely returning to their roots. If examined in its impersonal form YHWH says "the word of YHWH" was given to so and so but in its personal and living from the word is the Messiah so yes the Covenant (Yahushua/Word) was given to the gentiles just as Isaiah 42 declared pretty much included the "whole" of Y'sra'el but especially the ten tribes mentioned by names many times.

Yeshayahu (Isaiah) 42:7 To **open the blind eyes**, to bring out the prisoners from the prison, and them that sit in darkness out of the prison house.

The whole imagery is to the Jubilee and to a future release on the Jubilee. What does sitting in darkness mean? To sit without the Torah since Torah is light so those who sat in darkness were the gentiles who had no Torah because they were expelled from Y'sra'el for being disobedient (Originally Ten northern tribes of Y'sra'el) and now were all classified gentiles mingled in nations.

Tehillim (Psalms) 119:105 Your word is a lamp to my feet, and a **light to my path**.

If we search through the Hebrew history and the only person to open blind eyes both spiritually and physically was Yahushua. He even healed a blind man from birth and no man in Y'sra'el's history has ever done this before a very special miracle since no such miracle has ever taken place in Y'sra'el such as this. So why are you chasing after Rabbis who tell you Yahushua is not the Messiah? Do you know that they are not going to know corporately? Do you know this is meant to be for many reasons that will take a lot of paper to explain?

Yochanan (John) 9:1; 7; 11 And as Yahushua passed by,
he saw a man which was blind from his birth. **7** And said to him, Go, wash in the pool of Siloam, (which is by interpretation, Sent.) He went his way therefore, and washed, and came seeing. **11** He answered and said, a man that is called **Yahushua** made clay, and anointed my eyes, and said to me, **Go to the pool of Siloam, and wash: and I went and washed, and I received sight**.

Remember the authorities at the time in the Temple refused to believe that this miracle took place. They were Sadducees the typical Karaite Yahudim of today. The Karaites even today reject Yahushua and try to invent their own way of keeping Torah so what's new?

Now let us apply the criteria of Y'sra'el to the suffering servant in Isaiah 53 and we will examine if this can work as the Rabbis claim.

Yeshayahu (Isaiah) 53:3 He is despised and rejected of men; a man of sorrows, and acquainted with grief: and we hid as it were our faces from him; he was despised, and we esteemed him not.

The Rabbis of Y'sra'el especially ancient apply this to the House of Y'sra'el. OK loosely it appears to apply to the House of Y'sra'el who went into captivity because they were rejected because of disobedience and despised acquainted with grief we can accept that no problem. Now ask yourself who the 'we' is and who is the 'him' or 'they?' So if the House of Y'sra'el is applicable to the Ten tribes then when were they thrown out they never bore our sicknesses or our sorrows but the poor souls were carrying their own sicknesses and sorrows. Ok let us apply this to the Hebrew dispersal to Iraq and Iran. When did they carry our sicknesses and sorrows? Never!

Yeshayahu (Isaiah) 53:4 Surely he has borne our grief, and carried our sorrows: yet we did esteem him stricken, smitten of Elohim, and afflicted.

Now looking at the history of the ten tribes and the sins they had become accustomed to when did the house of Y'sra'el pay for your and my sins? Can blind lead the blind? Can a sinner carry sins of others?

They were sinners themselves and were thrown out of Y'sra'el by Elohim. They could not carry anyone's sins nor sorrows but their own and that is exactly what happened. They even had no authority to be in the place of the High Priest who could technically atone for Y'sra'el's sins upon his death so this verse in Isaiah rules out the House of Y'sra'el to be the ones to carry our sorrows and grief's at a personal level. It makes no difference which Rabbis applies this to the House of Y'sra'el, it's irrelevant. For your information Jonathan Ben Uzziel only applied part of the text of the verse below to the Messiah and not the rest of the chapter to the Messiah while Christians incorrectly assume that Jonathan applied the whole text quoting him. Jonathan ben Uzziel did not apply the whole text of Isaiah 52/53 to the Messiah, this is where Christians need to correct themselves.

This is where many Christians and Hebrew Christians

an oxymoron if you ask me make mistakes applying the whole chapter of Isaiah to the Messiah upon claims of the ancient Hebrew sources which is not true. Here is what was applied by Jonathan ben Uzziel to the Messiah only, in the Targum.

Yeshayahu (Isaiah) 52:13 Behold my servant Messiah shall prosper; he shall be high, and increase, and be exceeding strong:

From my perspective this prophecy applies to a person who is righteous and would be a future figure since Hezekiah was not that figure therefore it would not apply to him. Nor can we apply this to the righteous king Josiah because he was not a light to the gentile nations either but Yahushua was and He commanded His Torah keeping disciples to take the message of the Torah and the coming Messiah to the gentiles (The Ten tribes who became melo ha goyim meaning many nations) in Matthew 28:19 in the great commission which once again Christendom mistakes for any Tom, Dick or Harry.

Question 2) What did the ancient Rabbis and present Rabbis think of this prophecy?

Before I move on to other areas of this prophecy I am going to quickly answer this question. The ancient Rabbis did not have the belief as most Christian writers have stated today as I have shown you some proof above and more to follow below.

Some Christian missionaries claim that Rabbi Moshe El-Sheikh wrote in the latter half of the 16th century and believed in Isaiah 52/53 for the Messiah.

Our Rabbis of blessed memory with one voice accept and affirm the opinion that the prophet is speaking of the King Messiah, and we shall ourselves also adhere to the same view.

Unfortunately this is misquoted by Christians once again due to lack of proper procedure and testing. Yes the Rabbis have always affirmed Isaiah 52:13 for the Messiah but they do not apply <u>all the verses</u> of Isaiah chapter 53 to Him this is a grave mistake and the Yahudim themselves will not only correct you but make you look foolish if you imply that they accepted all of the chapter 52/53 to the Messiah. This is what most Christian scholars are doing both ignorantly misquoting Hebrew sources. We need to beware that we do not need approval of ancient rabbinic authority to justify Yahushua and His Messiahship but the authority of the Father in heaven alone. If you talk about false messiahs then the Hebrew Rabbis have picked many wrong messiahs one such picked by Rabbi Akiva was called Bar Kosiva. Another one was Sabbatai Zevi who was such a good messiah that he became a Muslim upon threat of his life by the Ottoman Turkish king.

Another fallacy in Christendom is that the Yahudim believed in two Messiahs. The Yahudim did <u>not</u> believe in two messiahs. Unfortunately when you pickup Christian literature you find many errors and omissions and wrong opinions on ancient material and this is likely down to one individual in the past making the mistake and the rest of the people like a herd quoting that one wrong person also making the same mistake. The problem is down to not being educated in rabbinic sources and how to read the literature because it contains very difficult reading and is written in many places with
idiomatic clauses and hidden phrases which a large majority of Christians do not understand.

This is termed Blind leading the blind even some of the most revered scholars amongst these have made errors including Yahudim who became Christians. Some of these converts spoke vehemently against the Torah the law of Adonai and others put Yahudim down generally for obeying the commandments. This is simply foolishness and not understanding the plan of our Father in heaven.

I do not want to shame people with their mistakes

because that is not what I am here to do but my job is to speak the truth in love and teach what is just and truthful.

Let me touch on one aspect of the two messiahs that many Christian historians believe that Yahudim believed. You may have heard of the term Messiah Ben Yosef and Messiah ben David (Dawud). Christians confuse this term with ancient rabbis believing in two messiahs or two separate individuals but this is not true and once again misquoted from ancient sources.

The rabbinic teaching on this was never seen as two separate individual persons or two separate appearances of the Messiah but <u>one</u> individual and <u>one</u> appearance only. According to ancient Rabbis He will either come as Ben Yosef that is if the Yahudim are not keeping Torah properly this is his appearance and if they obey Torah then he will come as Messiah ben Dawud as the King. Some Rabbis have gone one way or another however the Messiah has been illusive to them always. He will not come as one such as ben Yosef then the other this is interpolation of Christian authors desperate to convert Yahudim which do not need to be converted.

Please see my article on salvation of the Yahudim on www.forever-israel.com for blindness which is also very much evident in Christendom.

Here it is the complete quote from Sanhedrin 98a.

R. Alexandri said: R. Joshua opposed two verses: it is written, And behold, one like the son of man came with the clouds of heaven[34] whilst [elsewhere] it is written, [behold, thy king cometh unto thee ...] lowly, and riding upon an ass![35] — if they are meritorious, [he will come] with the clouds of heaven; [36] if not, lowly and riding upon an ass. King Shapur [I] said to Samuel, 'Ye maintain that the Messiah will come upon an ass: I will rather send him a white horse of mine.'[37] He replied, 'Have you a hundred-hued steed?"[38]

34 Dan. VII, 13.
35 ech. IX, 7.
36 'Swiftly' (Rashi).
37 This is more fitting.
38 [This jest is explained by Krochmal, (Hechalutz, I, p. 83) as an overt invitation to the Yahudim to help Shapur in his struggle with the Romans.]

If you look through Christian writings you find this is not how they presented it which caused confusion for people thinking that the Hebrew Rabbis have lied. It was simply glossed over as two comings or two persons while Judaism both ancient and modern sources the large majority have never stated it this way but there have been dissident voices that believed a different way. Don't you think if they had that understanding why would Isaiah ask "who has believed our report?"

I state the simple fact based on the prophet that means if Christians are true then the prophet Isaiah must be a liar? If the prophet Isaiah is true then the Christians have been misquoting Hebrew text all this time and persecuting Yahudim in the Diaspora trying to force Messiah down their proverbial throat. Now the Christians need to re-read the prophet who said "who (Y'sra'el) has believed our report?" This is clear Y'sra'el corporately had rejected the report but Christians in their foolishness are adamant that the prophet's report has to be accepted by the Yahudim. The reality is that it has not been accepted just as the prophet stated and it will not be until the Messiah returns.

Question 3) Why should the Yahudim leave Torah and become let us assume Christian which is a religion that has no respect for the law of Elohim the Torah given to Moses?

To understand this we must understand that the Christian theology is upside down. It's akin to a movie where you only see the last ten minutes and then by this you try to figure out what happened earlier in the film. Christians have a very bad habit of interpreting the bible backwards this means they will use Rabbi Paul's writings to interpret the passages in Torah or the prophets.

They will usually often use a letter of Rabbi Paul to determine if the Torah is valid, if circumcision is valid or not and everything they seem to look at is taken through the prism of the letters of Rabbi Paul. Rabbi Paul's letters are misinterpreted and then used to abrogate YHWH's holy words, the Tanach. Let me be blunt with you and make no mistake I do not give the same weight to Rabbi Paul's letters that most of you do because I do not live in Corinth or in Ephesus but most of the situation of Rabbi Paul really was applied to those regions and has nothing to do with us or our time. Do you live in Ephesus with Diana's temple? Then we must read them very carefully to a situation in past time. Certain precepts may carry in our time but not all.

Rabbi Paul is not Moses and Moses cannot be challenged even Yahushua gave him credit (John 5:46) so for me Moses comes first and foremost. If Rabbi Paul had contradicted Moses I would throw out his letters this is very simple for me because I do not allow a few Catholics to decide for me what is sacred. After studying his letters I found he does not contradict Moses but complements him. Moreover, his writings are very difficult even for the learned therefore they are easy to misinterpret and have been misapplied by Christians generally.

This also happened in the first century with allegations against him that he was teaching against Moses's law and it was taken very seriously so he was summoned by the Jerusalem Beyth Din so do not be haughty and think Rabbi Paul is your Elohim he is not. He certainly has become an Elohim for Christians while they arrogantly reject the law of Elohim and put Rabbi Paul above the Father in heaven is a sure recipe for disaster and total blasphemy. Muslims are right in that Christians follow after

Pauline Christianity model that is because Christians prove their behaviour through the prism of Rabbi Paul's letters misinterpreting and re-inventing everything as a new religion so can you blame them? I agree with them this is foolish.

Yesterday in a discussion with a Christian friend who was adamant that he does not need to obey the Torah he could not understand the difference between abrogation and fulfilment. It is true that England and the United States have some of the best schools in the world but it is also true that some of these children that go on to become high clergy in the Roman and Anglican churches actually do not know the difference between abrogation and fulfilment.

They do not know the difference between that which is clean and unclean and yet millions of you foolishly put your trust in these kinds of men. Even a pupil in the worst school in Lahore, Pakistan would be able to tell you the difference of these words. Abrogation is the law of something that no longer has any value so you would not even bother to quote it while fulfill means to bring something to pass or to fill up but the preceding revelation does not get abrogated or change. While the foolish in Christendom happily quote the verses from the Tanach but all the time picking and choosing what to believe.

Let me show you the Christian argument and read how foolish it
is.

Christian -> Paul said that we are no longer under the law and he said do not circumcise and he said do not keep the Sabbath.

Rabbi Simon-> You mean Rabbi Paul. First of all the Christians are so disrespectful to Rabbi Paul that he does not even call him by his respectful title. On top of this the Christian tries to make his own new fangled invented doctrine by twisting facts that he has no understanding but is adamant that he is right and you are wrong even if the entire testimony of the prophets is behind you. Let me show you how it goes.

Colossians 2:16 Let no man therefore judge ye in meat, or in drink, or in respect of a set-apart day, or of the Rosh Kodesh (new moon), or of the Sabbath days:

The Christian quotes the verse above and is adamant that this verse no matter what I would say he is not going to keep the Sabbath because Rabbi Paul said do not worry about it. No amount of discussion seems to remove his blindness brought about by ignorant Pastors and Bishops.

The foolishness is evident in the discussion. The Christian does not realize that Rabbi Paul was a Pharisee and died a Pharisee and did not convert into any new religion. It would be sacrilege for

Rabbi Paul to teach against the set Sabbath commandment by which righteousness was judged in the first century. Also with in the letter of Rabbi Paul which seems in the Christian's eyes weightier than Moses's Torah actually is a failure of massive understanding. Rabbi Paul used terms that were familiar in the first century that had meaning to the people hearing his speech. He is not saying for the believers to not keep the Sabbath or not to bother about new moons but is in fact cautioning against heathens who come challenging about the Sabbath rest.

The term "no man" is a loaded term in the first century and it has a mishnaic application of anybody who is not part of the community of believers therefore this "man" coming to challenge you or argue with you on the Sabbath according to Rabbi Paul would be a heathen or gentile and not a Yahudee. **The heathen "man" outside our community of faithful Y'sraelites is not to judge us on what we eat, drink or not.** What days we keep set-apart and why we keep is our eternal covenant with YHWH and our business and outsider may object to our days our meats and our way of life, that is not to be a concern to us for we are to remain faithful that is what Rabbi Paul is actually saying but look how the Christian ignorantly twisted facts.

However the Christian is adamant no, this is not what Rabbi Paul means. So now the Christians tries to redefine how Rabbi Paul thinks by superimposing his thoughts into Rabbi Paul's mind and at this point Rabbi Paul has become his father and the Christian man or woman who refuses to keep the Sabbath has forgotten that our Abbah is YHWH and not Rabbi Paul. Yes we can have spiritual fathers but when spiritual fathers override the commandments then they become idolaters so beware.

The letter to the Colossian synagogue was written somewhere around 62AD because of prevalent false doctrines that had started to enter messianic places of worship after the epistles of Ephesians and Romans. The Acts of the apostles were written somewhere around 60-62 AD also. Now two important things come to mind, one that Rabbi Paul has been shown to be Sabbath keeping in the book of Acts by Luke this means at least 32 years after the death and resurrection of the Messiah he did not abrogate Torah. Someone perhaps forgot to tell Rabbi Paul why are you being legal and keeping the Sabbath. Oh foolish Christianity when will you learn?

Second Rabbi Paul was an observant Pharisee of the tribe of Benjamin so he was obedient to the Torah then why would he be advocating breaking the 4th commandment? Rabbi Paul said in one of his other epistles **_First Corinthians 11:1_** *Be ye followers of me, even as I also am of Messiah.*

If Rabbi Paul was an imitator or follower of Yahushua then he would have kept the feasts and the Sabbaths because Yahushua did too therefore he would also be teaching it the same way. If he was not he would be stripped of all his titles and service and thrown out of the synagogue an appropriate measure for idolaters.

Shemoth (Exodus) 20:8 **[Dalet: Four]** Remember the Sabbath day, to keep it set-apart.

Do you see the Christian has totally ruled out Elohim himself and is quite happy to break the commandment based on a misreading of Rabbi Paul's letter?

Why I gave you this example is to show you that this is why a Yahudee cannot be a Christian because the term is an oxymoron. You are asking a Yahudee to convert and then to break the Sabbath and other important commandments which is sacrilege and Elohim does not allow such things.

The second verse that the Christian has hand picked again is another letter of Rabbi Paul. Surprise, surprise and you can be sure its time for another misreading and bad interpretation.

Galatians 3:10 (KJV) For as many as are of the works of the law are under the curse: for it is written, Cursed *is* every one that continueth not in all things which are written in the book of the law to do them.

Christian-> Paul told us not to keep the law and if you keep the law you are weak and under a curse.

Rabbi Simon-> How very interesting but unfortunately that is a complete misquotation of the text and bad representation of a Rabbi generally. Let us quote the verse out of the HTHS Hebraic Study Scriptures to see if this is what Rabbi Paul is saying or are you misquoting the text due to bad teaching.

Galatians 3:10 For those who are slaves to **Ma'aseh Ha Torah** (rabbinic customs), are under the curse: for it is written, Cursed is every one that does not act on all the things which are written in the scroll of the Torah.

Once again Rabbi Paul uses very loaded first century terms for which the Christian has no knowledge or rabbinic understanding and he invents his own misconstrued theology.

Rabbi Paul is directly making a cross reference to the Torah of Moses and saying exactly the opposite to how the Christian is misapplying it. This quote is taken from Deuteronomy 27:26, those that reject the Torah of Moses remain **under a curse** that includes Christians who remain rebellious today so the man who is under the curse is the Christian himself.

Ma'aseh ha Torah a Hebrew concept that Rabbi Paul is speaking about is a heavyweight rabbinic term which means works, which were setup by the Rabbis. More correctly called Oral Torah in which we have Gerizim, minhag, basically customs and traditions that are usually not in Scripture or are taken from passages in scripture to highlight or put a fence around a commandment. The word here Torah or Law can also be related to your local government laws, that say, what you do as a society to be an ordered society however Rabbi Paul is applying it to the laws in the Synagogue.

For us not to obey the commandments (short cut for Torah) is to dishonour the Father and the Son but the Christian is adamant that he does not have to obey the Torah and that whatever I say and however many prophetic witnesses I have from the scriptures they are wrong and he alone is right because his Pastor told him so. His Pastor's testimony seems to be heavier than Isaiah, Jeremiah and even Moses.

He even throws in a pun and says with a wry simile that Abraham even sinned and Noah sinned. I ask him can you prove that assertion. He says Abraham lied about his sister. However I told him Abraham did not lie Sarah was indeed his half sister but he is adamant that I do not know. I asked him where does he see Noah sinning in the past. He claims Noah being drunk in his home was a sin. I told him what Elohim does not call sin he should not either and label incorrect Christian theologies on the Patriarchs but he laughs as this is a joking matter. This discussion did happen with me in fact yesterday at lunch time about Noah and Abraham.

First John 2:4 He that says, I know him, and does not guard his commandments, is a liar, and the truth is not in him.

Its clear from John that not to obey is dishonouring Elohim, the passage shows us that a person has no knowledge or relationship with Elohim and simply living ignorantly who behaves this way hence no Yahudee should convert into Christianity but should believe in the Messiah Yahushua and be Torah observant just as Yahushua was.

In fact a similar and very foolish charge was put against the Yahudim by Justin Martyr in his dialog with Trypho the Yahudee. This is another one of the Christian heroes who was a Hellenist.

Let us look at the Debate with Justin and Trypho

Trypho the Yahudee was smarter than Justin Martyr yet Christians rate Justin Martyr and not Trypho, unfortunately Christians can be very dogmatic and biased. I am not surprised. I call Christians the kings of misquoting and misinterpreting the text of the bible. This indeed was also the problem with Justin Martyr.

Dialog of Justin Martyr with Trypho the Yahudee Chapter XI.—The law abrogated; the New Testament promised and given by Elohim.
"There will be no other Elohim, O Trypho, nor was there from eternity any other existing" (I thus addressed him), "but He who made and disposed all this universe. Nor do we think that there is one Elohim for us, another for you, but that He alone is Elohim who led your fathers out from Egypt with a strong hand and a high arm. Nor have we

trusted in any other (for there is no other), but in Him in whom you also have trusted, the Elohim of Abraham, and of Isaac, and of Jacob. But **we do not trust through Moses or through the law**; for then we would do the same as yourselves. (for I have read that there shall be a final law, and a covenant, the chiefest of all, which it is now incumbent on all men to observe, as many as are seeking after the inheritance of Elohim.

For the law promulgated on Horeb is now old, and belongs to yourselves alone; but this is for all universally. Now, law placed against law has abrogated that which is before it, and a covenant which comes **after in like manner has put an end to the previous one**; and an eternal and final law—namely, Christ —has been given to us, and the covenant is trustworthy, after which there shall be **no law, no commandment, no ordinance**.

Have you not read this which Isaiah says: '**Hearken unto Me, hearken unto Me, my people; and, ye kings, give ear unto Me: for a law shall go forth from Me, and My judgment shall be for a light to the nations**. My righteousness approaches swiftly, and My salvation shall go forth, and nations shall trust in Mine arm?' And by Jeremiah, concerning this same new covenant, He thus speaks: 'Behold, the days come, saith the Lord, that I will make a new covenant with the house of Y'sra'el and with the house of Judah; not according to the covenant which I made with their fathers, in the day that I took them by the hand, to bring them out of the land of Egypt'). [Bold mine]

He continues…

"For since you have read, O Trypho, as you yourself admitted, the doctrines taught by our Saviour, I do not think that I have done foolishly in adding some short utterances of His to the prophetic statements. Wash therefore, and be now clean, and put away iniquity from your souls, as Elohim bids you be washed in this layer, and be circumcised with the true circumcision.

For we too would observe the fleshly circumcision, and the Sabbaths, and in short all the feasts, **if we did not know for what reason they were enjoined you,-- namely, on account of your transgressions and the hardness of your hearts.** For if we patiently endure all things contrived against us by wicked men and demons, so that even amid cruelties unutterable, death and torments, we pray for mercy to those who inflict such things upon us, and do not wish to give the least retort to any one, even as the new Lawgiver commanded us: how is it, Trypho, that we would not observe those rites which do not harm us,--I speak of fleshly circumcision, and Sabbaths, and feasts?

So Justin Martyrs words are clear which most Christians utter in unwise ignorance just like Justin did who lacked broader understanding of the Torah being a Hellenistic follower of Yahushua. We often find the Hellenist missed the point entirely and misquoted and misinterpreted the Torah and the prophets and often mixed heathen accepted practices as biblical.

- For he said we do not trust through the <u>Law of Moses</u>
- He said the new replaces the old
- There is a new law that abrogates the previous law
- The Torah is for the Yahudim and not Christians as Justin saw it.
- The Torah was given because of the hardness of your hearts according to Justin.

I can tell you today that Justin and all those who follow after this kind of bad theology are not only mistaken but will pay for the mistake by having the kingdom revoked from them! Note kingdom not salvation. Justin and all others who reject the law of Elohim and replace him are in for a surprise and shock at the end of days.

All people whether Christian or others the misfits Hebrew Christians who teach people to eat pork and

do not keep the holy days of Elohim follow after man-made theologies will not get the first resurrection in the coming kingdom? For that please read my article "Will Christians enter the 1000 years millennial reign" study on www.forever-israel.com.

While most believers get all huffed and puffed about this it is important to recognize that the Rabbis are not in the place of Elohim so one cannot expect them to be right in everything they have said in the past. Clearly they were wrong but their ideas did have some merit. Judah was not meant to know this because this was clearly mentioned by Isaiah. Second a Midrash is not a bullet proof commentary but only a homily or a way of seeing text to understand it. There are many factors such as is it halacha in which case it will be binding or is it non-halachic in which it is not binding upon the community of the faithful believers. The texts of Isaiah 52/53 are non-halachic so any Rabbi who interprets or gives a commentary on that cannot be held to account because of the basis of it being non-halachic. All of you who run around trying to prove the Messiah by quoting Jonathan Ben Uzziel forget that his Targum is not halachic.

Now ask yourself the question could you recognize the Messiah if you stood there in the 1st century? This is demonstrated by the Messiah Himself that unless the Holy Spirit gave you a revelation the chance of you recognizing the Messiah would also be nil. Did the twelve recognize him? We are given testimony of Yahushua in the following text.

Mattityahu (Matthew) 16:16-17 And Shimon Kefa (Peter) answered and said, You are the Messiah, the Son of the living Elohim. **17** And **Yahushua** answered and said to him, Blessed are you, Shimon Bar-Yonah: (Simon son of Jonah) for flesh and blood has not revealed it to you, but my Abbah which is in the shamayim (heaven).

So Yahushua was anointed to do the will of the Father

in heaven. He did not come to establish a new religion but he actually was continuing in the same. All of Christendom therefore that refuses to obey Torah has strayed from the true path that have made their new religion according to Constantine and not Yahushua.

So we can see that the Messiah was going to turn around the House of Y'sra'el (Ephraim) back to Torah and specially sent for restoration and also to fulfil the promise given to Abraham that through him all families of the earth will be en-grafted into him.

Beresheeth (Genesis) 12:3 I will bless those who bless you, and I will curse him who curses you; and in you all the mishpachot (families) of the earth shall be en-grafted.

[4]In English it may not be so obvious but in Hebrew the verse for "In you ALL the families of the earth shall be blessed" reads "**Ve Nivrechu Bekah Kol Mishpachot HA-Adamah.**" The Hebrew word used here "Nivrechu" is translated as "be blessed", however the actual Hebrew word used for "be blessed" is not "Nivrechu" but "Yivrechu". In the Hebrew Rabbinic opinion this word is more correctly translated "intermingled" or to be "grafted in".

Question 4) The Messiah came for the lost sheep. Can we say the Yahudim who kept the Torah were those lost sheep?
The Yahudim were not the lost sheep because the Messiah tells you so.

Mattityahu (Matthew) 9:13 But go you and learn what that means, I desire mercy, and not sacrifice: for I have not come to call the righteous, but sinners.

Who were the righteous and who were the sinners?

Yahushua of course discouraged his followers to take

---

[4] Yeshua or Isa – True path for Salvation page 167 by Rabbi Simon Altaf

the message of his Messiahship back to the 1ˢᵗ century custodians of the faith namely Yahudim because he knew his Messiahship was concealed from Judah and that they were not meant to know nor understand as yet since he had to restore the 10 tribes first which task was not yet finished. Look at the Master's instructions to his disciples.

Mattityahu (Matthew) 10:5-6 These twelve Yahushua sent

forth, and commanded them, saying, <u>do not get into the way of the heathens</u>, and into any cities of the Samaritans do not enter: **6** But <u>go rather to the scattered sheep of the Beyth Y'sra'el (House of Y'sra'el: Ten tribes)</u>.

Could it be clearer that he did not want them to go to the gentiles but go straight to the lost sheep of the ten tribes only? No mention of go to the Yahudim and tell them because Yahushua indeed unlike Christendom had believed Isaiah's report that the Yahudim cannot see nor understand the deeper truth. Even today anyone who compartmentalizes Elohim cannot see the deeper truth.

Now I am going to show you what I consider to be the prophesies of the Messiah and I will just touch upon some more rabbinic opinion to show you that if you use rabbinic opinion then you can search for the Messiah all day and all night and never come to the Messiah. As far as I am concerned historically this is why the

Jews made many mistakes of selecting Messiahs but who were not messiah.

It is clear to me that Christendom has rejected Isaiah's report in ignorance with lack of understanding but also they have rejected eye witness testimony of the disciples of Yahushua in fact the most beloved Yochanan (John) the son of Zebedee who said the exact same words explaining what had happened.

Yochanan (John) 12:37-40 But though he had done so

many miracles before them, yet they believed not on him: **38** That the saying of Yeshayahu (Isaiah) the prophet might be fulfilled, which he spoke, who has believed our report? And to whom has the arm of **YHWH** been revealed? **39** Therefore they could not believe, because that Yeshayahu (Isaiah) said again, **40** He has blinded their eyes, and hardened their heart; that they should not see with their eyes, nor understand with their heart, and be converted, and I should heal them.

Whatever our argument against the ancient or modern rabbinic opinion but John is clear that Isaiah 53 was no other than the Messiah of Y'sra'el Yahushua who was hidden from the eyes of the prevailing Yahudim people.

Even Matthew the Yahudee stated this truth, note Matthew wrote earlier.

Mattityahu (Matthew) 8:17 That it might be fulfilled which was spoken by Yeshayahu (Isaiah) the prophet, saying, he took our infirmities, and bore our sicknesses.

Let us examine the verses Christians use such as Isaiah 52:13-14

Yeshayahu (Isaiah) 53:3 He is despised and rejected of men; a man of sorrows, and acquainted with grief: and we hid as it were our faces from him; he was despised, and we esteemed him not.

Christians apply this to the Messiah Yahushua but the modern or many ancient Rabbis do not. Rabbinic opinion varies and much of it applies this to Y'sra'el the nation. Would you ever find the Messiah with this opinion if applied to Y'sra'el? No chance of that ever happening so the Jews effectively sealed their own fate of ever discovering the Messiah. Blind leading the blind but is that not what John the beloved disciple of Yahushua said? Indeed and I am backing him up. However we must not confuse recognition of the Messiah with the Hebrew salvation because the two are mutually exclusive and this is where Christendom confuses the issue at hand which is not about their salvation.

[11] Here is a Targum on Isaiah 52 by Samuel Driver and Adolf Neubauer.

Yeshayahu (Isaiah) 52:13 -14 Behold, my servant shall deal prudently, he shall be exalted and extolled, and be very high. **14** As many were astonished at you; his disfigurement was more than any man, and his form more than the sons of men:

Targum
Yeshayahu (Isaiah) 52:13 Behold my servant Messiah shall prosper; he shall be high, and increase, and be exceeding strong:

Yeshayahu (Isaiah) 52:14 as the house of Y'sra'el looked to him during many days, because their countenance was darkened among the peoples, and their complexion beyond the sons of men,

As pointed out in the Targum verse 13 was applied to the Messiah and verse 14 was applied to Y'sra'el or the House of Y'sra'el.

Now coming to the question of the Arm of YHWH which is the second question mentioned by Isaiah the prophet in verse 1. To whom has the Arm of YHWH been revealed? We need to understand this is a metaphoric example of a special figure of speech of Elohim to reveal His Righteous Servant the Messiah. The Arm of YHWH was also referred to a person and not to Y'sra'el the nation because it was used to deliver Y'sra'el in times past too.

---

[11] Page 5-6 in "The Suffering Servant of Isaiah, According to the Jewish Interpreters" by Samuel R. Driver and Adolf Neubauer Originally published in 1877 and off copyright, (reprinted 1999 Wipf and Stock Publishers)

So Y'sra'el cannot be the Arm delivering itself. We find many usages of this type/shadow of the Messiah in this usage.

Shemoth (Exodus) 6:6 Therefore say to the children of Y'sra'el, I am **YHWH**, and I will bring you out from under the burdens of the Mitzrim (Egyptians), and I will rescue you from their bondage, and I will **redeem you with an outstretched Arm** and with great judgments:

Y'srael was redeemed from the Egyptians by a special provision. This is one of the places where YHWH revealed his special agent or the Messiah as an Angel thus the Father in heaven bearing His naked Arm a metaphor for the future Messiah the Tzadik Son. This Righteous Son of the Father was understood by King Solomon who asked two questions similar to Isaiah the prophet.

Mishle (Proverbs) 30:4 Who has ascended up into shamayim (heavens), or descended? Who has gathered the wind in his fists? Who has bound the waters in a garment? Who has established all the ends of the earth? What is **his name**, and **what is his son's name**, if you can tell?

Christendom still cannot answer that question because they think the Son's name is "Jesus" which is a five hundred year old invented and the name of the Father is "Jehovah" which is a 16th century invention. If we examine ancient Hebrew literature or the Hebrew text you cannot find these names however you do find YHWH and Yahushua so what is His name and what is His Son's name? YHWH and Yahushua.

This is the special Son that many in Judaism try to understand as The Tzadik or what we term as the middle - pillar and all kabbalists know what this terms means. It actually is a reference to the mystical Son or who we have come to know as the special anointed Messiah who facilitates entry into the Kingdom of Elohim.

Even the Covenant Covenant (NT) writers understood this term e.g. Yochanan (John) says the following:

First John 2:1 My little children, these things I write to you, that you sin not. And if any man sin, we have a Counselor *of justice* with the Abbah, **Yahushua** Messiah **The Tzadik**

(Righteous One):

Yeshayahu (Isaiah) 52:10 YHWH has made bare his Set - Apart arm in the eyes of all the nations; and all the ends of the earth shall see the deliverance of our Elohim.

One may ask when the Holy One bared His arm. This is a reference to the mystery of divinity when He revealed His Son Yahushua who is **the Arm of YHWH** who in times past was revealed as the Angel of YHWH in various places.

The Messiah is a green tree

Luke the Hebrew writer also confirms a unique prophecy that no other gospel writer touched upon

Luke 23:31 For if they do these things in a green etz (tree), what shall be done in the dry?

What does Luke mean by this?

The 'green' tree is a prophecy of the Messiah quoted from Jeremiah 11:16 and Psalm 52:8.

Yirme'yah (Jeremiah) 11:16 YHWH called your name, A **green olive etz** (tree)...

Tehillim (Psalm) 52:8 But I am like a green olive etz (tree) in the house of Elohim: I trust in the mercy of Elohim forever and ever.

While the 'dry' tree idiom can be used for a wicked man such as the anti-Messiah a Eunuch or even a childless man.

Here is what Alfred Edershiem a Hebrew man said about this.

(The Life & Times of Jesus the Messiah, Grand Rapids: Eerdmans, 1947, Vol. II, p. 588).

"For if Y'sra'el has put such flame to its 'green tree' how terribly would the Divine judgment burn among the dry wood of an apostate and rebellious people, that had so delivered up its Divine King, and pronounced sentence upon itself by pronouncing it upon Him!"

Now you see what Luke is referring to? He is saying if this is what happens to a righteous man who is the Messiah sent by the Father then what about the wicked one?

He is actually hinting that in the future because of the moral state of the nation they will accept the conditions and terms of the anti-Messiah while they have rejected the conditions and terms of the Righteous One from above.

This is also the hint that Yahushua was hung and killed on a green TREE and not on the pagan cross of Tammuz. Within the "dry" are two clear hints. One the coming destruction of Y'sra'el that was completed by 135 CE and the arrival of the anti-Messiah which is yet future and he will be a Muslim. Please see my book World War III unmasking the End-Times Beast and World War III – Salvation of the Jews from www.forever-israel.com.

Question 5) Does the Tanach back up a second return of Messiah?

To answer this question we have to see that if the Tanach speaks about the first coming and only for salvation and not for world government. Yes indeed it does the prophet Zechariah.

Zechar'yah 9:9 Rejoice greatly, O daughter of Tsiyon; shout, O daughter of Yerushalim: behold, your King comes to you: he is just, and having deliverance; lowly, and riding upon a donkey, and upon a colt the foal of a donkey.

This refers to the day Yahushua rode on the donkey into the city of Jerusalem, fulfilling the prophecy by Zechariah that the Messiah would present Himself as king. This is the only occasion that Yahushua presented himself as King. Just as Zechar'yah declared this coming was only for salvation not for world government which means that was reserved for His return.

Yochanan (John) 12:15-16 Fear not, daughter of Tziyon: behold, your King comes, sitting on a donkey's colt. **16** These things understood not his disciples at first: but when **Yahushua** was glorified, then they remembered that these things were written of him, and that they had done these things to him.

Ma'aseh Shlichim (Acts) 1:11 They said, You men of Galil, why do you stand gazing up into the shamayim (heaven)? This same **Yahushua**, who is taken up from you into the
shamayim (heaven), shall return in the same manner as you have seen him go into the shamayim (heaven).

When Yahushua returns he will return the same way He went up that means the Hebrew rabbinic understanding is wrong that the messiah will be born as a baby and save Y'sra'el and then marry and die. Such a messiah is prone to fail and history declares that such man-appointed messiahs rose and died which did no use to anyone.

Daniel's prophesies in Daniel 9:25-26 confirms the timeline of the first coming of the Messiah which clearly say he will not die for himself and the prophecy matches precisely to the day of his crucifixion but the Orthodox Rabbis simply reject it because they expected world peace and an everlasting government which is not meant for this coming but the second coming only. Note here it is important that the question the prophet Isaiah asked becomes true that no one believed his report meaning the leadership.

Once we have established the first coming then we can

see the second coming is when the world peace and the kingdom in Y'sra'el will start and there are numerous prophesies for that.

Yeshayahu (Isaiah) 11:10 And in that day there shall be a root of Yishai (Jesse), which shall stand for a banner of the people; to it shall the nations seek: and his rest shall be glorious.

This is yet future and is connected to the second coming of the Messiah.

Yeshayahu (Isaiah) 11:11 And it shall come to pass in that day, that **YHWH** shall set his hand again the second time to recover the remnant of his people, which shall be left, from Assyria, and from Mitzrayim (Egypt), and from Pathros (south Egypt), and from Cush (Sudan), and from Elam
(Iran), and from Shinar (Parts of Iraq), and from Hamath (Northern-Syria), and from the islands of the sea (Western nations).

Note the gathering of the tribes is yet future also so go and look at Y'sra'el and you will not find the ten tribes there. Even justice is no where to be seen in Y'sra'el but when the Messiah returns there will be Torah justice right now in Y'sra'el the secularist government does what it likes and oppresses who it likes they even refuse to listen to their own established high court. Y'sra'el's present government and the attitude of the people to their neighbours' is one of contempt and disgust. This type of government YHWH will break and remove such evil people and establish a Torah based government that will be a very different Y'sra'el.

Zechar'yah 2:11 And many nations shall be joined to **YHWH** in that day, and shall be my people: and I will dwell in the midst of you, and you shall know that **YHWH** of hosts has sent me to you.

These many nations that will join Y'sra'el in the future

are Ephramite nations who will be joined back to Y'sra'el and "I will dwell in your midst" tells us we will have our 3rd Temple fully functioning with sacrificial offerings which many people will come and make. The Shekinah will once again be in Y'sra'el. It's clear that none of these future prophesies have been fulfilled yet and so we wait for the return of the Messiah.

Recommendations

Whenever we examine any text in the accepted biblical literature and try to ascertain its interpretation we must always go back to the public eye witnesses at the time to confirm the prevailing view and understanding. We can certainly go to present day Orthodox Rabbis and ask them for their opinion but their opinion is only to be treated as opinion and not hard truth because of what Isaiah said. Secondly and most unfortunately the majority of the Orthodox Rabbis have always been hostile to the adherents of the faith of those who believe Yahushua is not just a man but a man revealed by Elohim and who embodies attributes of Elohim and is divine. Even leading Rabbis like Jacob Emden confirmed that Yahushua was indeed a good Rabbi sent to the gentiles.

We cannot like modern Judaism or Islam compartmentalize Elohim and put him in a tin can or cardboard box, put wrappers on the this and then decide what Elohim can and cannot do. I have to attest to you that both the Jews and Muslims in their zeal are guilty of doing this.

No man can decide for Elohim how he can and cannot reveal himself and then sell him as sweet candy to the world. This unfortunately has been the attitude amongst the two major religions and both have proved to be mistaken in their identity and view of Elohim but they still have not leant their lessons. While Christianity on the other hands takes it a step further and starts to divide Elohim into persons which I would suggest is also a mistake.

Elohim certainly chose a personal form to reveal His Son but we cannot say these are three persons. If the Holy Spirit is a person and is in everyone then how many persons? This is idolatry and the primary reason why Judaism to this day cannot accept the Christian view of Elohim. For your information the early disciples believed in a binitarian view which is the Father is Elohim and the Son is also Elohim but they did not give a form to the Holy Spirit.

So if we have the Father and the Son where is mamma?

In my personal opinion the Holy Spirit is the Mother or feminine side of Elohim. We have a complete eternal family living in eternity in complete love and harmony. The Father, the Mother and the Son. There can be no son without a woman being part of a relationship and there can be no relation without a compound unity of different people. This at least shows me that Elohim embodies within Himself all the attributes present in the creation of male and female. Elohim is the perfect patriarchal family.

Remember the world is patterned after an order that already existed in heaven. See my article on "Is the Holy Spirit masculine or feminine."

The divine everlasting light may choose to reveal self in a personal form this right belongs to Elohim and Elohim alone. It would be blasphemous to decide how Elohim can and cannot reveal himself to us whether in the form of a man or not. In ancient times the prophets saw Elohim in a personal form of a man.

Now how Elohim managed to encapsulate Himself in a male form we do not know. I believe this personal form is the Arm of YHWH or the agent function by which the divinity of Elohim reveals self to the ones receiving the revelation. The difficulty for most people is that since the creator who created the whole universe how can he reveal himself in a man? Also since its not the creator is in the universe but that the universe is in the creator then how can it be possible for him to come down?

To me these are our human barriers of understanding the divinity we try but fail but the divine creator who talks about himself as a family yet Akhad (United one) has revealed himself through His chosen Son who is also brought forth out of the bosom of the Father in heaven yet the Father has never at anytime in history revealed himself but the Son Yahushua indeed has manifested the Father.

We can either choose to believe scripture or reject this is entirely your right but it's also then your right to accept and take the punishment that will result from rejecting revelation of the most High and His voice.

Personal Revelation

Certain individuals from all walks of life are chosen and ordained by Elohim and not man. We find many examples in scripture e.g. Abraham was chosen and called. I believe I was also chosen one day when I was working in a merchant bank in my old faith of Islam when Yahushua spoke to me. Then many individuals enquire over whether the voice I heard was audible or non-audible but this is irrelevant. If the voice was meant for me then I was the only one who heard it. Is that also not what Rabbi Sha'ul said? Indeed for a Muslim it is a suicide to go home and tell his wife and family that he has heard Elohim and especially the Elohim of Y'sra'el is tantamount to the ultimate blasphemy. My family was equally shocked at my exposition of Elohim who can talk. Many people are happy at Elohim being dumb.

According to Islamic law a Muslim man's marriage is instantly annulled. His family can ostracize him and he can no longer inherit anything from his father. Certain radical elements of his family can even try to kill him for leaving Islam. All religions seek to impose themselves upon you but the faith of Elohim liberates you and does not shackle you in religious chains.

I agree that we cannot rely on personal revelation because this can be subject to the individual but we cannot ignore it either. Most of us like to rely on corporate revelation such as what happened in Y'sra'el to Y'sra'el but Abraham was not in Y'sra'el since Abraham was outside of the land born in South-Eastern Turkey when he received his individual and personal revelation and indeed it is by this revelation that the three major religions try to live interpreting his revelation in their own way of understanding but who is right? This can only be determined by the testimonies of Individuals whether we like it or not.

Can we deny the testimony of Abraham? Or can we deny the testimony of Moses. Can one say he was delirious and never heard the burning bush speak? How come no Hebrew Rabbi questions how a burning bush can speak? This though seems to be in the realm of fantasy but in reality it happened. History follows such individuals with consistent revelation.

How come we all question the Messiahship of Yahushua? Then if Yahushua's Messiahship stands out and stands to its claims then why choose man-made messiahs which all ultimately failed? The reality is that all Judaism's and even Islamic followers claimed Messiah's were false while the one Judaism claims to be false today is the real one. How ironic!!! While the one Islam claims as the real Messiah for them being Isa is also false because he is created and will ultimately return and get married and die a normal death. Do we seriously think that eternal government can rest on an individual who will die?

Yeshayahu (Isaiah) 9:7 Of the increase of his government and shalom (peace) there shall be no end,

No matter if you are a Yahudee or gentile but it is truly to live in fantasy to believe that one man who is not eternal can bring world government and rule forever through his earthly life of say seventy years.

Judaism also claims that the Messiah will be a military leader will come and marry and of course ultimately he will also die. This means Judaism will never recognize the true Messiah either in its current man-made theological model.

Sabbatai Zevi of Turkey a Kabbalist Rabbi who claimed to be the Messiah in 1648 was a false messiah and on death threats later became a Muslim. He was the laughing stock of all of Turkey.

There were others too...

[12]Menahem ben Judah revolt against king Agrippa II Simon bar Kosiva 135 CE proclaimed as the messiah by Rabbi Akiva. Simon was killed by the Romans.

Moses of Crete - 440 to 470 who after convincing Jews to walk back to Y'sra'el through the sea when many foolish people died by casting themselves in the water trying to part the water while Moses himself either perished in sea or fled according to Socrates.

Jacob Querido who also claimed to be the incarnation of the late Sabbatai Zevi around 1690, he was the brother of Zevi's last wife Jochebed who converted into Islam under the name of Aaisha and later this proclaimed Messiah Jacob also converted into Islam and took his followers to Mecca for pilgrimage. Can you imagine the laughter that the Muslims had at this farce? Incredible yet Judaism refuses to stop proclaiming false messiahs as the list is rather long and no doubt they will choose others in the future.

Löbele Prossnitz 1790 calling himself messiah ben Yosef found to be fraud of course because the real Messiah Yahushua is alive and well and at the right hand of Elohim.

The Muslims on the other hand also have had several false messiahs but of course are we surprised since the real one is up there with the Father in Heaven?

Muhammad Ahmad bin Abd Allah (The mad mahdi) 1844-1885 claimed to be the Mahdi (or the coming Muslim Messiah). He was killed by a simple typhus fever.

Mirza Ghulam Ahmad (1835-1908) through whom the Ahmadiya movement came about he was a false messiah.

---

[12] http://en.wikipedia.org/wiki/List_of_messiah_claimants

He claimed Yahushua survived the crucifixion and ran away to Kashmir in India and they have made a grave there in Kashmir and many of his followers still go there. Sunni Muslims hate Ahmadiyya's and try to kill them whenever they get a chance even today.

Rashad Khalifa (1935-1990) he found the submitters international movement. He claimed the number 19 of the Qur'an was divine and so it is believed he was murdered in 1990 in the Tucson Mosque by possibly one of his own followers.

There have been many false messiahs in fact tuppence a dozen and I am sure we will continue to see more in the future before the arrival of the REAL one.

I can tell you personally that when I met the REAL DEAL He spoke to me eleven years and eight months ago when he called me out of Islam but I do not want you to give value to this because this was my personal revelation from which I ended up losing my wife, children, home and other family. My suffering is not worthy and not important in the scheme of things but I mention it none the less because it has become an important part of my life and who I am. The thousands of answered prayers in my life by the Elohim of Y'sra'el and the miracles which He did through me I cannot ignore and just put it to chance.

He was not a Sabbatai Zevi who converted into Islam neither was he Moses of Crete convincing his followers to try to cross the sea nor Jacob Querido who converted into Islam and took his follower to Mecca for pilgrimage. My Messiah and My Master is very **REAL** and answers prayer everyday and only asks me to stick to the established faith of Y'sra'el. So if you want to know more about this faith of Messianic/Netzarim Judaism then by all means get in touch with me and join us see details on our information page at beginning of book.

Let me give you some examples of answered prayers.

Can I put it to chance in 2010 on the night I prayed for my ill son who was sixteen years of age on Passover night to be taken away and released from his pain and failing body because he was seriously and terminally ill? I can tell you I came home that evening
and prayed to the merciful Father in the name of Yahushua to take him away the same day. At 3am I had a phone call from my daughter crying that my son had passed from this life to glory and I was though sad but happy that the merciful Father had answered the prayer that took 5 hours to answer. Can you boast of such a response?

A student of mine phoned me last year in 2009 that he had been stuck in some court case for the last five years seeing no hope of it ever ending draining him financially and asked that if I could pray for him to be released from this bondage once and for all. I told my student go and it shall be done as you require it. He had his hearing in court in two weeks and the judged dismissed the case and he was set free after five years of hardship.

He phoned me on another occasion later because he had his driving test the next morning which he had failed six times already. I told him go and this time you will pass. He did his driving test the next morning and without a fanfare he passed the test.

He then asked me another time to pray for him for a house because he was living on rented accommodation. I told him so that you know that I have the authority and the prayer is not answered by chance not only will you get a house but you will get a house bigger than three bedrooms and the finance will be provided this year meaning in 2009.

I did not hear from him for a few weeks and then he phoned and told me of receiving £25,000 unexpectedly and to pray and confirm that he finds a suitable house. I told him go the house is waiting and it is a big house waiting for you so that you may know YHWH has spoken through me. He went searching and purchased exactly the house revealed to me which is a nice large 4 bedroom house in London to which I was invited to bless the house and put the Mazuza up on the doorposts and what a beautiful house it is. Praise YHWH for His mercy.

The confirms the authority YHWH has given me, in my prayers there is no claptrap of the church of jumping up and down on stage, calling down the Holy Spirit, speaking in tongues or rolling on the floor in laughter. I simply used the authority that Yahushua has given me and it was used to accomplish a good deed that blesses and glorifies Ha'Shem (The Name).

This brought Yahushua's words to pass that any prayer that you pray to the Father and ask in My name will be granted provided the one praying is indeed right with Elohim. Was He lying? My experience not only on this night but many many other times have proved that Rabbi Yahushua was honest and trustworthy and does indeed stand on the right hand of Abbah YHWH even today which really is to say He has been given the authority by Abbah YHWH. He does not literally stand on the right twenty-four hours because that is the duty of the angels but to stand on the right also reveals the side of judgment which means his judgments or rulings stand.

Yochanan (John) 15:16 You have not chosen me, **but I have chosen ye**, and appointed ye, that ye should go and bring forth fruit, and that your fruit should remain: that whatever ye shall ask of the Abbah in my name, he may give it you.

Can we all boast of such answered prayers? I can boast in Messiah and boast in the glory of YHWH but once again I urge you to pay attention to the voice of Elohim which is Torah in order to be effective in your life.

I do not to this day ask for money for answered prayers or send in donations just because I did something that helped another struggling man or woman in the kingdom while when you switch the TV Channels on to Christian TV the beggars are out begging for money and to give them your important tithes and love offerings which they can use to fill their coffers while they lie to you that we need it to do such and such work but most of the money is used to buy luxury goods for the individuals concerned. We are not talking of small money here but hundreds of millions of dollars.

Just look at the trips that Benny Hinn makes to top hotels staying in presidential suites costing $14,000 a night and rendezvous in private jets for important holiday destinations, big homes and expensive cars and a huge salary with it.

I hear in Africa also it is fashionable for preachers to buy three or four cars and build big homes, send kids to expensive schools while their poor African neighbours living in rural areas do not even have clean water or a secure roof over their head living in mud shackled huts.

[13] In 2009, Jesse Duplantis Ministries plane took a 17 day trip to Hawaii. The plane hopped from island to island. We spoke to one airplane operator who has the same jet as Duplantis. By his calculations, this Hawaii trip cost his ministry $40,000. That includes the cost of gassing up, flying, and storing the plane in Hawaii for 17 days.

[14] A fan of Thoroughbred horse racing, Robertson paid $520,000 for a colt he named Mr. Pat. Mr. Pat was not a successful runner. He was nominated for, but did not run in, the 2000 Kentucky Derby.

This is the kind of hypocrisy that exists amongst these types of Christians hence why Christianity is discredited and a false religion of Rome. This is why like my forefathers my faith is a faith of Torah deeds while most religions out there are religions of creeds including the Roman religion of Christianity.

Can the creator of the Universe reveal himself personally?

Just read the story of Abraham in Genesis 18, the story of Gideon in Judges, the story of Manoah the father of Samson to understand that Elohim is indeed able to do this. The wise must let Elohim do the bidding and we can observe, learn and enhance our knowledge about the wisdom and revelation of heaven but we cannot contradict or put Elohim in a tin-can and decide how he should reveal himself to the world.

Question 1) Who has believed our report?
Question 2) To who is the arm of YHWH been revealed?

In summary no one believed Isaiah's report by intellectual capacity and university degrees because we never discovered the Messiah by our intellect unless the Holy Spirit has revealed the Son from the eternal family. Elohim is a family and unless we view the family this way we will have a distorted view of who Elohim is which is prevalent amongst many.

[13] http://inthedustofyeshua.wordpress.com/2010/05/22/jesse-duplantis-living-the-high-life-of-greed-wealth-and-prosperity/
[14] http://en.wikipedia.org/wiki/Pat_Robertson#Business_interests

The Arm of YHWH has been revealed to the nations to gather the outcasts of Y'sra'el a task which is still not finished. First there is the spiritual task of returning them back to Torah then they will be returned back to the land. Elohim cannot violate his own covenant where he requires certain amount of obedience from us to obey the Torah which then allows us to live in the land promised to Abraham and if there is no obedience in the land then the land will spit us out and we end up back in exile again. Therefore this explains when entry is granted into the land why many gentile people will be learning Torah and how best to keep it (Isa 2:3) because they are still refusing to right now.

Conclusion

As I said earlier the only Yahudee that took my sins and yours was Yahushua and He is the **Righteous One** (Middle-Pillar) sent by the Father in heaven. We do not need to go running to the Hebrew Rabbis to confirm this truth because many of them could not agree on the passages in question because of the spiritual confusion that is running in the nations and also this is not an exercise of intellect.

If you want confirmation from a Hebrew Rabbi then I am confirming it because my eyes have been opened by the Ruach Ha Kodesh (Holy Spirit) unlike many others in my nation and I am of the same tribe as Matthew that is Levi a Kohen. At least we can see two witnesses here that prove to us from the timeline of Matthew of what was believed by the disciples and apostles of Yahushua. I am going to date the gospel of Matthew around 36 -37AD because Matthew the Levite recorded a very interesting discourse in Matthew 23 about certain Pharisees and the

Pharisees mentioned are actually of the school of Shammai which had a large group of Pharisees ruling during this era in the Temple.

The witness of John who was a close eye witness disciple of Rabbi Yahushua I am going to place his gospel before the destruction of Jerusalem that means before 70 AD. This at least gives us two credible 1st century witnesses that verify that at least even these two disciples and possibly several others other than the twelve may have accepted that the Servant that the prophet Isaiah spoke about was indeed Yahushua.

My final question to the Hebrew Rabbis who do not believe

How can the Orthodox Jews inherit the land considering that they were expelled from it because of disobedience? Are you not also expecting the Messiah to do what the Christians already claim in that he should bear your guilt vanquish your enemies and take you back to the land but you deny that? Does not Isaiah 53:10 say that His Soul was made an Asham offering which is only ever for sin? Did Y'sra'el ever offer an Asham offering for sins of the nations?

We know very well that this is not a free will sacrifice of the tabernacle and the Jews have never offered themselves as an Asham offering therefore who is the one who has become an Asham? This is no other than the Messiah. If I accept the theology espoused today by the Hebrew majority that Isaiah 53:10 is about Y'sra'el the nation then technically an Asham has to be slaughtered and killed. That means by extension all Jews have to literally die but even if one Yahudee is standing alive then this contradicts this theory. Furthermore, Jews have always had a presence in the land of Y'sra'el which means the modern theology of Y'sra'el being an Asham is self contradictory. Yahushua was indeed made an Asham, killed, literally died and then He rose by the will of Heaven which leaves no room for our argument and the final argument will be settled by Heaven.

The Jews also know very well that the Covenant with Elohim is a two way street, you obey Torah and setup a Torah government in the land but not give sides to an unrighteous secular government is an abomination before Adonai. The expulsion from the land only came about because of Torah disobedience hence the one righteous individual that will be sent by Abbah in heaven will be the one to end our exile and before that we are not to live in the land.

The rights or deeds to the land are eternal but the stay is dependent on our conduct. Therefore the Hebrew Rabbis have already setup a false trap for themselves expecting the Messiah to fulfil the righteous requirements which they are not able to fulfil themselves and then rejecting Him.

Vayikra (Leviticus) 18:25-29 And the land is defiled: therefore I do visit the iniquity there upon it, and the land itself vomits out her inhabitants. **26** You shall therefore keep
my statutes and my judgments, and shall not commit any of these abominations; neither any of your own nation, nor any foreigner that lives among you: **27** For all these abominations have the men of the land done, which were before you, and the land is defiled; **28** Do not make the land vomit you out also, when you defile it, as it did the nations that were before you. **29** For whosoever shall commit any of these abominations, even the souls that commit them shall be cut off from among their people.

This is precisely why a righteous individual such as the Tzadik Son which is the anointed one, the Messiah is needed to take us all back to the land. This means if we do not agree to the terms of the Messiah you will stay outside the land because our sages teach that we are forbidden to enter the land by force. Remember the three oaths and the curses that ensue we do not delay the coming of the Righteous Tzadik the Messiah.

Any Hebrew sovereignty during the time of the Exile delays the arrival of the Messiah

Rabbi Chama Bar Chanina said: The son of David (Messiah) will not come until even the most insignificant form of government no longer exists among the Hebrew People. Rashi explains this as follows: "That there absolutely no sovereign governmental body of the Hebrew People shall exist, even the most minor or trivial type of regime". (Talmud Sanhedrin 98a).

Therefore many Zionist Jews today are guilty of breaking the oaths promising to take people back to Y'sra'el and to start to form a Sanhedrin and try to resurrect the 3rd Temple and take part with the unrighteous secular government of Y'sra'el. Did not our blessed sages teach that not even the miniscule government needs to remain for the Messiah to return? Some of you who live in the land illegally lie to the people and mislead them. Did Rabbi Akiva not made a similar mistake? On top today's so called claimed children of Y'sra'el or not. The majority of the real children of Y'sra'el remain outside the land who are Black Hebrews while the Caucasian claim of being the sons of Jacob is simply false because Jacob was blacBe warned because the Master YHWH will not tolerate it and throw out the rebels first. While you are guilty of breaking the oaths in which you take part with the government of Y'sra'el that cannot even hear the cry of the poor and is totally secular and unrighteous government and many of you take land illegally from the Palestinians who Elohim said will remain for now but you use expulsion by force and deceive them by building access roads, taking land by stealth. The land which the Holy One said is not to be taken back yet which is for the moment given to the gentiles until the time of the return of Messiah who will settle all disputes.

And those of you who say we can go up to the land and take it by force I have this to say.

Mishle (Proverbs) 12:15 The way of a fool is right in his own eyes: but he that hearkens to counsel is wise.

Chapter 6

Yahushua the Divine Son of Elohim?

Many people continue to have problem with Yahushua being divine and confuse the term Son of Elohim with the ordinary human being the same type of son rather in comparison to Yahushua who is the Only Son and divine. Many who do not accept His divinity continue to face dilemmas in their outlook on life and fail to understand who the Creator is. It is very difficult to try to understand how an infinite Creator can have a Son and one who is purely a special type of light that is totally incomprehensible to us and indeed our coming into contact with such a being in His infinity can kill us instantly or burn us to cinders. The dilemma is very difficult for humans to accept this pure light which we are not able to see or touch then we rationalize and argue over how can this type of substance or light source dwell in a limited human body.

Our science has completely failed to understand the dimension where Elohim dwells since it has no known model to apply to that particular light and to examine it in a laboratory environment.
Therefore they have concluded at random there is no Elohim. They ignore the vast creation and the contradiction in their statements which fails to take the various stages of the creation model. Their hypothesis of creation occurring by itself over billions of years fails miserably since it is only a model with man-made introduced set values to arrive at the set conclusion to make them happy in fact their system is flawed.

Methushelah lived the longest to 969 (Gen 5:27) years and after his death of this great man the Tractate of the Talmud (Tractate Sanhedrin 108b) notes that the sun rose from the west and settled in the East for seven consecutive days to give people the opportunity to repent before the flood came but the people were not interested in repentance and went about as if nothing was going to happen. The same is true today! Does Science know of these extraordinary events? No. Does science know that YHWH stopped the sun and moved time back for a day (Joshua 10:12)? No. So how can people rely on such science that can only see the present and has no knowledge of the past? Therefore it is my firm belief that the present scientific model is both in error and completely flawed which views times and dimensions according to a man-made model and has no recognition of Elohim or His supernatural laws which have overridden natural laws on many occasions in the past.

Even the Muslim holy book the Qur'an speaks of this phenomena because it was common knowledge in the Arabs and it was passed to the Muslims through the Yahduim where even Muhammad calls his elohim the Lord of two easts and two wests trying to make him the same as YHWH.

Sura Alrahman 55:17 (He is) The Lord of the two Easts (i.e. the two extremes from where the sun appears to rise in summer and in winter) and the Lord of the two Wests (i.e. the two extremes where the sun appears to set in summer and in winter).

If you ask a Muslims why this is then I guarantee you that most do not know what this Sura refers to and what it means. To get the true story you have to go to the Bible and see what happened just before the flood of Noah and it is there that we find truth.

For a discourse on the Hebrew and the sun rising from the West and setting in the East for seven days see the discourse with Rabbi Hai Gaon in the 10th century (Steinschneider, Hebraische Bibliographie, Vol. XVIII, PP. 61ff).

Well in order to understand this we have to go back just before the flood. After the death of Methushelah seven days before the great flood it became chaotic. The sun started rising out of the West and settling in the East. Many people were worried and perplexed as to what was going on since Elohim wanted people to take note and repent but repentance was not forth coming. There are several questions that then arise. What happened to the earth's tilt? Did the earth rotate differently? How were days and nights determined?

Therefore to understand Elohim is beyond our understanding it is not that He inhabits the universe like limiting himself as an object that the scientists are searching for but cannot find and that the universe dwells in Him the incomprehensible being full of grace and truth. Unfortunately the scientists are searching for the wrong thing hence they will not find their answer in science. Science is very limited and will never break the barriers of Elohim. Science only examines today what is in front of it and applies its calculations to that object then extrapolates backwards and often gets things wrong because events have taken place by Elohim which were supernatural and science cannot take those things into consideration since it has no knowledge of them.

We also find the Hebrew people had awareness that YHWH is a special kind of being and that they cannot see Him and live this is why they were scared to look upon Him when He did descend from the third heaven in a human angelic body.

Shoftim (Judges) 6:21 -23 Then the Malakh **YHWH** put forth the end of the staff that was in his hand, and touched the flesh and the matzah (unleavened cakes); and there rose up fire out of the rock, and consumed the flesh and the matzah (unleavened cakes). Then the Malakh **YHWH** departed out of his sight. **22** And when Gideon perceived that he was the Malakh **YHWH**, Gideon said, Alas, O Master **YHWH**! **Because I have seen the Malakh YHWH face to face** . **23** And **YHWH** said to him, Shalom (Peace be to you); **fear not: you shall not die.**

Gideon understood that looking at the Mighty One would kill him so he was afraid to look at Him. The Torah had set a warning that anyone who sees Him shall/will surely die

Exodus 33:20 But He said, You cannot see My face; for no man shall see Me, and live.

In Hinduism it is accepted that the deities they worship can become humans or become animals for them to interact with them or even stones. In Islam it is incomprehensible to accept that Allah their deity can descend and become a human being. Even in Judaism this concept is not well accepted. So how does Judaism explain the manifestations of YHWH as an angel coming to Gideon or to Abraham? They usually suggest that this is just an emanation of the Holy One or that the angel has a special character and the Holy One has put His name upon the angel and this particular angel is a special one caring the name referred to as the Angel of the Covenant. This still does not explain why a man or woman in ancient Y'sra'el would render worship to an angel and why the angel speaks in the first person and the third person calling himself YHWH and yet directing the sacrifice to YHWH in the heaven. This can only be because of the two powers in heaven which were clearly understood by the ancients. One was called the Father and the other the Son. This was the view of the early disciples of Yahushua which we refer to as binitarian view of Elohim.

Let us look at this conversation of Gideon and the Malakh YHWH. (Angel of the Covenant)

Judges 6:12 And the Malakh **YHWH** appeared to him, and said to him, **YHWH is with you**, you mighty man of valour.

Note the Angel is YHWH yet he is speaking in the third person about YHWH saying to Gideon "YHWH is with you."

Judges 6:13 And Gideon said to him, Oh **my Master**, if YHWH be with us, why then is all this befallen us?...

Gideon is speaking to the Angel and not seeing that the angel is YHWH but calling him my master in Hebrew Adonai and also speaks in the third person about YHWH being not with them.

Judges 6:14 And **YHWH looked upon him**, and said, Go in this your might, and you shall save Y'sra'el from the hand of the Midianites: have not I sent you?

Is not YHWH supposed to be in the 3rd heavens then how can the Angel at Gideon's time now be looking at Gideon and become YHWH in the first person? The text in the Hebrew is ויפן אליו והוה

רמאיו.

V, Ypan Eli' v" Yahuweh, v'Yomar.

Literally the text in Hebrew says "And the face of El (YHWH) was upon him and YHWH said. It is unmistakable that the Hebrew text here describes the Angel as YHWH looking upon Him and answering Gideon. We just cannot get around the text and pretend that YHWH is aloof in the third heavens and this is just a simple created messenger who has come to give a message.

Judges 6:16 And **YHWH** said to him, surely I will be with you,..

Again YHWH in the first person speaking to Gideon but looking like an Angel. We see this first person and third person switch in the bible in many places.

Note now Gideon speaking to the Angel in the first person as if he is facing YHWH.

Judges 6:22-23 And when **Gideon perceived that he was the Malakh YHWH**, Gideon said, Alas, O Master

YHWH! Because I have seen the Malakh **YHWH** face to face. **23** And **YHWH said to him**, Shalom (Peace be to you); fear not: you shall not die.

Gideon now realised he was speaking to YHWH and not just an angel but look YHWH tells him "do not fear you will not die". So here is a very interesting confirmation and confrontation with YHWH as like an angel but Gideon does not die.

This was not uncommon and this does not mean that the angel was a created being to simply carry a message. We know that nothing living dares to carry the name of YHWH and pretend to be speaking as Him. We find Yahushua in the body of a man doing the same so let us examine that case.

John 20:17 Yahushua said to her, Touch me not; for I have not

yet ascended to the Abbah but go to my brothers, and say to them, I ascend to <u>my Abbah</u>, and your Abbah; and to **my Elohim, and your Elohim**.

People who do not believe in Yahushua's divinity often offer this as proof text that Yahushua is not divine because He said that He was going to ascend to His Eloah and your Eloah. On the surface this seems to be a plausible argument, however the people who insist on this often have a flawed case as I will demonstrate in this chapter because this speech is similar to that which was taking place between Gideon and YHWH where YHWH in the form of an angel looked like human being for all practical purposes and talked to Gideon in the first and third persons. John's gospel here shows the same colouring because of its Hebrew origin because it's a Hebrew gospel and not Greek. It carries the same tones. His speech was in the first and third person's (Mine and your's). My Eloah and Your Eloah does not negate the fact that Yahushua is divine.

Next one must ask how can Yahushua ascend to the Father in heaven and by what power? Is he Spock who is being transported up, the beam me up Scotty kind in the movie Star Trek or is he a very different type of being?

Note if Yahushua had the power to ascend up as He did in Acts 1:9 then what is He? Is He a plane, helicopter or missile? Well He had no gas bottles strapped to him and yet people saw him ascend up and taken in the cloud. Let us assume for a minute that Yahushua is a very ordinary human being just like you and me, well if he is and that is what the anti-divinity crowd are making Him to be then He cannot offer His body as a sacrifice.

The anti-divinity crowd are happy to accept His sacrifice which for a human is forbidden and idolatrous (Lev 18:21). How come these people never deal with this objection and issue of great concern? What about the fact that all humans have sinned at some point of their life and are not sinless? How do we deal with the Yetzer Hara (Evil inclination) that entices one to sin? Could a human then be offered as a sacrifice for sin who himself is sinful? All these questions demand meaningful answers which you will not get from the anti-divinity people.

There are several reasons why Yahushua's death can be accepted to atone for the sins of the House of Y'sra'el.
1. His body was specially designed in heaven by the Father and cloaked with heavenly dust which is uncorrupted. We are told this truth in the Torah in Exodus 24:10 see below.
2. He was born without human intervention and without the need for male sperm with a supernatural birth.
3. It was also revealed in the Covenant Covenant writings that He never sinned when He was upon this earth no not even once.

Exodus 24:10 And they saw the Elohim of Y'sra'el and **supporting his feet with great strength** there appeared to be a brilliant white sapphire and standing above it **a pillar of strength as a bone (body)**, his essence pure as heaven.[15]

Notice He has feet and that is what the elders of Y'sra'el saw. Well if there were feet then there must also be a body to go along with it.

His body is described as a bone in the Torah in the HTHS translation. So this body or bone was designed for the Son by the Father to reveal His Son to the world.

When Satan was banished from the heaven after he was tainted by sin he was shot down by the lightening of Elohim and Satan fell to the ground with his wings being burnt. That would bring down some ash upon the earth also along with him other rebellious angels were thrown out which would cause sin and rebellion to enter the world at that stage. Note by clothing Yahushua's body in heaven the Father prevents taking corrupted soil.

Luke 10:18 And he said to them, I saw Shaitan (Satan) fall as lightning from the shamayim (heaven).

Yahushua's sacrifice was acceptable because His body was of a special covering of non-human origin and belong to the heavenly Temple.

As can be **seen above** numbers 1 & 2 lead us to conclude that He was not tainted with Yetzer hara (the evil inclination) by which man is inclined to sin, which brings us to the conclusion that His

---

[15] The bone or the body (Ivrim-Hebrews 10:5) they saw was Yahushua the middle-pillar communing with Moses and the elders of Israel.

body can be offered as a sin offering to atone for Y'sra'el's sins. We have already proved in this book that He was the rightful High Priest from the House of Tzadok. He did not come to sit upon the earthly throne as a King in the first coming because the issue of Y'sra'el's sins had to be dealt with first.

Corroborating evidence that Yahushua was both the Son of Elohim and Elohim

Looking at the rules of kinship

I have on numerous occasions in this book documented the rules that priestly and princely clans followed.

Why does Yahushua in the flesh as an angel (Jud 6:14) is called YHWH and subsequently calls another entity YHWH in the Heavens which we know is our Abbah YHWH (Jud 13:16). He explicitly tells Manoah to offer the sacrifice to YHWH in heaven.

Judges 13:16 And the Malakh YHWH said to Manoah, Though you detain me, I will not eat of your lechem (bread): and if you will offer a burnt offering, **you must offer it to YHWH**. For Manoah knew not that he was the Malakh YHWH.

We can see that in many world cultures today some cultures have made the Holy Spirit a literal heavenly woman and worship statues who look like women. While we also see a myriad of deities in various cultures believe to all be Elohim. However it is certain in my mind that all these people corrupt the main principles that are to be seen spiritually but they make them into the physical and thus end up in idolatry.

We know that It was a common custom in Abraham's African ancestors the Horoites to place wives in the north/south divide axis. North represents the Heaven in the Bible.

The Horoites have known to live in the southern regions of Y'sra'el Beersheba being one of them. It was in Beythlechem where Abraham's mother was married to his father Terach while Terach already had another wife in the North so Abraham's mother was the wife on the southern axis. In fact she was also a Horoite the daughter of one man called Joktan.

Abraham married his cousin Keturah from the mother's side who was the daughter of Joktan and she named her firstborn son Joktan (Gen 25:2) following the kinship pattern from her mother's side who was Abraham's cousin/sister bride. Sarah was from the father's side which was the ruler clan so her husband Abraham would be the next prince in line. Abraham's two wives in the north/south divide was Sarah living in Hebron and Keturah living in Beersheba the area of the wells. Horoites people travelled and controlled waterways and this can be seen in Abraham's family also where they dig wells. Abraham's father came from the river Euphrates an area in Turkey where also was a major waterway.

One of Abraham's grandfather was called Na'hur (Gen 11:22) then we have his father Terach born through him followed by a son that Terach calls Na'hur. Do you see the pattern? These were all Horoite clans. Even Yosef the son of Jacob was buried back in Y'sra'el territory which was then Horoite place of burial.

Even Moses's sister Miriam according to rabbinic sources husband's name was Hur and her son's name was also Hur.

Ask yourself why? How about kinship patterns revealing another interesting kinship pattern of the Horoites.

The Horoites were priestly clans and only married in priestly families. They kept to close kinship patterns and followed in the lines of their forefathers. The Y'sraelites i.e. Jacob was Abraham's grandson therefore directly a descendant of the Horoites. Josephus the historian calls Keturah a Horoite. She the daughter of a Joktan and called her firstborn son Jokshan (Gen 25:2). Her children controlled the regions in the south. She lived in Beersheba and named after firstborn son Jokshan after her father

Joktan the son of Eber.

The Horoites were the conquerors of Egypt and founded the Assyrian Empire.[16]

[17]Besides being the name of Abraham's father, Terah is also the name of an Arabian tribe (Terabin) that dwells chiefly between Gaza and Beersheba. This information links Terah to the clans of Joktan and Sheba, from which he took his wife, Abraham's mother. It also suggests that Terah's mother was a daughter of a Horite chief named Terah. She named her first-born son by Terah after her father, according to the cousin bride's naming prerogative. The idea that the people of Esau, referred to as Edomites, supplanted the Horites is hardly possible if Esau and Jacob were Horites who married Horites.

Horite identity was figured through the mothers and is already evident at the time of Peleg, Noah's great great grandson. Peleg was one of 3 sons and 3 sons in Genesis always points to a tribal unit. The Horite tribal unit is indicated by the clans of Peleg, Joktan the Elder, and Sheba the Elder. Yet we are told that Peleg's generation marked a time of "division." The division involved geographical separation of the Horite clans, but it did not involve a change in their kinship pattern. Through intermarriage of the Horite rulers, their Afro-Asiatic worldview diffused across the ancient Near East and became the foundation for the biblical worldview.

[16] Josephus antiquities. Lib. I. Cap. 16.
[17] http://jandyongenesis.blogspot.com/2009/05/horite-territory.html

Note when Yosef was in Egypt he did not just marry any woman in Egypt but the daughter of a priest. (Gen. 41:45). Isaac married a Horoite bride the descendant of Na'hur and Terach. The southern bride of Abraham Keturah was a direct descendant of Sheba who was also the forefather of Bathsheba (Hebrew meaning the daughter of Sheba) (2 Sam 11:3). In I Chronicles 3:5 she is called BathShua. These people link directly to today's Arab clans in the middle-east. Unfortunately Christians who often see the Arabs pitted against the Jews fail to see that there is a very close kinship tie and it was the Arabs who came first and not vice versa, look at the first Arab ancestor Joktan (Gen 10:25) and even Abraham is related to him because Joktan was his father in law and the father of Keturah. Jacob from whom we today get the Jews people are all directly related to the Arabs. Actually the truth be told the Arabs are older since Joktan is the first Arab mentioned who lived in these regions of the Middle - East however YHWH chose Jacob and gave Him the Covenant through his grandfather Abraham to carry the mantle to all future generations while the Arabs were not chosen for that task such as Ishmael who actually was half Egyptian. Both Jacob's children and Keturah's Arab children were black and not Caucasian.

These people were the black Africans who travelled to the west and later became many Y'sraelite tribes and even later many nations.

Abraham was chosen by Elohim out of these Horoite clans and we have historical evidence that they lived in Beersheba and in the Southern regions of Y'sra'el. Abraham was indeed a prince and called one by the people living in Y'sra'el. (Gen 23:6). No one in the world just wants to give land away free and yet we have here people who wanted to give Abraham a place for Sarah's tomb free recognising him as a prince but Abraham paid for the land and took the whole field (Gen 23:6) to secure it for his future generations.

If we follow this pattern then we begin to understand that pattern of the Horoites actually is one which has its roots in heaven. YHWH has revealed this pattern in himself but we need to see since YHWH is light then how do we as humans understand this pattern. We will now examine this a little. Please do not confuse this with many elohim but we serve the one El who is revealed in these facets which we use our human reasoning to understand. The Sonship of Yahushua fits in this category. Remember I told you about the ruling class placing their son as the next ruler well so it did begin in heaven.

Yahushua was the model for mankind

Ezekiel 23:1-4 The word of YHWH came again to me, saying, **2** Son of man, there were two women, the daughters of one mother: **3** And they committed whoredoms in Mitzrayim; they committed whoredoms in their youth: there their breasts were handled, and there *lovers* fondled their maiden nipples. **4** And the names of them were Aholah the elder, and Aholibah her sister: and **they were my *wives***, and they bore sons and daughters. Thus were their names; Shomeron is Aholah, and Yerushalim Aholibah.

Note YHWH calls the two portions of Northern and Southern Y'sra'el my wives. These are on the North/South axis as I revealed the pattern to you earlier. He said they are from one mother. In other words they are sisters. Remember the half sister pattern of Sarah and sister/cousin pattern of Keturah. This is being hinted at here using Y'sra'el as an allegory or Drash to tell the story.

YHWH has used anthropomorphological terms to describe Himself with His two wives and the relationship. The wife in the North was the Ten tribes of Y'sra'el and they would have had the greatest blessing had they endured to love YHWH and serve Him faithfully. The chance was afforded to the Southern wife Yahudah also but she also failed. If you have read carefully so far then this pattern is what we see the Horoites clans practicing who were Abraham's ancestors.

The pattern is hidden in heaven

We can never claim to know all about Elohim because if we did then we would be in the place of Elohim. Elohim forbid we are not. However we can apply certain assumptions and look at some cryptic scriptures and come to some understanding from what we know in the Bible taken to its logical conclusion we do see a pattern in the heavens of a Father, the Mother and the Son with seven other subordinate Spirits of Elohim.

Revelation 4:5 And out of the throne preceded lightnings and thundering and voices: and there were seven lamps of
fire burning before the throne, which are the **seven Ruachot of Elohim**.

Scripture are replete with these examples.

Zechar'yah 4:10 For who has despised the day of small things? For they shall rejoice, and shall see the plummet in the hand of Zerubbab'el with **those seven; they are the eyes of YHWH, which run to and fro through the whole earth**.

The Seven eyes point to the seven Spirits which are subordinate to YHWH. We will find out who and what they are soon.

I believe that if we use our human understanding and model then I can clearly see that the pattern of two wives and a ruling son actually came from heaven. The Horoites people believe in the sun as Elohim and ascribed a son to him with two crowns. We do not know for sure how they came to this belief however we do know that Yahushua is the son from the principle wife the Ruach Ha Kodesh in the Northern axis which is the place of the throne room. I call her principle wife purely from a human perspective. Elohim is light therefore I am merely trying to understand the light so please do not confuse this with a literal woman and literal man type pattern having sexual relations to bring forth a son.

Scripture tells us there are seven Spirits of Elohim which are described as His eyes which scripture I gave you above in Zechar'yah but also the hint is in Zechar'yah 3:9.

Zechar'yah 3:9 For behold the stone that I have laid

before Yahoshua; upon **one stone shall be seven eyes**: behold, I will engrave an inscription there, says **YHWH** of hosts, and I will remove the iniquity of that land in one day.

In the hidden mystery I see a hint (remez) of seven hidden Spirits of Elohim. I know I may be one of the few people to write about this but there are things that many do not understand and do not have the revelation from Elohim but since Elohim has given me certain understanding of His sacred words I begin to appreciate this revelation more and more.

Do we not sometimes question where did the man come from and where did that woman come from. What about marriage, sons and daughters? These patterns are established in heaven and that is where they come from within Elohim.

We would have to be deceptive to ignore what Elohim has revealed to us because our earthly pattern of marriage came from heaven so if it did then why would marriage not exist in heaven on a spiritual plane?

In Malachi 2:15 this mystery is part revealed what I am trying to express in words. YHWH is one yet YHWH is composed of Ten.

Malaki 2:15 And did not he make them one? And the rest of the Rachamim (Spirits) are **his** also. Why then Akhad? That he might seek a righteous seed. Therefore take heed to your ruach (spirit), and let none deal treacherously against the wife of his youth.

From the Aramaic, this shows us the seven subordinate Spirits of YHWH, which are also mentioned in Proverbs 9:3, Zechar'yah and the book of Revelation. All seven spirits were trying to bring the righteous Son Yahushua in the world. The Father in heaven is the **original** patriarch and that is why we see this pattern in the world also ending at the end of days in Isaiah 4:1 which shows seven wives to one man.

We know that the only Spirit of YHWH that calls Yahushua her Son is the Ruach ha Kadosh known as The Holy Spirit.

This is what I term the kinship pattern of heaven principle to be the northern wife and I see her Son Yahushua to be the one established as King or ruling prince.

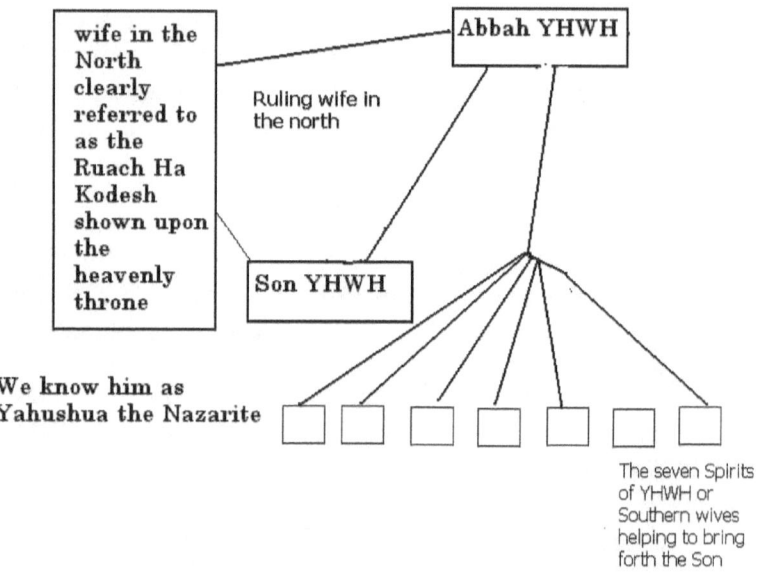

The other seven Spirits are never given the same mention and are not mentioned being in the northerly realm so they must be in the opposite realm which is south therefore the head of the seven Spirits is going to be the Southern bride of YHWH and we can see that this pattern clearly revealed in the two division of Y'sra'el.

Note why no mention of YHWH's southern bride and her children because the ruling King was already chosen from the North or that being Yahushua our Master Messiah.

There was a book written by the disciples of Yahushua called the book of the Hebrews in which there is an explicit mention of Yahushua as the Son of the Holy Spirit. We only have a few surviving quotations from it and in that the Holy Spirit the feminine side of Elohim calls Yahushua her Son which brings me back to the conclusion why Yahushua is indeed the spiritual divine Son and why as a ruler King He is established on the Holy mountain of Tsiyon (Psalm 2). We can ignore this pattern, even refuse to believe it but it will forever remain true.

It came to pass when YHWH was come up out of the mayim (water); the whole fount of the Set-Apart Ruach (feminine) descended and rested upon him, and said to him. 'My Son, in all the prophets was I waiting for you that you should come, and I might rest on you, for you are my rest, you are My first begotten Son, that reigns forever.' (An ancient copy of the letter of Hebrews that is now lost).

Jerome quoted from this in 342-420 CE. Origen also quoted from it in 185-254 CE. This gospel is lost but only some quotations exist. (Messiah Volume 3 Page 199 by Avi ben Mordechai)

One wonders Wow if this is true then what about haStan does he copy the pattern or has two wives in the North/South axis as YHWH has revealed?

Whether you believe it or not the answer shockingly is YES. Let me show you his two wives. Remember these things are at times hidden in scripture so you need revelation to see these and not theology from some seminary.

Zechar'yah 5:9 Then I lifted up my eyes, and looked, and, behold, there came out **two women**, and the wind was in their wings; for they had wings like the wings of a stork:

and they lifted up the barrel of liquid between the earth and the shamayim.

These are the two wives of Satan on the North/South axis. Let us follow the story to the conclusion. The stork is an unclean creature according to the rules of the Torah hence we are given some aspects of what is going on.

Zechar'yah 5:11 And he said to me, To build a house in the land of Shinar : and it shall be established, and set there upon her own base.

In order to build a house you need a son so who is Satan's son?

Take a guess.

The land of Shinar is not just southern Iraq but extends all the way to Turkey which is North of Y'sra'el and follows Nimrod's kingdom which was vast. Since he was the son of Cush his kingdom extended to Africa where he originally came from. We can be certain that Satan also has a Northern wife because this is where he has his throne and this is also the place where his son will come from known as the Anti-Messiah powered by Satan. Scripture places him in the Assyrian regions and calls him Gog from the land of Magog (Ezek 38:2) which is south-Eastern Turkey.

Revelation 2:12-13 And to the messenger of the Y'sraelite congregation in Pergamos write; These things said he which has the sharp sword with two edges; I know your works, and where you dwell, even where Shaitan (Satan)'s seat is…

Pergamos is in Turkey including the seven congregations mentioned in the book of Revelation.

Yahushua indicated that Satan's seat or throne rests in Turkey so we can see Satan has established his Northern axis there so what about his southern wife?

Satan's southern wife inhabits the land of Saudi Arabia. Proof is here.

Revelation 17:1-3, 9 And there came one of the seven heavenly messengers which had the seven vials, and talked with me, saying to me, Come here; I will show to you the judgment of the great whore that sits upon many waters: **2** With whom the kings of the earth have committed fornication, and the inhabitants of the province of the Middle-East[19] have been made drunk with the wine of her fornication. **3** So he carried me away in the ruach (spirit) into the desert: and I saw a woman sitting upon a scarlet coloured beast, full of names of blasphemy, having seven heads and ten horns. **9** And here is the mind which has wisdom. The <u>seven heads are seven mountains</u>, near which the woman sits.

This woman is described as a whore since this is Satan's wife and is said to reside near the seven mountains which are in Saudi Arabia. Remember that the Master YHWH has His holy mountain in Saudi Arabia also and not in Egypt where most Christians flock to. The place was discovered by an American Christian and a researcher by the name of Ron Wyaat in 1984 in the town of Al Bad, where you will discover Jebel el Lawz the REAL mountain of YHWH.

[18] World war III – Unmasking the end times beast page 81 by Rabbi Simon Altaf.
[19] See footnote Rev 11:10.

[20]

In the picture the giant sixty foot rock from where Moses gave water by hitting the rock (Exo 17:6) that still exists there and the Saudi authorities have now closed the place to visitors. You can see from the Bible it can be proved that Satan also tried to falsify YHWH's idea of the North/South Axis.

Now coming back to the story of Gideon this is why in the scriptures we see the Angel of YHWH assuming the name YHWH and calling out to the Father in heaven as YHWH. So YHWH calls out or points out to YHWH.

The demonic realm does not care about etiquettes or what university degree a person has or what political position he is in.

In other words demons do not care about how many academic degrees you hold. When this realm speaks it speaks frankly of its intentions. This is why when people get possessed by demons they are quite frank that they do not want to leave that person's body.

If they hate you they will say it. We find that in the spiritual realm demons recognise Yahushua.

Mattityahu 8:29 And, behold, they cried out, saying, what have we to do with you, Son of Elohim? **Have you come here to torment us** before the appointed time?

[20] http://www.arkdiscovery.com/mt_sinai_found.htm

They ask him that has he come to torment them before the appointed time? The demons are asking Him this question because they knew that Elohim had appointed a set time to punish them. **Note they see Him as Elohim**. The argument that they are calling him the Son of Elohim so he must just be an ordinary human like Adam is baseless. Could we show even one prophet in the Tanach who had a similar speech with demons? The demons call him Son of Elohim so some argue that this is probably why he was just a human. This is not true. What comes out of Elohim? Only Elohim can come out of Elohim. Here is proof text.

John 1:18 No man has seen Elohim at any time; the **only One Himself Elohim**, which is in the bosom of the Abbah.

Yahushua came out of the Father's bosom and no one had seen the Abbah but only Yahushua and even in the future no one will see Abbah YHWH. Can you see Elohim and live if you are just a human being? The text in Exodus 33:20 confirms that you cannot.

In scripture the demons have never called anyone else the Son of Elohim either.

Exodus 33:20 But He said, You cannot see My face; for no man shall see Me, and live.

So if Yahushua was an ordinary human then how was it possible for Him to be in the presence of the Abbah before the foundation of the world? How can the Abbah be love (First John 4:8) if He had no one to love in eternity? Let me explain this.

In order to say that you are "love" you must demonstrate that love because it is a relational attribute. So the text of the Covenant Covenant tells us that Yahushua was there in the beginning in the following verse (John 17:24) and the Father loved him. This is clear proof that the only reason Yahushua did not die when He was in the presence of the Father is because He is of the same substance. Like begets like therefore Abbah YHWH did beget His Son (Ps 2:7) Yahushua.

John 17:24 Abbah I want those, whom you have given me, to be with me where I am; that they may behold my glory, which you have given me: for you loved me before the foundation of the world.

Yahushua is worthy of receiving worship because He is Elohim revealed in the flesh.

John 1:14 And the Word was made flesh, and tabernacled amongst us, and we beheld his glory, the glory as of the only begotten of the Abbah, full of grace and truth.

If we set our differences aside we know that none of the above texts I have pointed out just resolve to a human being. There is certainly a lot more because I have only scratched the surface of the divine Sonship and the divinity of the Messiah.

Since Yochanan did not have a problem in the first century writing about the begotten Son of Elohim this shows the Hebrews though do not claim to understand everything but took things at face value because this was not theological stuff that people were trained with but rather this was revelation that some people clearly received while others struggled with it.

So if you are struggling with this truth then that is OK because in a time appointed by Elohim He can give you the revelation of this. If you do not see this it would be ludicrous to say that your salvation is at stake since the Bible makes no such stipulations. As long as you believe in Elohim and obey His Torah then the rest will fall into line because by definition you will accept the Messiahship of Yahushua and that calls the end of any other speculation. Note even if you accept Yahushua and rebel against the Torah you actually forfeit your salvation so do not believe in the lie that you can reject the law and accept the Son to receive salvation. The two are one and the same. That is grace. You cannot have one without the other. It's like having a car but no tyres but both go together. Christians at times are confused about this but the scriptures are not. No where in scripture is the Torah relegated to the ground or discarded. Only foolish people believe this.

Matthew 16:16-17 And Shimon Kefa (Peter) answered and said, You are the Messiah, the Son of the living Elohim. **17** And **Yahushua** answered and said to him, Blessed are you,
Shimon Bar-Yonah: (Simon son of Jonah) for flesh and blood has not revealed it to you, but my Abbah which is in the shamayim (heaven).

The above verse was in response to a question about who Yahushua was. Shimon recognised through the revelation that he received that Yahushua was the Messiah and the Son of Elohim. We are not talking about an earthly created son but the divine Son which means Elohim or the Father in heaven and begotten like for like so Elohim had brought out His son from within His bosom. Well the Son came out of the bosom then where did the Holy Spirit the Mother come out of? She was brought forth first and then the Son was brought forth next. This is in like fashion when the man was created in the garden and out of him the second woman was brought out. The heavenly pattern was simply being revealed that everything came out of the Father, first the Holy Spirit, then the seven subordinate spirits followed by the Son of Abbah YHWH. We are shown this in the book of Proverbs king Solomon a wise man who understood these mysteries.

Proverbs 8:22 YHWH constituted[21] me[22] in the beginning of his way, before his works of old.

24 When there were no depths, I was brought forth;[23] when there were no fountains abounding with mayim (waters).

The application of verse 24 is to the Holy Spirit first and then to the Son. Note the Holy Spirit is the feminine character of Elohim.

32 Now therefore hearken to me, O you children: for blessed are they that keep my ways. **33** Hear instruction, and be wise, and refuse it not.

So it is the Mother that is saying listen to her and refuse not her instructions (Torah) but where did She get her Torah? This is from the Abbah YHWH the source of all things living and the Torah is a living entity because it is out of the Father's mouth but revealed both in a written form and in the physical form of the Son.

---

[21] More accurately constituted see Genesis 1:2.
[22] Talking about the heavenly Mother the Ruach Ha Kodesh.
[23] First the Holy Spirit was brought forth and then the Son Yahushua.

34 Blessed is the man that hears me, <u>watching daily at my gates</u>, waiting at the posts of my doors.

So how do you hear her and what does the term "watching daily at my gates" means? Shema Y'sra'el YHWH Elohenu YHWH Akhad. We pray this twice daily and looking up to the authority in heaven which is the plurality of YHWH. So the term watching at my gates is an encrypted idiom which points back to Yahushua her Son and Abbah YHWH's Son. **He is the Gate of**

Heaven.

35 For whoso finds me finds life, and shall obtain favour of **YHWH**.

How do we find her?

She has already told you whosoever watches at my Gate (calling to Elohim to reveal His salvation in His Son). There are seventy primary arch-angels who are established to watch over the nations and all of these have authorities (gates) to direct people to the heavenly throne where Yahushua is established as the King over all earthly kings.

Proverbs 9:1 Wisdom has built her house, she has made for herself seven columns:

How does wisdom build her house? Remember the analogy of Satan and his son. So wisdom which is an idiom of the Holy Spirit and Torah begot a Son and it is the Son who is the builder hence why Yahushua said the following:

Mattityahu 16:18 And I say also to you, That you are Kefa_(Peter), and upon this rock I will Rebuild my congregation; and the gates of She'ol shall not prevail against it.

Yahushua was/is the Rock, who himself is YHWH and not Peter. Peter is not the first pope either because he was a Yahudi and the Jews become Rabbi's not Popes. The reference for the Rock is for Yahushua which once again validates His divinity from Deut 32:3-4.

What is wisdom and what are the seven columns?

Wisdom (Cochmah) is established in the two primary letters of Yud and Hey which make Yah in turn is linked to Torah revealed upon the earth but in heaven wisdom is personified in the Ruach Ha Kodesh (Holy Spirit) which was first begotten by Abbah YHWH so in essence wisdom came out of Father in heaven which was then revealed in the Son begotten of YHWH through the conception that took place in heaven through the Holy Spirit because like begets like and on earth the vessel that was chosen was Miriam the daughter of Eli who brought out the physical manifestation of the Son of Elohim. So wisdom Cochmah brought forth the Son who brought from the wisdom upon the earth which reflects back to Abbah YHWH in heaven as He is the Alef or source of all things that live.

36 But he that sins against me wrongs his own soul: **all they that hate me love death**.

This is indeed the Holy Spirit in speech saying that the one who hates me hates himself and the one who sins against her (meaning refusing Torah of Elohim) refuses eternal life and the result of rebellion to Torah is death.

Yeshayahu (Isaiah) 66:24 And they shall go forth, and look **upon the carcasses of the men that have transgressed against me**: for their worm shall not die, neither shall their fire be quenched; and they shall be an abhorring to all flesh.

What the Holy Spirit teaches is confirmed both in Isaiah and Mark 9:48.

Mark 9:48 Where their worm dies not, and the fire is not quenched.

What about the book of the prophet Isaiah that shows there is only one person up there and not two or three or ten in the divine council of YHWH, how do we deal with this mystery?

Yeshayahu (Isaiah) 45:22 Look to me, and be you saved, all the ends of the earth: for I am El, and there is none else.

The Unitarians use this text to say look there is only person there in the heaven so how do we deal with this seemingly anomaly? We are interested in the two Strong's words reference 413 and 589.

Strong's 413 the Hebrew word Al for unto, upon, against, among etc.

Strong's 589 the Hebrew word ani for I, We, Us.

The word Ani can be used for US or WE this makes for an interesting reading and suddenly shows us that the Father up there is not alone as we have conceived but the Son is there with Him.

A variant reading of the Isaiah passage could easily be as follows;

Yeshayahu (Isaiah) 45:22 Look **upon us**, and be you saved, all the ends of the earth: for **WE ARE EL,** and there is none else.

In the above Hebrew where the word I AM EL the word "am" is introduced and is not in the Hebrew and could very well even have the word ARE which is more consistent with the sentence structure but so as not to cause misunderstanding YHWH is described in the plural as Elohim. It could easily say WE are El and will be consistent with the term Akhad or the oneness of Elohim. This is because within the substance of YHWH which no man has ever seen or will ever see they are ONE.

Many ancient cultures ran away with the idea of a mother Elohim and erected statutes of deities looking like women while it is a reality that there is a feminine side of Elohim so it is out of the Male (Father) and the female (Mother) that we are revealed the Son Yahushua (Luke 1:35). We can see this clearly in the dialog with the Angel of YHWH that reveals Himself both as YHWH and at the same time redirects worship to YHWH.

So we have a sort of two pointers to YHWH. Do we see this in the Torah? Yes Indeed in the text of Genesis 19:24 where one YHWH standing on the earth rains fire from the YHWH in heaven.

Genesis 19:24 Then YHWH rained brimstone and fire on Sedom and Amorah (Gomorrah), from **YHWH** out of the shamayim (heavens);

As I explained earlier these are the two Powers in heaven mainly seen throughout Scripture. We see a picture of the Abbah, and the
Son. Greater, Elder, YHWH (The Father), and the Son who is also YHWH, under the authority of His Abbah in heaven.

It shows us the authoritative structure of heaven. We also have the Ruach Ha Elohim or the Holy Spirit the feminine side of YHWH and the seven columns or seven feminine Spirits of Elohim mentioned clearly in Scripture. Combined together these make up Ten which we see in the sefirah. They can be seen as the Menorah with seven upper columns and three legs that support the structure. In the Sefirot we can see ten clear attributes of Elohim which again relate to various propositions of what Elohim is according to Torah.

It needs to be understood that Yahushua left His crown up in heaven and chose to become a servant in the likeness of a man and therefore this was completely His own undertaking to redeem Y'sra'el and it's strayed sheep (Phi 2:5-8). Now that He is glorified He is our Elohim and it is only fit that we worship Him and give glory on to the Father in Heaven who sent His Unique Son to this sinful earth.

Religion in Crisis
Between the 6th Century CE to the 10th Century CE there were Jews scribes who looked at the Tanach and had

decided that they could correct Elohim. That he must have made a mistake. They started to alter texts where YHWH was mentioned by the four sacred letters and started replacing it with Adoni (Lord or Master) in order that how can the ancients call Elohim directly by name. These were not the only alterations done. Other places alteration were done to hide or obscure some passages where Elohim appears to have a mouth or eyes. They felt he was appearing to be human like so this must be changed. However each of these markings was documented and hence can be referenced in the Hebrew copies of the scriptures from that time period which allows us to see why this was done.

One of the key texts I want to look at is Psalm 110. In this are two clear references to two YHWHs in heaven. How could they be two? The only way this would work is if as we understand it now one was the Son and the other the Father. The first century believers knew and believed in the two Powers of heaven but they never referred to them as the trinity. This term was coined much later.

Let us examine the text in the Second Edition of the HTHS Study
Bible. First I will show you the King James Version so you can see the differences as they also appear to have swallowed the bait.

Psa 110:1 (KJV) The LORD said unto my Lord, Sit thou at my right hand, until I make thine enemies thy footstool.

Looking at the verse above Judaism then contexts that this is the Master YHWH speaking to King Dawud who is the King. Well their work was made easy as a scribe had already by his own pen adjusted the passage that connected to verse 1. That key verse was verse 5.

Psa 110:5 (KJV) The Lord at thy right hand shall strike through kings in the day of his wrath.

As you can see the term in verse five is "Lord" which in

the underlying Hebrew is Adoni. However this was not always the case. By making the term Adoni you could then argue that verse 1 of Psalm 110 is where the Almighty is talking to King Dawud however what if this verse five was not Adoni? Let us examine this.

Abrahamic-Faith Netzarim Hebraic Study Scriptures
Psalm 110:5 YHWH at your right hand shall strike through kings in the day of his wrath.

Do you see it? The actual Hebrew text there was the sacred name YHWH which was switched around in 600CE to Adoni. This way it could be made to appear that Yahuweh is simply referring to a human king. However what do you do when you have one YHWH speaking to another? That is why the scribes felt they needed to make that change. How can here be two YHWHs? Well one is Yahushua who declared that only He has seen the Father and no one else.

John 17:25 O righteous Abbah, the world has not known you: but I have known you, and these have known that you have sent me.

The English word 'known' is the underlying Hebrew Yada which means to have a relationship like in a marriage or where you personally know the person closely. This is what Yahushua had declared. This would be considered a blasphemy if you put yourself next to the Father in heaven and this is exactly why Yahushua was sentenced to death see Matthew 26:65. They accused him of
blasphemy because He had declared himself to be Elohim. Many stumble at this even today but right now if you are reading this text you will have seen why.

Now let me show you what the underlying ancient Hebrew of Psalm 110:1 actually said from the HTHS Bible.

Psalm 110:1 YHWH said to my Master,[24] sit at my right

hand as an appointed witness,[25] I will make your enemies your footstool.

Yahushua is the appointed witness commissioned by the Father in heaven thus we can clearly see the two Powers active. The ancients had no problem with such concepts but the moderns today try to make sense of this by giving it names such as the trinity. However it is not the trinity but a dualist power or imagine a King with a co-regent. How can they be two yet one? In essence Elohim at the base level is a Ruach (a Spirit) so they can easily be one but in order to reveal the son to humanity he was clothed in heavenly dust so that he became the primordial man or the prototype for Adam called Adam Kadmon. There is no doubt in my mind that Yahushua whose voice I have heard more than once is indeed YHWH the Elohim of Y'sra'el.

Conclusion

Yahushua therefore was revealed as the Son of Elohim and Elohim. Like begets like and we are shown this in the things of this world and nature so the patterns follow whether here on earth or in heaven. It is when we corrupt the patterns then we end up with problems. The world continues in oblivion in its course to destruction its time we submit ourselves to Yahushua repent and learn to live according to His Torah or face the consequences!

---

[24] Prophetically this is speaking about the Messiah Yahushua. The Targum of Jonathan says YHWH said to his word. So Abbah YHWH says to His word, which is Yahushua from John 1:1. Confirmed in Heb 1:13. This is not the Solomon, King David's son, he would not call him master but this is Abbah YHWH speaking to His Son Yahushua.
[25] See appendix HB29.

Chapter 7

Understanding the two Houses of Y'sra'el and who are the Gentiles?

One question that I was asked by my Student Rabbi Michael to go into a bit more detail about the two Houses and who are true gentiles so this is for my friend, brother and student Michael and for anyone else who cares to listen and understand who these people are likely to be and what nations they will come out of. Many two House adherents have their compasses stuck at Europe and America because for them the Ten tribes are likely today to be in Europe and the US. Some believe they are in Burma.

From here on we will refer to the Ten tribes just as Ephraim. In order for us to successfully find the Ten tribes we first have to identify who were the <u>ancient</u> Y'sraelites and that is the key factor at identifying the scattered Ephramites.

It is widely though incorrectly accepted that the House of Judah has returned to the land of Y'sra'el and many Messianics confuse the House of Judah's return with the House of Ephraim yet we find that the complete return of the House of Judah and even the House of Ephraim has not happened at all and is yet future.

Will the real Ephraim please stand up?

It is true that when we start to uncover the truth we will be dealing with highly controversial materials and even some things taboo and many people will be shaken at the core of their belief systems when they are found not to be aligned with the deep mysteries of the scripture of the Hebrews.

Any servant of the most High is to speak the truth in love and rebuke gently and shake the ground and not backtrack. The prophets of Y'sra'el who were the servants of Elohim did not shy away from showing truth but were generally criticized for being too truthful. I want to challenge the traditional held views and to show you what is widely believed may not always the absolute truth and needs correcting.

Let us examine the prophecy in Hosea to see if this sheds some light on this subject.

Hosea 11:10 (KJV) They shall walk after the LORD: he shall roar like a lion: when he shall roar, then the children shall **tremble from the west**.

When the two House adherents look at this prophecy this is the one they will look at and they immediately come to the conclusion that the ten tribes are going to return from the Western lands. There are many problems with this view first people do not return from rich and prosperous lands for no reason so in order to fit this theory then they have to artificially make America and Europe bankrupt financially to make it look like now they should return or to show that anti-Semitism will increase so that people can return out of fear. However the real factors of the return are neither anti-Semitism nor bankruptcy of these lands but solely the hand of YHWH.

For the verse of Hosea or Hoshea they have also failed to take in the full context of this verse and miss the very next verse which it relates to.

Hoshea 11:11 They shall **tremble as a bird out of Mitzrayim** (Egypt), and as a **dove out of the land of Assyria**: and I will place them in their houses, says the YHWH.

This verse continues from verse 10 so one can see that if the sons of Y'sra'el or the ten tribes come in from the Western lands such as America and England then why is Adonai calling them out of Egypt? Do you see the problem? America is not in Assyria and neither is Europe in Egypt or the Middle-East.

It is particularly noteworthy that some of the Ephramites but not all travelled West from the East and then spread in the Western hemisphere nations such as the UK, Europe and US, Australia and New Zealand etc but this has nothing to do with British Y'sra'el or that all of the US is Manasheh, which cannot be concluded from Scripture or history unless you want to call the US the Assyrian Empire and it is certain that a few errant teachers are teaching this today.

So if the US is definitely not the Assyrian Empire which was domiciled in the Middle-East then we start getting the bigger picture, which is that Ephraim is largely domiciled in the Muslims lands. How do we know this? Hosea is not the only prophet telling us this information but there are some other prophets too which are important witnesses. They are domiciled in nations in and around the middle-east including Africa. So where should we be looking for the sons of Y'sra'el? Not in Europe and the US. So do you see a nation of fair Caucasians around the Middle-East? So for this we have to identify the colour or ethnicity of ancient Y'sra'el?

Will the real sons of Tsiyon please stand up?

The sons of Tsiyon...

Lamentations 4:2 (HTHS) The precious sons of Tsiyon, comparable to fine gold ...
Lamentations 4:8 (HTHS) Their visage is **blacker than a coal**...

They are black like coals so what colour is coal, please tell?

Does this mean Caucasians are not Jews or the sons of Tsiyon? Not at all because of earlier exile and migrations much mixing had already occurred but the number of

Caucasians is however not in large numbers as many believe. We are looking at the majority not the minority. King Dawud was ruddy which means of mahogany complexion and the son (King Solomon) he produced with Bathsheba was jet black. The Hebrew word for red that is used in the Bible is Admonee (Strong's H132) while it correctly means mahogany coloured and not just red. People automatically assume this means white. It does not. The Hebrew word used for white in the Torah is Laban who was also the brother of Rebecca while nothing that one he was an African and albino and two the same word is used for the word in leprosy for white spots on the skin.

Leviticus 13:4 If the bright spot be white (Laban) in the skin of his flesh,

This tells us the colour of judgement in scripture was white. We also note that in African culture they often paint their faces with white paint to depict evil spirits.

Many Africans in their ancient portraits are of this mahogany colour and hue. If we look back at the American history Malcolm X was of this colour and his nickname was red.

While many forget there was large scale conversions to Judaism in Russia bringing in Caucasians which the Jews do not deny. Even people in Yemen converted in large scale to Judaism and indeed a man or woman can convert into Judaism and can become a proselyte and still be fully counted as a Yahudi but it does not mean that they have to be biological Hebrews to start with. This is not about black or white supremacy but scriptural facts and facts alone will dictate who Y'sra'el is. It's quite clear that in Europe many Caucasian Jews have carried the mantle of the Torah hence one cannot deny them their heritage and their zeal for Torah however it is to be understood that many of these are really the sons of Japheth and not Shem.

Note in the conversions it was the Caucasian Jews who would have helped convert others like Russians and Yemenites. Since the large scale ten tribes were in exile already at that time and were non-Hebrew so our concern is more with the scattered ten tribes. How could the Jews convert anyone if they were mostly in slavery themselves which means they have to be free and have the resources to do the conversions which indeed Judah did have. We know the longest slavery that continued was of the black people and no other race. This also indicates the southern two tribes also had mixing and may have been of darker origin to start with but later mixed to incorporate other colours of the nations.

A 10th century author states "All of the Khazars are Jews. But they have been Judaized recently." - Ibn al-Faqih,

"One of the Jews undertook the conversion of the Khazars, who are composed of many peoples, and they were converted by him and joined his religion. This happened recently in the days of the Abbasids.... For this was a man who came single-handedly to a king of great rank and to a very spirited people, and they were converted by him without any

recourse to violence and the sword. And they took upon themselves the difficult obligations enjoined by the law of the Torah, such as circumcision, the ritual ablutions, washing after a discharge of the semen, the prohibition of work on the Sabbath and during the feasts, the prohibition of eating the flesh of forbidden animals according to this religion, and so on." - Abd al-Jabbar ibn Muhammad al-Hamdani, in his early 11th century work *The Establishment of Proofs for the Prophethood of Our Master Muhammad*

We can see a mixing of races started to happen when Y'sra'el was dispersed.

This may be a shocking picture for you but this is

actually the true picture as we see that the ancient Assyrian Empire ruled lands that today are all occupied by the majority Islamic peoples and another important region that contains a lot of the sons of Y'sra'el is Africa. Please note a majority of the ancient Hebrews were of non-white origin and not Caucasians as depicted today but due to mixing many other colours were added later.

This also proves that when a Muslim comes to faith why he will immediately go back to the Torah without any arguments while the Western Christians are not really happy to be Torah obedient because they are a product of Greco/Roman culture and are not really Hebrews biologically as many think. Some may have biological lineage but the majority definitely have no link. The other big problem they have is with leadership and do not want to be under an authority structure but rather everyman is his own boss attitude which is contrary to scripture. Scripture has the structure of the Patriarch and everyone else below him fits in but the world has a hierarchical structure contrary to scripture.

We though know that there are Caucasian Jews but historically when were the Caucasians ever slaves in the past? Did you see a white slave in a white home in the 12th, 13th or 14th or 15th century? If not then this indicates that the only people that were solely in slavery and for hundreds of years were the black people and they were put down and even today in many areas black people are not thought of as good. This is a racial stereotyping that exists in various cultures where a black person is considered less intelligent and more into the ills of society. Also note many ill advised people think slavery is now finished but do not realize there

are still black and other slaves in Arab lands which are openly bought and sold in underground slave markets in Sudan, Lebanon and other middle-eastern countries.

Debarim (Deuteronomy) 28:32 Your sons and your daughters shall be given unto another people, and your eyes shall look, and fail with longing for them all the day long: and there shall be no might in your hand.

Historically speaking the **black people** lost their sons and daughters who were captured as slaves and taken away from their lands. The whole episode started with the large clans in Y'sra'el due to their disobedience known as the Northern ten tribes. So many Messianics who are totally if not partially ignorant to history and scriptures come up with contrived theories of the ten tribes returning. Let's see if Adonai says this is the case.

Ezekiel 37:12, 21 12 Therefore prophesy and say to them, Thus says the Master **YHWH**; Behold, O my people, **I will open your graves**, and cause you to come up out of your graves, and bring you into the land of Yah'sar'el (Y'sra'el). **21** And say to them, Thus says the Master **YHWH**; Behold, I will take the children of Y'sra'el from among the gentiles , where they be gone, and will gather them on from every side, and bring them into their own land:

Has this happened yet? Many would like to think so but this is still yet future and is nothing to do with born again syndrome of the Christians. When did YHWH raise the skeletons of the dead Y'sraelites from the graves and take them back home? Never!!! So how could we say this is present day Y'sra'el? It cannot be because all these people are dead and will be literally raised to make them return home. In fact they are not dead in Y'sra'el but their dead carcasses lie in graves in heathen lands.

Here is another shocker because many of these were people of colour.

First witness

Miriam the sister of Moses

Bmidbar (Numbers) 12:10 And the cloud departed from off the tabernacle; and, behold, Miriam became leprous, white as snow: and Aharon looked upon Miriam, and, behold, she was leprous.

Note Miriam Moses's sister became white as snow upon her punishment. This clearly shows that Miriam was not Caucasian in which case when she became white as snow this shows the colour of the plague. Assuming Miriam was a middle- eastern colour which possibly could be light or dark black then what about Moses her brother?

Second witness

Exodus 4:6 (KJV) And the LORD said furthermore unto him, Put now thine hand into thy bosom. And he put his hand into his bosom: and when he took it out, behold, his hand *was* leprous as snow.

What colour is snow? Does this show that Musa (Moses) was another colour perhaps other than what is depicted in the movie the Ten Commandments? Popular stereotypes are often wrong.

When Musa saved Zipporah from the shepherds (Exo 2:17) who did she say saved them from the shepherds?

Exodus 2:19 (KJV) And they said, **An Egyptian** delivered us out of the hand of the shepherds, and also drew water enough for us, and watered the flock.

Zipporah said **an Egyptian** saved us? Did Moses show his passport and nationality or was it from his appearance that Zipporah concluded that he could be an Egyptian? Did Zipporah conduct an interview of Moses? No. So we can conclude based on the evidence supplied that people knew **the skin colour of the Egyptians was dark**. So what colour are the Egyptians? As a South-Easterner I can tell you instantly when I see a South-Indian or North-Indian because I can recognize them from the shading of the skin colour and I can even tell you when I see a Sri Lankan so likewise Zipporah was not incorrect in her assumption to place him from Egypt though He was

Hebrew of course but black. Many of the Africans also travelled to the East to India and Pakistan we find many dark coloured people there some

dating their migration thousands of years ago. In Pakistan they have majo daro and Harappa where we have the artifacts of these ancient civilisations.

Was there a mixing later? Yes. So what would the mixing produce? People of all shades. The colour white is not the original colour of the Hebrews but white people did come out of this mix no doubt later after the exile as the tribes mingled and married into other tribes and cultures so we cannot rule it out entirely.

Third witness

Genesis 42:8 (KJV) And Joseph knew his brethren, but **they knew not him**.

Do you see that Yosef's brother did not recognize Yosef and thought he was an **Egyptian** so what colour was Yosef? Now answer the question again what colour are Egyptians? Clearly Yosef not only had their colour but also looked like them. Most likely black.

Now one final piece of evidence before I move forward. King Solomon the wisest man of the East was the product of the union between King Dawud and Bathsheba. The Hebrew term Bat-Sheba means the daughter of Sheba. Let us examine this a little more who is Sheba to identify Bat-Sheba.

Beresheeth (Genesis) 10:7 The sons of Cush were; Sheba, Chavilah, Sabtah, Raamah, and Sabtechah; and the sons of Raamah were Sheba and Dedan.

Note Sheba mentioned in Genesis is the son of Cush. What colour is a Cushite person from Sudan? The Cushi people have lived in the upper and lower Nubian regions even today and I have shown you that Bathsheba King Dawud's wife was an ancestor of these people. Therefore now ask yourself what colour was the wisest man of the East King Solomon? **Can we really put down black people as unintelligent? Well history and the scriptures show that the wisest man to live was of very dark skin in fact black as black can be or black as coal because he was also the son of Tsiyon.**

Evidence from the Covenant Covenant

Acts 21:38 (KJV) **Art not thou that Egyptian**, which before these days madest an uproar, and leddest out into the wilderness four thousand men that were murderers?

Rabbi Paul is mistaken for an Egyptian 2000 years ago so what colour are Egyptians today? Let me give you an answer that the historians suggest. **The ancient Greek historians such as Herodotus, Diodorus Siculus, and even Aristotle have written that the ancient Egyptian people were black-skinned. This may put us a step closer to identifying the real lost tribes.**

The million dollar question then remains if these people are not Caucasians as many were led to believe and let us assume they were black-skinned according to ancient historians near the time meaning all shades of black and even brown then **where should we be looking for the true Y'sraelites or the ten tribes, Europe, America or the Islamic and African lands?**

The logical place exactly as Yahweh tells us is the Middle - East and surrounding nations only such as Africa which is the largest place of their domicile . Now the verse below should make perfect sense. Most people are identifying the wrong people with Ephraim that is their problem. They have what I can only term an identity crisis. Most migrations happened in these directions and a few to Western Europe.

Is it any wonder YHWH calls his dispersed ones from Africa?

Tzephan'yah 3:10 From beyond the rivers of Cush (Sudan) my worshippers, even the **daughter of my dispersed**, shall bring my offering.

By the way scripture can refer to a wife as daughter also so the wife of YHWH that was cast out and divorced was the House of Y'sra'el the ten tribes which here He calls the daughter of my dispersed perfectly legible Hebrew term. Even Today Africans use the term daughter interchangeably for a wife.

Now answer the question about who retained the Hebrew culture Western Europe, America or Africa and the Middle-East?

The prophet Tzephan'yah is our proof that the ten tribe members were headed into Africa because the book of Tzephan'yah was written around 640 BC and at this time historically the tribe of Yahudah had not dispersed but Ephraim had so where did they go to? We are told that they were taken into Assyria but they also dispersed into the African states because the center of all these states was Egypt and that was the connection to all of Africa so you could say Egypt was the heart and soul of Africa which was under the Assyrian tutelage. The next most mentioned place in the Bible is Cush which is Sudan right next to Egypt where you will find the Nubian people. Therefore the rivers that this prophecy in Zephaniah speaks about are beyond the Nile deep into the African regions south of Y'sra'el. How do we know this? Let us get our second witness from Isaiah 18.

Yeshayahu (Isaiah) 18:1-2 Woe to the land shadowing with wings, which is beyond the rivers of Cush (Sudan): **2** That sends ambassadors by the sea, even in vessels of bulrushes upon the waters, saying, Go, you swift messengers, to a nation tall and smooth skinned, to a people terrible from their beginning onward; a **nation mighty and subjugating others, whose land the rivers divide**!

Bingo, do you see our connection to the Assyrian

Empire with Africa? People mistake this for America while it has nothing to do with them but YHWH is actually asking messengers from deep in Africa to go up to **the two rivers both the Tigris and Euphrates** so the nation its speaking about that subdued other nations just before Isaiah was writing was not Babylon but **the Assyrian Empire**. Now you may ask why it cannot be Nebuchadnezzar's Empire instead.

Simple because Isaiah was warning Judah to repent and they had not dispersed yet and hence Jerusalem was still intact while it is Isaiah who himself tells us the character of this nation in verse 5. Isaiah was writing in around 740 BC and it was around 745 BC that Tiglath-pileser III of Assyria began his reign. Note the ten tribes had not dispersed in 740 BC but later in 722-24 BC.

Yeshayahu (Isaiah) 18:5 For afore the harvest, when the bud is perfect, and the sour grape is ripening in the flower, **he shall both cut off the sprigs with pruning hooks**, and take away and **cut down the branches**.

This prophecy where he who cuts down with pruning hooks and takes away the branches is all about YHWH's judgment on his people who were cut down and taken away.

The vine is Y'sra'el and the branches are the people of Y'sra'el, this is not just talking about one or two grapes but whole clusters of grapes that were cut down which were going to be matured. The king of Assyria came cut them down and took them away. He indeed will come a second time in the future but this time the results will be different. So the prophecy is double for both past and future. Why we know that it was Assyria because they would conquer a nation and take away its inhabitants to disperse them in other areas so that a rebellion could not form against them and they would place their own people in the conquered lands. This indeed happened and is how we end up with the hybrid Samaritan people.

We can pin it down to the Assyrian Empire even through the prophet Zephaniah who speaks about the same people in verse 10 and when Zephaniah wrote this it was around the year 640 BC and this is the active time of the Assyrian Empire and it was not until 605 BC before Nebuchadnezzar would rise up for the Babylonian or Iraqi Empire.

This proves that many people in the African regions such as Zimbabwe, Rwanda, Nigeria, Republic of Congo, South Africa and others are Hebrew people by origin and biology, one day soon they will also get to know who they are and worship YHWH the true Elohim. Many ancient Hebrews were black and or darker skinned people as illustrated earlier. The word Mitzraim for Egypt actually means **burnt-face**.

Hoshea 11:11 They shall **tremble as a bird out of Mitzrayim** (Egypt), and as a **dove out of the land of Assyria**...

Anyone with an ounce of common sense and Hebrew wisdom can add two and two and prove that Christianity as we know it today is the product of the Greco/Roman religious model still carrying the idolatries of their past and has nothing to do with the true faith of Y'sra'el and I mean absolutely nothing with the Hebrew faith which

is very much patriarchal since Christianity rejects any form of patriarchy it cannot hold the authority it claims.

What do you call a son that rejects his father as his father? The Hebrew word appropriate is mumzair. Christianity rejects Judaism from where it usurped its authority so therefore it can no longer be considered part of the faith of Y'sra'el. The Y'sraelites never worshipped icons and bowed before statutes because when it did happen by idolatrous Y'sraelites it was always considered profane and punished by Elohim as such. The same punishment would be meted out to Christianity because its time of grace has run out. YHWH has already brought a foreign nation the radical Muslims to enact his judgment because the Christians refuse to listen to His voice. The radical Islamists are already being used as instrument of his judgment both in the idolatrous west and east.

Debarim (Deuteronomy) 28:64 And YHWH shall scatter you among all people, from the one end of the earth even unto the other; and there You shall serve other elohim, which neither You nor your ahvot (fathers) have known, even **wood and stone**.

Do many people in Africa serve wood and stone? Yes many animists do. Do Christians in the West serve wood and stone? Yes many Roman Catholics bow before statues of Mary which is idolatry. What about let's say people in the US and Europe? Indeed they also serve wood and stone because they have erected false idols like golf stars, football stars, baseball players, singers and Hollywood stars as idols of their heart. They are more interested in their day to day activities rather than the creator of the earth. These are man-made idols of wood and stone as well. In essence wood and stone does not necessarily always apply to statutes it can apply to anything we have erected that has no eternal value. Football players' cricket stars singers and actors who we may chase after have no eternal value so they are also classed as wood and stone. Because we refuse to obey Torah therefore Adonai has confounded us and left us to our own devices as punishment and even our prayer is an abomination to him until the day we repent and return to his Torah with a sincere heart.

The Roman religion of Christianity that poses as the truth but in reality to practice the truth you have to leave Christianity and practice the Torah the outer Messiah which means you have to leave church and join a Messiah believing synagogue or other fellowship.

Don't be surprised when Christians tell you that the law of Adonai that is Torah is abrogated this they have been taught to parrot and in my opinion this is tearing down the Messiah himself by rejecting His Father's law/Torah. And that includes all Jews who have entered and supported this lie and call themselves Christians are destined to fall with humiliation one day when they realize they supported a lie of Satan that says Adonai's law is no longer of any use.

Their lies of grace are just another form of self deception and bigotry that they live under while acting in all sorts of sins of the flesh. I saw it first hand in Nigeria when a Christian woman refused to give another Christian woman a seat in the bus on which she had her purse refusing to lift her purse. I asked her to show the woman love she did not understand perhaps thinking I was a Muslim taunting her. What I meant was to show the woman mercy whom she would not let sit on her empty seat where her purse an object of no worth had more importance just because it had her makeup and some Nairas (Nigerian currency) in it than a human being who should not be treated in such a way and deserved more respect.

I have seen English people with no religion in the UK show more mercy to people in trains and buses to give up their seats than these types of Christians. The Christians want all the mercy but I have seen some of these people being the most unmerciful to their own co-religionists. They will do wrong against them and will think they can just go to church on Sunday hide in a corner and ask forgiveness from Adonai but the man or woman they have hurt they will not bother to go to.

Yahushua said treat others as you want to be treated (Matt 7:12) and this was one instance where it was easier to read and listen to a sermon about it which most Christians happily do but when it actually came to real life this was obviously not applied. She refused to do that and sent the young woman in the back seat. This kind of hypocrisy I see in Christians all the time. Am I surprised? No I do not expect anything better from people who reject

Adonai's law whether in Nigeria, Pakistan, the UK or the USA. For men who reject His Torah is rejection of his mercy upon us because without it we have no life and no direction and no Messiah.

Then later before the bus was about to move off for our journey she asked everybody to pray for safety while the foolish woman did not know the time of her visitation and that where the priests of the Most High set their feet angels are there to protect them and they do not need to show the public signs of fear and artificial meaningless prayers. Sadly Christendom has many such hypocritical people and it's from here we can assess the truth versus what is masqueraded as truth.

Kefa (Peter) said it appropriately of this type of self deception evident in Christendom.

Second Peter 2:14-15 Having eyes full of adultery and that cannot cease from sin; beguiling unstable souls: a heart they have exercised with covetous practices; children of a curse: **15 Which have forsaken the right way**, and are gone astray, following the **way of Balaam** the son of Beor, who loved the wages of unrighteousness;

Just because you claim to believe in the Messiah of Y'sra'el and give him the name of **Jesus** it does not make that name or that religion true. Or the statement they claim that we believe in the Bible later retracted to we do not want to obey Torah because it's for the Jews (Jews). Well if it's for the Jews then the whole Bible is for the Jews not just the Torah then why obey a few letters of Rabbi Paul even incorrectly or was he not a Yahudee affirming the LAW of Adonai?

Some Christians claim because of miracles Christianity is true. Its foolishness to think that because of miracles Christianity is true ignoring there are many miracles in Netzarim Judaism we do not count ourselves worthy to publish these on TV and newspapers and sell them in bazaars. Miracles do not prove a faith but how we live and humble ourselves before Adonai does reveal and prove our faith. In fact the biggest miracle worker Yahushua said the exact opposite.

Matthityahu 12:39 But he answered and said to them, **an evil and adulterous generation seeks after a sign**; and there shall no sign be given to it, but the sign of the prophet Yonah:

This shows how little Christians know about their scriptures.

Yahushua did many miracles and even raised the dead but did all of Judea follow after him? No, when he spoke about eating his flesh (keeping the commandments) drinking his blood (keeping the Covenant Covenant) they all ran away (John 6:66) . So much for miracles hey and they were called His disciples or had become His disciples did not last other than the twelve, of which one fell.

Jacob said you show me your faith (and your miracles) I show you my works (Torah). Are you willing to take up the challenge of Jacob, I would challenge any Christian to take up this challenge and do what Jacob said.

The biggest miracle in our lives in Netzarim Judaism is people trying to obey Torah given upon Mount Sinai 3500 hundred years ago. Could you enact a bigger miracle than this? While Christendom can name it and claim it all day but there is little respect for Adonai's law and obedience in their lives which is many miles away which puts them squarely in the lawless bracket. What would you call a person who lied? A liar would be appropriate. What would you call someone who does not obey, guard and protect Adonai's holy Torah? Rebellious and rebellion is the sin of witchcraft (First Sam 15:23) so what is Christianity into? Witchcraft and witchcraft is forbidden in the Torah.

I did not define the term but Master Yahushua indeed did.

Mattityahu 7:22-23 Many will say to me in that day,

Master, Master, have we not prophesied in your name? And in your name have cast out demons? And in your name done many wonderful miracles? **23** And then will I profess to them, I never knew ye: depart from me, you that work Torahlessness (lawlessness).

They knew about Him like you know a superstar but He had no relationship with them because they were into witchcraft as demonstrated above. There will be many Christians on the day of resurrection not granted entry for remaining in continual Torah Sin. The second qualifying text is first John 3:9. Also read Matt 5:19.

Just look at the pagan temple today known as the Church they accept homosexuality which was the filth that the Greeks and Romans practiced while Adonai calls it an abomination Lev 18:22. Their marriages were a sham just like the marriages in the west of one wife and one boyfriend on the side even today there are many homosexuals amongst these people. The act of monogamy is shambolic in the West because while the man has a wife he may have a mistress on the side too for the odd days when he is bored. This by the way is perfectly acceptable to these folks and is considered playboish charming and entertained in the western culture while heaven forbid if you ever choose biblical polygamy they will put you down for it while we know our Patriarchs and subsequent generations of Y'sra'el practiced polygamy many times having two wives in the North/South divide according to the Horoite priestly clans.

Only Satan opposes Adonai's law so we can see in whose spirit these people walk certainly not the Set-Apart Spirit that leads to Torah and not away from it but they walk in the demonic spirit that leads to rebellion. You find most of the activist against biblical polygamy to be women. Am I surprised? No, not really since the first woman ran away and the second woman fell into the deception of Satan and gave Adam the fruit of the tree from which we still suffer today. Note the tree of knowledge and evil was never spoken of after this event, do you ever wonder why? Because we have internalized the tree of knowledge and evil in humanity and we think we know better and refuse to come to the Torah of Yah.

I do not shy away from interpreting the text of the Bible the way it should be done hence why I was given the task to translating it and we have the Abrahamic-Faith Netzarim Hebraic Study Scriptures.

The culture of Hebrews of Y'sra'el was both polygamy and monogamy so anything that Elohim said is good these rebellious ones will say is evil. Many Christians including the half way house Messianics who love to put on a Tallit but miss the substance of Torah living and do not even know that Adam had two wives try to justify their model of western monogamy in the garden. I call this the pinnacle of stupidity in the western world.

Well if YHWH the Father is a patriarch and the Holy Spirit is the feminine Spirit the picture of the Mother and we also have the Son then what are the seven other feminine Spirits of Yah? Polygamy or monogamy? This is the picture of a complete patriarchal family.

The heavens carry the pattern we can believe it or reject it but it makes no difference to the heavenly Temple.

Watch out for these signs amongst the heathens including ignorant Messianics who also have nothing to do with true spiritual Y'sra'el since they can place their Tallit upon themselves but their practice is still from the pagan temple of Christianity that today has further subverted the authority of YHWH by choosing to place women as Bishops and homosexuals as clergy.

Here is what one follower of this had to say on the BBC.

[26] 13th July 2010 BBC News

One liberal priest - Canon Robert Cotton - said he was worried that the Church could turn into a sect, refusing to listen to the wisdom that was available in the outside world.

Only paganism seeks for the wisdom outside in the world while the real wisdom is in Adonai's voice the Torah that He commanded us never to depart from.

Any Hebrew man or woman will not have a problem with Patriarchy of Adonai of Y'sra'el and any man or woman who claims to follow Torah but shuns patriarchy is to be avoided as Korah and not even engaged in a debate. One can choose to live with in the norms of the Torah this choice is conferred unto Y'sraelite men and women and is perfectly acceptable and good but one who shuns our patriarchs, our patriarchal marriage lifestyles directly attacks our Patriarchs Abraham, Isaac and Jacob and our matriarchs Sarah, Rebecca, Rachel and Leah.

Note these were loved by YHWH and Jacob fathered the twelve righteous sons of Y'sra'el from four wives and not one. These people who live in what I can only term la la land need to wake up from their stupor who do not know Y'sraelite Torah practices.

Who was the first woman? Certainly not Chava because she was produced from Adam's bones and flesh while the Hebrew text in Genesis 1:27 says the following:

---

[26] http://www.bbc.co.uk/news/10616553

ויברא אלהים את־האדם בצלמו בצלם אלהים ברא
אתו זכר ונקבה ברא אתם:

Gen 1:27 So Elohim created ha'Ahdham in His own image, in the image of Elohim He created him; male and female He created them.

So if he created them both then both were created from the earth while if you remember Chava was not created from the earth but created from Adam. My point is made that the first two humans were made from the earth which indicates there were two women in the garden and not one as most have believed so what happened to the original woman created from the earth? For further answers get yourself the HTHS Bible and look up the answers there. This subject is too big to start at the end of this book however I have given you the literal Hebrew and its translation.

I certainly will recommend for you strongly to avoid any such people who deny Elohim or His ways of life. Muslims are welcome who are willing to learn, discuss and debate for they already accept many Torah precepts but Christians need to prepare to learn and do not forfeit your rewards and eternity for the sake of your foolish pastors who has accepted the teachings of the pagan temple .

Ephesi'yah 5:11 And have **no fellowship with the unfruitful works of darkness**, but rather reprove them.

There is no blessing being in their camp. We are commanded not to be in fellowship with people who reject Torah unless they want to learn Torah and we were simply paying a visit to teach them then yes you can do so as such.

Only Satan wants to break patriarchal authority structures no servant of the Most High dares will. We are commanded to accept these structures and understand them. We may not be in perfect alignment in how our people practice these things but we are commanded to love our spouses and treat them with the utmost respect but certainly not kissing their feet (submitting to them). Any home where the woman rules will be a broken home with the children scattered all over the place with no blessing from above. Welcome to the Western culture where the woman rules the home and man the pattern of haStan.

Now we may begin to grasp why the true Y'sraelites have still not returned to the land. The majority of YHWH's people will come out of the Islamic and African lands in the future and they will be very middle-eastern looking and all shades of black and brown. If we examine Afghanistan alone then we know out of the twenty million people there majority of which are bloodline Judah and are actually Y'sraelites but today living as Muslims. We have the prophecy of Isaiah 54 to back this truth. Now how does it feel to know that Rabbi Paul was not the Caucasian you find in book covers but more likely an Egyptian looking man? Can you imagine the shock and horror on the faces of most Western Christians? I can already see it.

Yeshayahu (Isaiah) 54:1 Sing, O barren, you that did not bear; break forth into singing, and cry aloud, you that did not travail with child: for **more are the children of the desolate than the children of the married wife**, says YHWH.

It says "more are the children of the desolate than the married wife". The question then must be who is the desolate and who is the married wife?

Judah is the married wife and the one that is desolate or the second wife of YHWH is Ephraim (polygamy not monogamy) which apparently has more children literally. Today the Western world through monogamy a pattern they established from the Greco/Roman world they restrict themselves to a few children so this shows it cannot be the present day Christians since they are stuck with one or two children with this view.

On the other hand Judah imposed a self imposed ban on polygamy so went into having monogamous marriages only which is one of the Torah patterns of marriages. We find the groups such as the latter day saints (Mormons) followed the laws of polygamy to certain or lesser degree and were shunned by the local society. This is clearly an established pattern of scripture but the only trouble is they did not do the other precepts of scripture and only made this a point of practice to attain heaven. In fact their founder Joseph Smith was killed by the people around him for hatred and jealousy. This should explain why Judah went into self imposed monogamy to avoid hatred of the pagan Europeans including from Christians who did not follow the Hebrew scriptures to the letter but the invented creeds and religion of the Roman Emperor Constantine.

Judah went into what is termed self imposed ban. The edict was set by Rabbi Gershom ben Judah to have one wife to protect the Jews from European bigotry and hatred and so we can see that she (Judah) was not going to be able to have many children with this style of living clearly marked in the prophecy of <u>Isaiah 54</u> while this is not true for Ephraim who would not follow any man-made ban. Even today the tribe of Lemba in Zimbabwe practices both polygamy and monogamy. The Igbu (pronounced ebo) people of Nigeria which are the tribe of Gawd practice both polygamy and monogamy. The Zooloos which have many Y'sraelites among them Jacob Zuma the president of South Africa practices polygamy. Note the African continent is covered with many Y'sraelites but no one ever bothers to check this fact out. The Western races do also have Y'sraelites due to mixing but they are few in number. This is how black Y'sraelites through the slave trade ended up in America and Europe and then became believers. Now you know why they went back to the ancient faith even if it was not entirely practiced right? They are heading back home soon but this was indeed the first step of their reawakening by finding their Messiah. The most diligent and committed Netzarim today are the black people and the middle-Eastern people, Western Caucasians unfortunately do not even come to the number two position yet but may speed up in the future in their zealous adherence to the Torah.

However the only other people in the world to accept polygamy in large scale are the Islamic lands though they also practice monogamy as well but in either marriages Muslims will have at least 6 to 20 children each which proves the prophecy only fits with the Islamic lands and African lands and there is no chance for this fulfilment to be found in the Western lands that is because that is what Hosea is telling us and Isaiah backs this fact up. You may well ask what about the fact that it says Ephraim will come out of the West and are not the Islamic lands in the East? We must look from Y'sra'el's vantage point not where we are living in the West.

Hosea 11:10 They shall walk after **YHWH**: he shall roar like a lion: when he shall roar, then the sons shall come **trembling from the sea**.

It matters little if you use the translation of the King James Version of west or my translation of the word Yam for Sea where Y'sra'el was dispersed beyond the ocean. If Ephraim is literally west of Y'sra'el even then it does not contradict across the seas because if you look below in the picture of the map West of Y'sra'el is **the African and Islamic countries** which ties in with what I have said earlier. We look from Y'sra'el and what is important prophetically that the five nations that are listed below which are prophetically important are Egypt, Libya, Tunisia, Algeria and Morocco.

How many are Islamic? All of them. They are part of the end time enemies of Y'sra'el.

It is still not the United States or Europe even if the historians claim Dan is the Danish and the US is Manasheh I am afraid you will have to put those details on the back burner because right now what I am saying versus what they are saying can be tested against the prophet Isaiah and prophet Jeremiah including Ezekiel. Time will prove that I am right.

Are the people of Netherland a Muslim land? No. Is American Muslim? No. America is furthest west from Israel but the West to Israel is always identified scripturally with African nations west.

For those who do not know the geography of Y'sra'el need to understand that if we used the scriptural definition West here then it takes us into the African Continent in which we cross the sea and we end up in greater Africa with many Islamic lands and Isaiah has already clarified some of these lands so there is no contradiction. Also note we find Portugal and Spain west which also have a large contingency of Y'sraelites.
27

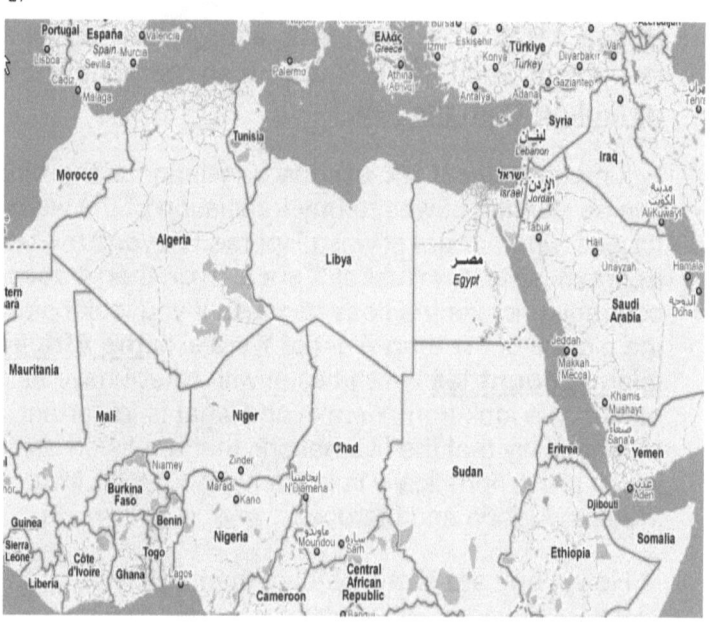

This is why the prophecy makes perfect sense in Hoshea verse 11 which talks about Egypt. **Why Egypt?**

The first Exodus happened out of Egypt so the second Exodus must also and has to involve Egypt in some way for the children of Y'sra'el to be removed from there twice as everything almost happens twice.

Yahushua's two comings, Moses two ascensions, the two giving of the Torah's, the two Temples, The two

Menorahs, the Two crossings of Y'sra'el upon water, the two entries into the land of Y'sra'el and the two Exodus's also. We note a thematic pattern of two's in scripture can we really deny this?

We cannot continue to ignore the African nations as insignificant and irrelevant. Unfortunately they were only backward because of their disobedience to YHWH but now that the times of punishment are over they have a chance to prove themselves and excel in the world.

[27] http://maps.google.co.uk/maps

Y'chezk'el (Ezekiel) 37:21 And say to them, Thus says the Master **YHWH**; Behold, I will take the children of Y'sra'el <u>from among the gentiles</u>, where they be gone, and will <u>gather them on from every side</u>, and bring them into their own land:

Note most of these people had died in heathen lands. YHWH will do the resurrecting first mentioned in Ezek 37:12 and then they will start marching back to home to the land of Y'sra'el. This means resurrection comes first for those that would have died at the arrival of the Messiah and then comes the return. Many Jews who have returned today and live in a secular non-Torah government are actually against the law of Adonai and oaths which our forefathers took not to return in large numbers and take the land of Y'sra'el by force or go to wars with gentile nations. Y'sra'el has so far gone to war six times with gentile nations (radical Islam) and this was against the oaths but since Y'sra'el broke the oath then they have to fight to keep themselves alive.

YHWH's covenant with us is a two way covenant. The Jews are not promised the land for their genetic makeup. The land was promised to Abraham as <u>an everlasting possession</u> but the promise attached a condition that required the Jews to be Torah obedient in order to <u>retain</u> the land. Whenever the Jews broke the Torah then Adonai threw them out of the land. The land will spew out the people who are rebellious to the law of the holy One of Y'sra'el.

Vaykira (Leviticus) 18:28 Do not make the land vomit you out also, when you defile it, as it did the nations that were before you.

This is why gentiles can convert into Judaism by taking the oath to renounce all idolatries and obey the Torah. This should explain why we are still in exile today. We have to repent and then wait for the Messiah to come back to take us home. We are forbidden to take the land of Y'sra'el by force or to go to wars with the gentile nations yet this is completely ignored by the present lawless political Zionist government of Y'sra'el and also Christians who dogmatically think they are serving the Holy One by taking the

Jews back actually breaking the oaths taken. What a stupidity at large scale ignoring the warnings of our sages.

These oaths can be referenced in the Talmud Kesubos 111a.

According to Rabbi Teitelbaum, out of the three oaths the second oath is relevant concerning the subsequent wars fought between Y'sra'el and the Arab nations. He viewed the political Zionist State of Y'sra'el as a form of "impatience" and in keeping with the Talmud's warnings that being impatient for Adonai's love has led to much "grave danger". The Hasidism Rabbis know that the constant wars in Y'sra'el are a fulfilment of ignoring this oath. I would second this that ignoring the oath and trying to do your own redemption is tantamount to usurping the authority of YHWH and has cause a curse instead of a blessing.

[28] Rabbi Judah ha Nasi sent two rabbis on a tour of inspection to the city and this is what was conveyed.

In one town they asked to see the "guardians of the city" and the city guard was paraded before them. They said that these were not the guardians of the city but its destroyers, which prompted the citizens to ask who, then, could be considered the guardians. The rabbis answered, "The scribes and the scholars," referring them to Tehillim (Psalms) Chapter 127.[29]

We are moving towards the redemption of the whole of Y'sra'el but there is much work to be done amongst ourselves to organize and to prepare for the future. Scripture tells us the following:

Yirme'yah (Jeremiah) 50:5 They shall **ask the way to Tsiyon** with their faces toward it, saying, Come, and let us join ourselves to **YHWH**

In other words they will ask the **halacha (Torah) of Tsiyon**. They will turn their heads and then agree to walk in that halacha where they live and then their redemption will take them to Y'sra'el. No pre-tribulation rapture and no fanfare.

---

[28] http://en.wikipedia.org/wiki/Neturei_Karta#cite_note-whatnk-2
[29] What is the Neturei Karta? (NKUSA) Accessed: December 24, 2006

Yirme'yah (Jeremiah) 50:4 In those days, and in that time, says **YHWH**, the children of Y'sra'el shall come, they and the children of Yahudah together, going and weeping: they shall go, and seek **YHWH** their Elohim.

Why would they be weeping? This is because those that will be alive will realize they were **into pagan idolatry such as Christianity** and other religions. At this time they will say goodbye to all these idolatries and then will go back home by the hands of YHWH.

Note now Ephraim is walking together with Yahudah but before this they had refused to walk with Yahudah this is because now they agree with the rulings and the laws of the Torah which were enacted by Yahudah with which they had vehemently disagreed earlier.

So now that we know who is Ephraim then who are the gentiles?

Well right now we know that even Ephraim fits into the category of gentiles but when we assuming remove Ephraim then it is fairly straight forward to know the gentiles.

The bible itself describes the people as gentiles such as Muslims they are gentiles and not Y'sraelites.

Zecar'yah 14:14 And Yahudah also shall fight at Yerushalim; and the wealth of **all the nations** round about shall be gathered together, gold, and silver, and apparel, in great abundance.

These are all Islamic countries that are qualified as gentiles but now we know we have the Y'sraelites in their midst but after they are removed the only ones that will be left are true gentiles.

Apart from that if we do not consider the mixing then anyone other than Y'sra'el or who is not from the twelve tribes would be considered a gentile.

The other rule of thumb I would apply is anyone refusing to submit to YHWH's Torah will be called a gentile.

May the Master YHWH bless you all who choose to follow him.

Points of imminent action

- Repent in front of Elohim and drop all your idolatries today and join a Torah and Messiah loving synagogue. You can contact me or the nearest person in your country we can certainly recommend good synagogues that believe in the Messiah and keep Torah, write to me or see the information page at the beginning of the book.

- Start learning to keep the 7th Day Sabbath on Friday sunset to Saturday sunset this is the seal of our faith and we must have it to be called Y'sraelites and is a Covenant.

- Start obeying the seven annual feasts. You can keep the other feasts such as Purim and Chaunkah as it's a mitzvah (Good deed) to keep them but the seven are mandatory.

- After getting practiced for at least for a year the males must get circumcised physically to enter the Covenant of Abraham. Without this you cannot keep the feast of Passover and partake in the meal.

- Drop all the unclean foods mentioned in scripture and stick to the healthy option listed in Leviticus 11 on which foods to consume. Pork is out so is shellfish, crabs, oysters out but Lamb, beef, chicken and fish with fins and scales is in. This type of diet will also give you long life and cut your risk of disease.

- Prayer three times daily as did the disciples of the Master. Weekly Sabbath and feast assembly prayers are very important for your spiritual growth.

- Men and women both to wear head-covering in Synagogues worship and during prayers mandatory no excuse.

This is only a short list but this is a good start. I pray that you choose to obey Elohim and not to run after modern day Christianity which has perverted the ways of Elohim.

Rabbi Simon Altaf Hakohen

Other Titles by Rabbi Simon Altaf that can be obtained from http://www.forever-israel.com

Beyth Yahushua – Son of Tzadok, Son of Dawud

Would you like to know the identity of Yahushua's family? Did He have brothers and sisters, did He get married, are not Rabbis meant to marry, was Mary Magdalene His wife? All these answered in the book. Are you fed-up of hearing objections such as if you do not know who Matthew, Mark, Luke and John are then how can you claim to have the truth?

Do you feel frustrated to go to your Pastor only to be told he does not know?

What caused Rabbi Paul to persecute perfectly normal Hebrew men and women who simply practiced Judaism? Who was Nicodemus, what relationship did Yahushua have with Lazarus? Did Yahushua have relatives? For too long He has been portrayed as the wandering man with no belongings and no family and living wildly, picking up food from the trees, fields and women offering him handouts.

This picture is both misleading and deceptive. Do you want to know the powerful family of Yahushua, fill the gaps, who were Mark, Luke, Matthew and even John? What connection has Joseph of Arimathaea got with Yahushua and why would a rich man like him be willing to give his own expensive tomb for Yahushua's burial?

Do rich men do such things, if so then why was the rich man in Matthew 19:21 unwilling to give away all his money? Did Yahushua carry the
curse of Jeconiah (Jer 22:24-30)? The answer that Christendom gives is the curse lifted because of the virgin birth or the lineage switch. Did it? Answer NO. Christendom's answers on this are wrong. What about the genealogy of Luke and Matthew why two fathers of Yahushua Heli or Jacob in Matthew 1:16 and Luke 3:23? Will the real father of Yahushua please stand up!

Who were the Hebrews, what is the West in Hosea 11:10?

Hos 11:10 (KJV)...then the children shall tremble from the west.

If we believe popular opinions then they are all in Europe and America but the reality is very different. This book is a wake up call to the last generations.

This book will give you new insights and the rich history of Yahushua.

Islam, Peace or Beast

Have you ever wondered why radical Muslims are blowing up buildings, bombings planes and creating havoc? We illustrate in this book the reality of radical Islam and the end of days that are upon us. Why are our governments reluctant to tell us the truth we uncover many details.

World War III – Unmasking the End-Times Beast

Who is the Antichrist, what countries are aligned with him and many of your other questions answered. All revealed in this book. Which might be the ten nations of the Antichrist? What did the prophets say on these events?

World War III – Salvation of the Jews

How will the salvation of the Jews come about, will they convert to Christianity or will Christianity be folded into Judaism?
Will the 3rd Temple be built before the return of the Messiah? Analyzed and explained with the correct sound hermeneutics.
Will we have a war with Iran and when? Considering the pundits have been wrong since the last 3 years and only Simon has been on track up to this time. What signs will absolutely indicate impending war with Iran calculated and revealed.
When will the Messiah return, what signs should we be looking for, is it on a Jubilee year?
Will the Messiah return on the feast of Trumpets fact or fiction?
Will America win the war in Afghanistan? Yes and No answer with details.
Who is the prince of Ezekiel and why is he making sin sacrifices. Can one call these educational? Read the correct answers...
Should we support the Jewish Aliyah to Israel or is it forbidden to enter the land for permanent stay under a secular godless

government?

Rabbi Simon is the only Rabbi to look at the thorny issues that no one has addressed to date while many people mostly run with popular churchy opinions colored by bad theology by picking and choosing verses in isolation. Is modern Zionism biblical? Is Israel right to take over territories occupied by Palestinians today? Should people be selling up homes to go and live in Israel? All these thorny questions and even more answered in this book the sequel to the popular prophecy book World War III - Unmasking the End-Times Beast.

Yeshua or Isa – True path for salvation

Ever tried to witness to your Muslim friends and were mocked? Do you have Passion for the Muslims to be saved? Want to know how Jesus Christ is Yeshua and not Isa? This book helps you to build a solid bridge with the Muslims. It clarifies your theological doubts and helps to present Yeshua to the Muslims effectively.

Dear Muslim – Meet YHWH the God of Abraham

Truth explained best seller step by step detailing and unveiling Islam! This book is designed for that friend, son or daughter who is about to convert into Islam but needs to read this first. This is the one stop to saving their souls. Don't procrastinate get it today.

The Feasts of YHWH, the Elohim of Israel

Have you ever asked why the feasts were given to Israel? Their meaning and their purpose is all explained in this detailed book that delves into the signs of the Messiah and the fulfilment of the feasts and how the return of the Messiah is revealed in the feasts from a Muslim angle the first of its kind.

What is Truth?

Have you wondered what is truth and how we measure it? How do we arrive at the conclusion that what you have is truth? How do you know that the religion you have been following for so many years is the original faith? We examine these things.

Hidden Truths Hebraic Scrolls Tanak 7th Edition

The Bible more myths busted. Packed absolutely full of information - no Hebrew roots Bible even comes close this is guaranteed and these scrolls are the difference between night and day, see for yourself!!! The politically incorrect guide to the Elohim of Israel and the real chosen people of YHWH. Are you willing to listen to what YHWH has said about our world and how He is going to restore all things back including His real chosen people hidden to this day?

Many texts uncovered and explained in great details accurately and many corrections made to the many faulty translations out there making this a real eye-opener text.

- ➜ Was Chava (Eve) the only woman in the garden? We reveal a deep held secret.
- ➜ Where did the demons come from?
- ➜ Ezekiel refers to some of Israel's evil deeds in Egypt explicitly uncovered which are glossed over in the King James Version.
- ➜ Who are the Real Hebrews of the Bible, which people does the land of Y'sra'el really belong to? Time to do away with the deception.
- ➜ Did Abraham keep the Sabbath? We show you when and where.
- ➜ But I thought Keturah was Hagar, another error of Judaism corrected.
- ➜ But I thought Keturah was married to Abraham after Sarah's death, no not really. A very bad textual translation.
- ➜ Who was Balaam, a profit for cash as are many pastors and Bishops today doing the same thing running and chasing after the Almighty dollar?
- ➜ Who were Abraham's ancestors, Africa or Europeans?
- ➜ Why did Isaac marry at forty years of age, what happened to his first wife? Rebecca was not his only wife, an error and ignorance of Christendom exposed?
- ➜ Where is Noah's ark likely to be? Not Ararat in Turkey or Iran another error.
- ➜ Who are the four wives of Abraham and who is the real firstborn? Not Ishmael and not even Isaac. Was Isaac his only begotten son another error?
- ➜ All the modification of modern Judaism of the scribes has been undone to give you what was the real text including the original

conversation of the Serpent with Chava (Gen 3) unedited plus Abraham's conversation unedited at last in Genesis 18.

The legendary Rabbi Simon Altaf Hakohen guarantees that this will teach you to take the best out there and open their eyes in prophecy, historical argument and theology. He will personally mentor you through the texts of the Torah, the prophets. Does any Bible seller offer this extent of training? We do. And Rabbi Simon is available at the end of an e-mail or just a telephone call away for questions that you have all this time.

Sefer Yashar (The Book of Jasher)

The book of Yashar has been translated from the original sources and with added commentary, corrected names of Elohim with the sacred names and with other missing text from the Hebrew. This will add to the gaps in your knowledge from the book of Genesis such as the following:

- What happened to the people at the time of Noach?
- Who were Abraham's ancestors?
- Did Abraham have two wives or four?
- What relationship did Abraham have with Eliezer?
- Why did Isaac wait for forty years before his marriage?
- Why did Sarah die suddenly after Isaac's departure to be sacrificed?
- Did Moses marry in Egypt before running away?
- And many other questions now answered.

Chanoch (The Book of Enoch)

The book of Enoch details the fall, the names of the angels, what happened and what was the result of those fallen. He also reveals the birth of Noah and some very important details around this. And many other important details to complete your knowledge.

Yahushua, The Black Messiah

Have you been lied to about the true identity of Yahushua? Have you been shown pictures of the idolatrous Borgia Cesare and may have believed that this Caucasian hybrid was Yahushua What ethnicity was Yahushua and what race of people did He belong to? Is it important that we know His ethnicity? What colour was Moses, King David and King Solomon? We examine and look at the massive fraud perpetrated upon the western nations by their leaders to hide the real identity of the true Hebrew Israelite people and race which are being restored in these Last Days. Would you like to know because it affects your eternity and His true message then get this book now.

Hebrew Wisdom – Kabbalah

The book's purpose is to illustrate basic principles of Kabbalah and to reveal some of the Kabbalah symbolisms. We look at the Sefirots what they mean and how they apply to some of the teachings. We also look at the first chapter in Genesis and examine some of the symbols there. We examine the name of Elohim in Exodus 3:14 and see what it means.

The Apocrypha (With Pirke Avot 'Ethics of The Fathers')

Read the fifteen books of the Apocrypha to get an understanding of the events both of the exile and of Israel's early history. Read Ethics of the Fathers to understand rabbinic wisdom and some important elements of the story of Genesis. The tests, the trials and the miracles of the Temples. Without these books the story in the bible is incomplete and has gaps which these books will fill up and give you a more complete understanding.

Forever-israel Siddur transliterated Hebrew with English (Daily life prayers 7th Edition)

Many times we wonder what prayers should we do when we go to bed, when we leave our home in the morning and how do we pray daily? What prayer should I do if I have a ritual bath? What prayer is for affixing a Mezuzah? Each year you wonder how to do the Passover Aggadah and what is the procedure. This book also covers women's niddah laws to give you understanding into women's ritual purity. Unlike other prayer books Rabbi Simon Altaf actually bothers to explain small details that are important and often ignored. This is one book you should not be without. The festival readings and the 72 names of God are included in the text.

World War III, The Second Exodus, Y'sra'el's return journey home

How will the genetic Hebrews be taken back to the land? Are the present day Jews in Y'sra'el of ancient stock? Is there any prophecy of foreigners invading Y'sra'el and inhabiting the land? How will Elohim have war with Amalek and wipe them out and who is Amalek today? Why is the Church so confused about bible prophecy?
How will the end come and why is the world hiding the identity of the true Y'sra'elites? Will there be a rapture or marching back on foot? What happens if we die in our exile? And many more questions answered. The time has come to expose the errors of others.

What Else Have They Kept From Us?

This book is as the result of an e-mail conversation with a lady who asked me some questions and one of her questions upon my answer was "What else have they kept from us?" This was the question that led to this book because instead of answering people with small sections of answers I decided the time had come that a book had to be written to answer and address everything as it happened from the start to the end so that many may see that the deception is real and it's a deep cunning deception which starts from your TV screens, in your newspapers followed by wherever you go in your daily life.

How would a person know that they are being deceived if they do not know what to look for? Its like a Ten Pound note well if you saw the original then you have something to compare the false note with but what if you were <u>never</u> presented with the original and always had the fake in your pocket then you will likely think the fake is real and this is how it is with Christianity today that is simply mixing paganism with truth. A false Ten pound note or a bad tender which will give you no value when you redeem it as I uncover it in the pages of this book. Who was Yahushua, the real Hebrews and Israel.

Patriarchal Marriage, Y'sra'el's Right-Ruling Way of Life, Methods and Practice

How did the Y'sra'elites live? What form of marriage did they practice and how did they practice it? This book is about to show you what was God's design from the beginning and how the Y'sra'elites lived within God's required parameters. Today these things appear mythological but here we show you the methods and ways of how this lifestyle was practiced and is being restored in these last days, while the much touted gentile monogamy is wrecking lives destroying families and society around us. How many marriages are breaking down as a result of the wrong model and how many children are living fatherless lives, while women live husbandless and unfulfilled lives. This book will show you why the Greek and Roman monogamy model with a husband and a wife and a bit on the side does not work. While Elohim's model of plural marriage is an everlasting model that not only works but saves many children from losing their father's and women from losing good husbands.

The Scroll of Yahubel (Jubilees)

The information that is missing in the Torah has been put in here to aid us in understanding the book of Genesis more. There are gaps in Genesis with what happened with Noakh? What was going on in Moses's time? This scroll allows us to piece together that information that is so important for our understanding. True names edition with many corrections made.

Who am I?

A Children's book to help the black Hebrew children with identity and direction in life. Many Hebrew children while looking for identity easily stray. While they search for love they end up in gangs to prove themselves and search for that missing something. When they do not find love in their homes due to broken homes often venturing out with devastating consequences, getting involved in criminal activities to prove themselves ruining their lives. This book's purpose is to help these children and even adults find themselves to teach them who they are and to find sound direction in life to secure you to the God of our ancestors where you belong. This will help change many lives.

Hidden Truths Hebraic Scrolls Compendium Guide Chumash Torah

For those who have the Hidden-Truths Hebraic Scrolls this is a must buy to give you a deeper understanding under the text and its meaning where the footnotes are expounded upon further in various books of the scrolls. To learn the secrets of the Torah. All the Parshas expounded for further understanding. It also contains all the parsha notes.

Hebrew Characters, The Power to have prayers answered

Have you ever tried praying and find that either your prayers take very long time to answer or they don't get answered at all? In frustration you ask other friends to pray for you in hope that you may get an answer from God soon. I have given considerable thought about the condition of our people and how many languish in poverty, in situations where they seek for help because they are given false dogmas, put in religious bondage and slavery of the mind and heart.

Many times they make their own lives harder because they have spent so much time in the nations that they just want to live like the gentiles and not Hebrew as they are unaware how to benefit themselves that await them. I know it can be a lonely road at times. Our Abbah in the heavens feels our pain while we live in exile He sends the Shekinah to be with us. He longs for us to return back to the contracts that we may receive all the increases and benefits that are only meant for us.

However we pass our life by with this that and the other person who gives us no joy but we think maybe if we carry on suffering things will change for the better but things NEVER change. This book was written to help for a time such as this to better the lives of our people. To empower them with the right petitions to give them benefits and increases in employment, love, marriage and sickness. This will help you break the spells of witchcraft, dealing with jealous people around you and personal anger issues. This will help you deal with demonic presences in your homes. This will show you how to receive a timely answer to all your prayers. I have used these methods for my students all over the world which have proven successful for them and have greatly benefited them.

It takes many generations for a right-ruling priest to be born in our generations. How many generations our people have suffered the scourge of the curses for not obeying the Torah? Many are still suffering. The Most High is going to raise his priests one by one until we get our restoration complete. Rabbi Simon is of the priestly family born to help his people.

The Kohen is meant to be a benefit to the people of Y'sra'el and is one of the person's that has been given the authority to stand between the heavenly court and the earthly realm. Christian clergy has been lying to you for so long that you don't know what is good for you anymore. The Melekzadek priest's job is not to stand between the heaven and earth as you have been wrongly taught, his job is to be a King and serve justice on the earth with the Torah. While the Christian clergy teaches everyone can be a Melekzadek this is not the truth. Only the Kings of Israel can right hold that title, it's not for anyone else.

There is only one everlasting priesthood and that is the Lewitical one. This book has been written by a Lewitical priest of Beyth of Tzadok, its time you reap the benefits so decide wisely. Even if you are a gentile looking to become part of Israel by conversion the opportunity is open to you to obey the Torah and join us.

I want you all to benefit and to receive what rightly belongs to you.

I could have sold this book for $100 a piece because everything in this manual would forever change your life once you put it in practice but I decided not to do that as my purpose was not that.

However this book is kept at a low price not for $100, no, not even $50 but for a price of $27 only this will forever change the way you think and pray. I am practically giving this away for you to better your lives. The rest is up to you.

Now that I know I am a Hebrew

You don't just wake up one day and say You are a Hebrew. Being Hebrew brings many processes that need to be completed before you are finally cleaned up as the Abbah desires to fulfil your responsibilities. This book is in the hope to help many of our people who are Hebrews and desiring the change to rid them of idolatry and clean up to present to the Abbah a sacrifice with sweet aroma so that they may serve Him faithfully according to His desire! Are you willing to make the sacrifices required to follow the God of Israel?

Religious Confusion and the Everlasting Path to the Torah

Everyone claims their religion is the truth or you will go to hell. The Torah makes only one claim that God is interested in our world affairs.

All those that are confused about which religion to follow there is only one voice of God and that voice is found in the Torah of Moses. For your eternal rest and peace in your life choose the Torah. This book helps you to make the wise choice to help your life. Everything around you is compromised and the entire man made religions claim to truth is nothing but smokes and mirrors to cheat people out of their eternal destiny. Turn back to the Torah to find your eternal future and hope.

To Purchase more books for study and reference

The Hidden Truths Hebraic Scrolls Tanak or Complete Bible can be ordered at the URL below. www.forever-israel.com. Note the excellent translation of bible which reflects our mission to Africa and to Israel worldwide and the true genetic Hebrews mentioned in the bible who live in the western word such as in Europe, Americas and in the Caribbean islands including many other countries like Brazil, India, Iran and Pakistan.

Why buy these books?

These books will answer questions you haven't even thought to ask yet and to polish you on how to serve the God of Israel.

Beyth Yahushua – the Son of Tzadok, the Son of Dawud

Islam, Peace or Beast

World War III – Unmasking the End-Times Beast

World War III – Salvation of the Jews

Dear Muslim – Meet YHWH the Elohim of Abraham

The Feasts of YHWH, the Elohim of Israel

Testament of Abraham

What is Truth?

Hidden Truths Hebraic Scrolls Tanak 7th Edition

Hidden Truths Hebraic Scrolls Torah

Hidden Truths Hebraic Scrolls Brit Ha Chadasha (NT)

Hidden Truths Hebraic Scrolls Study Bible Complete

The Torah Chumash is a commentary in addition to the popular translation of the Hidden Truths Hebraic Scrolls translated by Rabbi Simon Altaf revealing some deep secrets with all the Parshas

Sefer Yashar (The Book of Jasher)

Seferim Chanoch (The Books of Enoch)

Yahushua, The Black Messiah

Hebrew Wisdom – Kabbalah

The Apocrypha (With Pirke Avot Ethics of The Fathers)

Forever-israel Siddur transliterated Hebrew with English (Daily life prayers 7th Edition)

World War III, The Second Exodus, Y'sra'el's return journey home

What Else Have They Kept From Us?

Patriarchal Marriage, Y'sra'el's Right-Ruling Way of Life, Methods and Practice

The Scroll of Yahubel (Jubilees)

Who am I?

Hebrew Characters, The Power to have prayers answered

Now that I know I am a Hebrew

Religious Confusion and the Everlasting Path to the Torah.

www.ingramcontent.com/pod-product-compliance
Lightning Source LLC
Chambersburg PA
CBHW030239170426
43202CB00007B/55